# CHANGE*d* AGENTS

## Nine years in Nepal

*Nick & Ros Henwood*

**www.henwoodfamily.co.uk**

Grosvenor House
Publishing Limited

Nicholas and Rosalind Henwood are hereby identified as the joint authors
of this work in accordance with Section 77 of the Copyright, Designs
and Patents Act 1988

The book cover picture and all illustrations are copyright
to Nicholas and Rosalind Henwood

This book is published by
Grosvenor House Publishing Ltd
28-30 High Street, Guildford, Surrey, GU1 3EL.
www.grosvenorhousepublishing.co.uk

A CIP record for this book
is available from the British Library

ISBN 978-1-908447-56-2

Scripture quotations are taken from the Holy Bible, New International
Version (Anglicised), 1986, Hodder and Stoughton Ltd, Kent, UK.

*For Ann,*
*in memory of Doug, who prayed*

# CONTENTS

v

# FAST ACTION REPLAY

Even though they are more than ten years ago, the first moments in Nepal are etched on our minds. Rich colours, city grime and a warm welcome at the guesthouse opened our initial chapter, 6-months of language and orientation in Kathmandu. The first days flew by as neighbouring shopkeepers, colleagues and new church friends cheered on our attempts at speaking Nepali.

As weeks became months the honeymoon ended. We queued for hours to obtain driving licences and in our naivety, were taken for a ride by traders who sold metal plates and pans.

We moved to the village of Amppipal where we lived in the 'Old Dispensary' a mud and stone house with a rusty corrugated iron roof. Despite the rats, it became our home. We sensed that God intended us to be there. The move gave us a chance to make a new start and avoid repeating mistakes we'd made in Kathmandu. Nick began some friendships with Nepalis that were to deepen over the years. For Ros, relating to Nepali women proved more difficult. Most of those she met day to day were uneducated subsistence farmers. We continued our language study – especially enjoying proverbs and stories. Church services demanded intense concentration. Our relationships with English-speaking expatriates were uplifting.

We found roles for ourselves, with our neighbours and Nick's colleagues at the Community Health Programme, and with church and expatriate friends. Nick in particular;

1

found he was becoming less of a doctor and more a trainer of others as he worked within a Christian mission and development agency. Ros developed skills in raising toddlers where there was no library or swimming pool, only steep muddy paths and free-range livestock. As the girls grew, she took responsibilities at the tiny project primary school – supporting short and long term teachers and teaching older children. We tried to keep on communicating with our family and friends in the UK. Occasional visits home were whirlwind tours, but at those times, two supporters - Doug and Ann pressed us to turn our experiences into a book.

Padam, Nick's inspiring boss, died unexpectedly. So Nick led the programme for two years and postponed his year's public health study in London.

In London Nick's class comprised of 40 students of almost as many different nationalities. As they studied together every class member brought experiences of working in developing country settings. The year also gave us student-rate opportunities to peer from the gods at West End shows and see more of Nick's parents. We weighed up possibilities for a next assignment and took up a new challenge – leading a tuberculosis and HIV programme with a secular French humanitarian agency.

On return to Nepal we began to realise the size of the task. Negotiating government agreements and our own visas took more than a year and ongoing interactions with health officials never ended. But the new programme was launched, and the Nepali team grew over the next three years to 25 capable men and women who trained health post staff and community people in TB and HIV. We were a springboard for ten drama troupes that promoted health awareness through street theatre.

In Tansen, a small town quite near to Nepal's Indian border, we were members of a vibrant Nepali church. We felt at home there. Our language skills were sufficient for us to participate more, Ros in our home group, Nick up-front through Bible teaching.

In this chapter we thrived in new roles and found we could relate confidently with Nepali friends and colleagues. Our 'homestead' included a large vegetable garden where inquisitive neighbours advised us which plants to grow, and the girls kept rabbits. Our swing was a magnet for local children.

Ros completed a degree in theology by correspondence and chose to explore the ways new believers in Jesus relate to their Hindu families at the annual Dasai festival.

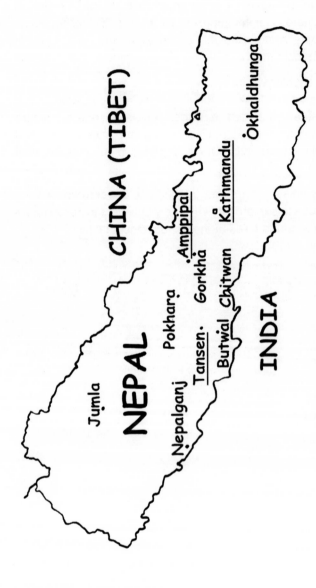

*Over nine years, we lived in Kathmandu, Amppipal and Tansen, in the Central and Western regions of Nepal.*

Over time Nepal's national security deteriorated. Strangers to a village, who would have received a warm welcome ten years before, engendered suspicion. Plain clothed Maoists and plain clothed army look alike, of course. Although we were privileged as foreigners, we did not escape demands for funds, and were fearful of rebels' threats. Curfews and armed patrols were part of every-day life.

As we neared the end of our stay we no longer knew where to call home. Our daughters had lived almost their entire lives in Nepal. We pondered and listed out things we would and would not miss as we moved on to England, as well as aspects of the UK that we looked forward to and those we were apprehensive about. It seemed appropriate to make another new start there, not least to give our girls a chance to discover their parents' 'home' culture.

Today we live in Leicester – a multicultural city. Our neighbours work at keeping parts of their Asian and African-ness alive while cheering for England at cricket. Our journey has led us through Asia to little Asia. We're glad you are travelling with us. We thought we'd be change agents on the way. Perhaps we have, but it's certainly true that we ourselves have been changed. As you read, may you be too.

Nick and Ros Henwood, June 2008, Leicester, UK

# Chapter 1

# DESTINATION NEPAL

**Thrust into a new world and learning to survive...
Kathmandu greets the senses**

Ros –

Amid black exhaust fumes the taxi swerved to avoid dogs
in a back alley. We didn't know where we were going, but
hoped the driver did. We'd expected someone to meet us at
the airport. When no one came, we phoned from an unlikely
courtesy phone and our contact told us to get a taxi to
'Thapathali'. Taxi drivers and hotel touts buzzed around the
airport entrance. Little boys tried to assist with our suitcases
and then pestered us for a tip.

A smiling hostess flagged our vehicle down outside the
guesthouse. Moments later we stood on the dusty grass
inside the walled compound. We were dazed and exhausted.
After the overnight flight and a five and three quarter hours
time zone change, we didn't know whether we were hungry
or sleepy. We sat down for the evening meal regardless.
Afterwards I remember the hostess gently lifting Lydia into a
swing and rocking her, while she sang "I see the moon".
There was at least one familiar thing as we looked up to the
night sky.

Nick –

On that first evening I took a walk from the guesthouse into
unlit streets to find a nearby hotel with an international

telephone. Car horns, piles of rubbish and ancient temples –
sounds, sights and smells - jostled for my attention. The acrid
exhaust of 2-stroke auto-rickshaws made me cough. A riot of
jammed vehicles at a main road junction revved their engines
and tooted. Their lights illuminated the scene a gloomy
yellow. I reached the hotel and made a 2-minute call to my
parents: "We've arrived in Nepal!"

We slept off the jet lag. Two days later I set out boldly to
explore old-town Kathmandu. It teemed with life. Cotton and
silk in a rainbow of colours, and brass cooking pots burst out
on to the streets to advertise each merchant's wares. Shoppers
chatted, laughed, drank tea, bargained and bought items on
display. The things for sale at a hardware stall covered every
inch of shelf and wall space. Pedestrians of all ages flocked
through the narrow streets. Porters carried stacked-up bales of
cloth, or a new refrigerator on their backs. Cycle rickshaws
inched their way through the crowd. My senses saturated, but
understanding nothing of the banter and exchange, I made my
way through Kathmandu's temple square.

Where the road widens at a junction, vendors had laid their wares
on the pavement. A boy sat behind a stall selling sticky doughnuts.
He fanned them to keep the flies off. On another corner stood an
ancient pagoda-shaped Hindu temple. Its exquisitely carved
wooden beams supported a roof of red clay tiles.

The road led on over a bridge. Tailors lined the footpath.
Each worked at his foot treadle sewing machine. A man
sitting next to his outdoor barber's chair offered me a haircut
and head-and-neck massage.

The revered Bagmati River flows under that bridge. It stank.
Its banks were covered with domestic waste and human filth.
Its dark grey water oozed through a clogged mass of plastic
bags. With guttural exertion, a man cleared his throat and
spat a gob of sputum on the pavement.

Two cows stood idly in the middle of the road. Another sat, calmly chewing paper refuse in front of a vegetable stall. She eyed the cars that wove their way past, unconcerned by the jam she was causing. Temples could be seen everywhere in Kathmandu. Women carrying plates of rice, flowers and red powder edged forward in a queue to make their offerings to the stone statue inside another shrine. Children clanged the clappers of heavy bells hung on the temple steps. Three yards away a red-smeared stone bull looked forward nobly – identifying the place as a temple dedicated to Shiva.

As we settled into new routines of living in a bustling Asian city, and began learning to speak Nepali, we made time to explore. In one corner of Kathmandu artisans cast and finished bronze Buddhas and Hindu deities inside numerous grubby workshops. We observed that many Nepali houses have a place for worship that feature such images. Everywhere I looked the secular and sacred seemed jumbled together.

The apparently casual attitudes of Hindu and Buddhist worshippers struck me. As we walked through temple courts in a run down quarter of the city we had to dodge children playing football and ease our way around rice and lentils spread out in the sun on straw mats. One of the temples was adorned with cooking pots and pans – nailed up to its beams. Women and girls, sedate in pristine saris, carried plates of rice, fruits and flowers through the muddle to make offerings to their gods.

Overlooking the city from the northwest stands the imposing Buddhist 'stupa' at Swayambunath. Following a guidebook tip we hired a taxi to take us there to observe early morning worship. It encompassed both physical and spiritual actions. The huge white dome (stupa) is crowned with the painted eyes of Buddha that gaze in four directions. Each morning between 6 and 8 o'clock it's a hive of activity. Women worshippers, wearing brightly striped Tibetan aprons, and young monks in red and yellow robes process around the site's perimeter, spinning the hundreds of prayer wheels - some as big as cars. Spinning the inscribed wheels is regarded as an act of prayer. Moreover worshippers hold 'prayer tops', or strings of beads, resembling rosaries, as aids for prayer. Overhead strings of flags, like bunting, are said to utter the prayers printed on their yellow and white cloth as they flutter in the breeze. Some worshippers make slow but steady progress as they repeatedly prostrate themselves to the ground every few steps. I saw profound perseverance.

*Swayambunath. You look up, and
Buddha's eyes peer down.*

To reach the stupa itself, you have to climb up a long steep flight of steps. Looking up, reaching up, climbing up... but what can be found at the top? The empty expressions of worshippers I observed suggested that they found little. I perceived religious zeal but felt sad because people seemed to be trapped in it.

## Mind your P's and Q's; pots and pans and social cues

Ros –

Ideally we would have learned about Nepal from Nepalis. To some extent we did. But it was not full immersion. We lodged at the mission guesthouse with fellow language learners from Norway, Germany, Australia and America.

Meals were served three times a day in the communal dining room. When the bell went, we scrambled to locate a high chair and two empty spaces before someone said a prayer of thanks over the food. Lydia, our one and a half year old daughter, quickly picked up the most frequently sung Nepali grace "Danyabad Yesu" – 'Thank you, thank you Jesus'. Meal times were a strain. It was hard for me not to criticise, at least inwardly, other parents' styles of disciplining their children. But I could not have coped with shopping and cooking. New sights, sounds and impressions sapped my energy.

We were linked to an 'Umbrella Organisation' comprising several Christian agencies. The Umbrella's impressive infrastructure freed us to pursue language study. We did not have to procure our own visas. We accessed money through the mission banking system. We bought stamps and posted letters at headquarters.

Jesus promised that when we leave things behind for his sake he will provide abundantly. In the mission guesthouse, we moved into a large bedroom with a bathroom attached.

The room boasted a little loft annex, which we used as a prayer place. We had a home from home.

The experienced coordinator of our language and orientation programme impressed me. She did not give advice. She listened and responded but she let us explore and develop a new lifestyle for ourselves, at our own pace.

We were beginners. We could not trust ourselves with even the simplest tasks. We had to relearn how to brush our teeth – to use purified water, not water from the tap. (We debated endlessly the best way to achieve this. Some boiled their water; others filtered it; some filtered and then boiled; others boiled and then filtered. There were different types of filter too...)

One day a trader invited me into his carpet shop for a cup of tea. I refused. I didn't want a carpet, and wasn't sure whether it would be safe to drink the tea. Afterwards I learned that Nepali tea was always safe to drink as the water, milk and sugar are boiled up together, killing all germs. The glass in which teashop tea was served however was not always as clean as I'd have liked. Some expatriates dripped a little tea over the rim of the stainless steel beaker on to the ground, and then drank from that edge. I soon came to enjoy Nepali tea, as long as I did not compare it with a cup of Earl Grey from a teapot.

Getting around was a new experience. I remember our first ride in a black three-wheeler motor rickshaw. We ducked under the low doorframe, perched on the narrow bench, and closed the makeshift black cloth door with a flimsy catch. The high- pitched engine squealed into life. It lurched and shuddered its way up a hill. Air rushed through the open sides of the vehicle, and we peered out through the low window in front. When we reached our destination we had to calculate the fare - the meter rate plus 40%.

I brought only two calf-length skirts with me from England as I intended to buy clothes locally. But it was three weeks before I found someone to accompany me on a shopping trip. She helped me buy matching 'kurtar sariwal' - sets of long tops with baggy trousers and scarves. I purchased a sari, along with material for a petticoat and blouse, and a length of cloth to sew around the hem. I returned to the guesthouse triumphant, eager to show Nick my new outfits. Then I discovered that without a drawstring I could not put on the 'kurtar sariwals'. I had to wait a few more days to procure one. We took the cloth to a tailor who sat behind a glass-fronted counter in a bare and gloomy room on the side of the street. He measured me for the blouse and petticoat, and we agreed a price and a collection day. Nick's clothes were simpler. He took a shirt and a pair of trousers he'd brought with him from England for the tailor to copy. He also took a pair of shoes for the cobbler to duplicate, but the resulting pair was too narrow and too short. I don't think the cobbler could believe how big Nick's feet were.

It did not take long to feel out of touch with home. English newspapers were unavailable and the guesthouse had no television or internet. So we tuned our short-wave radio to the BBC World Service.

We arrived in Nepal with three suitcases and a travel cot. We intended to buy equipment for our home locally. But we had no idea how much time and energy this task would consume. One Sunday afternoon Nick and I, with Lydia in a back pack, stood before the narrow counter of a stall, bemused by cluttered plastic buckets, hanks of rope, and metal spoons.

Someone tapped me on the shoulder, "Namaste".
I turned round to see the smiling face of a Gurkha soldier we had met on the aeroplane.
"Tulsi! Great to see you. Let's have some tea."
"I'll help you with your shopping – I know what to look for."

He examined the plates one by one for defects, felt their weight, and bartered for a fair price. He was an angel sent to help us that afternoon. Another time we bargained for saucepans, a pressure cooker and a stove. We returned to the guesthouse tired but satisfied. When we unwrapped our newspaper parcels however, we discovered that several extra pan lids had been added alongside the saucepans (which were sold by weight). The valve on the pressure cooker didn't work and the pressure stove was faulty. Nick reluctantly returned to exchange the defective goods. We learned to check all purchases before leaving the shop, even light bulbs and balloons.

We didn't recognise social cues. We received a wedding invitation. We had to find out what we were expected to wear, what would be an appropriate gift, and when we should arrive. We hoped to meet up with our Gurkha friend for a meal. Two weeks in advance we sent a letter to arrange a date. When the day arrived he didn't turn up. We realise now how culturally inappropriate our expectations were. Most invitations we have received from Nepalis have been given just a day or so ahead of an event.

"Have you had the family planning operation?" a taxi driver asked. I was taken aback. It appeared acceptable to ask questions we reserved British avoid: How old are you? Where did you buy that coat? How much did it cost? And we did not know how to greet others. A 'Namaste' with palms held together and lowered gaze was usually appropriate. Young men walked hand in hand down the street quite naturally. But we never saw a married couple show affection in public. For a young couple to share a portion of ice cream in a trendy Kathmandu restaurant was pushing boundaries.

Confusion and mistakes occurred. Some months on, when an English friend visited us, Nick didn't know how to greet her – after hesitating, he hugged her. One evening we went out for a meal with friends. I automatically reached for Nick's hand as we walked along. I was hurt when he rebuffed me, and declared that we should no longer hold hands in public. I understood his reasoning: he wanted to avoid offending others. Years later, holding hands when we returned to England felt almost conspiratorial.

We got sick. I don't remember ever seeing Nick ill in England, but he suffered bouts of diarrhoea and sickness in Kathmandu. I remember appreciating the return of my appetite after a few days feeling very off-colour, and the relief when a meal stayed down. The pollution in Kathmandu was inescapable. Shirt collars were filthy after a day. Dust filled our noses and throats. I could not shake off a phlegmy cold. Lydia fell and cut her lip on the edge of a concrete step. It bled profusely. I felt guilty that we had not taken her to hospital when the lip became 'blobby'. We quickly got tired, and were often in bed and asleep by nine. Indeed after several late nights, we developed symptoms of minor illness. Our moods swung up and down as never before. We became tense about minor decisions. I wanted to buy some shampoo. Nick insisted that Nepali women use soap to wash their hair and bodies. I risked alienating myself from them by purchasing expensive imported shampoo. I refused to wash my hair with soap. I went out and bought a bottle of shampoo in defiance. Nick conceded that it was the best shampoo he had ever used.

We rapidly became institutionalised. One Saturday when we signed out of the guesthouse lunch, it felt daring to buy our own bread and spreads. I remember the night we went out to a popular Nepali restaurant. It was a stark room with white walls and ceiling. Most of the tables were already taken. We ordered soup and main courses. Immediately after the soup arrived, so did Nick's chow mein. We sent noodles back, saying we wanted it after we had finished the soup. The waiter promptly whisked it on to the windowsill. After he cleared the soup bowls, my curry appeared, and the waiter retrieved the stone-cold chow mein from the windowsill for Nick.

We took Lydia out to the zoo. She attracted more attention than the rhinos and crocodiles. Despite my protests Nepali visitors pinched her cheeks. One boy grabbed her teddy and dangled it out of her reach. I could see why the cages had notices saying 'don't tease the animals'.

We approached overload with so many things to discover, but we had help. Our orientation course leaders asked us to set goals over a five-month period, in areas such as survival, family life, language learning, and future roles. I wanted to build up a bank of activities for Lydia. We wanted to speak about our family and work in Nepali. We needed equipment for water purification. When we broke the tasks down into manageable chunks we could tackle them, and celebrate when we achieved them.

Just when we thought we had mastered some of the skills of living in the city, we went on a two-week orientation to a Nepali village. To prepare us, an extrovert language teacher mimed, Mr Bean-style, a trip to the pit toilet. He deliberately emptied his trouser pockets of money and keys before squatting down to do his business. He took a jug of water in with him to splash himself clean using his left hand. I made a mental note to take a roll of toilet paper with me to the village. A female teacher advised us to obtain a wrap-round skirt made up with an elastic top, for washing at the public tap. I admire Nepali women, who manage to wash themselves discreetly under their loose clothing, and then dress without getting their fresh clothes wet.

In the village we stayed with an extended family of sixteen. We spent five hours a day at language learning. At seven each morning, long after the family had risen, we emerged from our bedroom. After a glass of hot sweet tea, our language lessons began. At ten o'clock we went to see if the rice was cooked. It seemed a long wait, we were hungry. We poured water from a jug over each other's hands, removed our shoes, then stooped through the low doorway into the kitchen, and sat down cross-legged on a rice straw mat. Our dishes were piled high with rice. Lentil soup was ladled out into a separate bowl. The hostess then spooned vegetable curry and spicy chutney on to our plates. We said a thank you prayer, and began our meal. When I ate with my hands I seemed to spill rice everywhere. Trying to feed an unrestrained one-year old, while sitting cross-legged on the floor in a rather awkward wrap-round skirt, proved a big challenge. The hot afternoons in the village were punctuated with a snack of sweet tea and popcorn, roasted soybeans, or beaten rice and vegetable curry. We spent free time walking in the village, showing Lydia the farm animals, washing at the tap, rinsing out nappies, and attempting conversation with neighbours and members of the household. We knew our privacy would be invaded. In fact people were not as intrusive as I had feared. Our possessions provoked much curiosity. Without asking, a family member picked up Nick's wallet and rifled through it. Another examined our camera.

In the evenings we sat on the veranda smothered in insect repellent waiting for our second rice meal of the day. Despite the lack of variety I looked forward to rice and lentils again – Nepalis eat this staple 'dal bhat' twice a day, every day. However, the gaps between meals seemed long. After the evening meal we brushed our teeth on the veranda, like when you're camping.

A highlight of that family's week was when several households gathered in a neighbour's home to watch a

Nepali soap opera on TV. Young and old sat hypnotised by the drama on screen. I couldn't follow the plot, but appreciated the slapstick humour.

## Back to the beginning

Ros –

"Is God calling you overseas?" The words on an advert for Wycliffe Bible Translators hit me between the eyes. I was 16, reading a Christian magazine, and sensed that God was indeed calling me. These words determined the direction of my life.

It was natural that Bible translation grabbed my attention. The story goes that, on holiday in France aged seven I asked, "Why can't I speak French, Daddy?" A little later I sold my doll's house to buy a English-French picture dictionary. The first person I witnessed using foreign languages at work was an airhostess, and for a long time it was my ambition to become one too.

From a young age my parents took me to church. I wriggled in the awkward wooden pews and envied my father's ability to kneel comfortably. I stumbled through the Lord's Prayer, confusing trespasses with trespassers. I remember how earnestly I emphasised "thy *will* be done", though I'm not sure what I thought a 'thy' looked like.

My mother used to deliver church magazines faithfully to a neglected council estate in the parish. I hated this chore – with the stiff letterboxes and the yappy dog that leapt up and bit my wrist as I opened a gate. But Mum was modelling God's mission heart for the poor.

The highlight of the church year in my childhood was the Easter 'project' week. The Church Mission Society produced resources to help children discover different parts of the world. One year we dressed up in colourful scarves thinking about Sierra Leone. Another time we bartered with tokens for currants, peanuts and sugar in an 'Iranian' market. These projects captured my imagination, and began to open the world up to me.

Though I remember praying and reading the Bible regularly from a young age, it took some time for my faith to travel from my head to my heart. I had always thought that Jesus rising from the dead was the most important part of Easter. Then one day I heard someone speak at a Christian Union meeting at school. She explained how Jesus died on the cross to take away the barrier of sin that separates us from God. I realised that I could no longer 'ride' on my parents' faith. I needed to decide for myself if I wanted to follow Jesus. Aged 17, on December 2nd I attended a 'let God speak' evening in the Colston Hall in Bristol with my church youth group. That evening I opened myself up to God's Holy Spirit and God graciously showed me how much he loved me, individually. My journey of faith took a leap forward. I found a new ability to pray aloud, and a closer intimacy with God. I started to go on long walks praising God in a new language he had given me. This gift of God to speak a 'tongue' that, unlike the foreign languages I was learning, I could not explain, was strangely liberating.

My first opportunity to combine my passion for languages and overseas mission came during my gap year, when I spent a month on an Operation Mobilisation summer team in Austria. Their suggested reading challenged my untried faith – I felt uncomfortably like the 'chocolate soldier' in one of their books, unready for the battle ahead. During the month we lived together in an international team, selling books, and singing German choruses door-to-door. It was a positive experience: I got to know Finnish Christians, ate oats for breakfast and tried to cook Yorkshire pudding for the team. A beautiful posy of wild flowers in a wicker vase, bought from the common purse for my birthday was a touching gesture.

I studied French, German and Maths at A level, but wanted a new challenge as I thought about university. After my gap year including travel to Austria and Greece, I started at Exeter College, Oxford, reading German and Modern Greek.

## Nick's Journey

Nick –

Although the youngest of three, in much of my childhood it felt like I was the only one – somehow my older brother and sister had already gone on ahead too far at primary school, and moved on to attend different secondary schools to me. Scouting gave me opportunities to brush with dangers and squeeze down potholes, explore mines and climb granite rock faces on our summer camps in Wales. As a junior Scout leader I learned to stand back and allow boys to develop skills for themselves.

Accompanying my parents to church grounded my faith, and singing in the church choir taught me disciplines of music as well as giving me an identity there. Larking around the back of the church hall on club nights aside, I grew in my understanding of Jesus in a setting where wise leaders of the youth group permitted us to discuss anything – and find out about ourselves in the process.

As a 16 year old I played Jesus at the annual Good Friday play, which that year explored the 'stations of the cross' – events and sayings in Jesus' life from his trial before Pilate to his dying on a cross some three hours later. In our play I let my wooden cross crash to the ground and fell down on top of it. At that moment I found myself praying, "Lord Jesus, I am ready to follow you".

Between 14 and 18 I attended a boy's school. It introduced me to physics, to monitoring the weather, to sailing and to back-stage antics. The head teacher encouraged me to aim high, and as a crescendo I was successful in securing a place to read medicine at Oxford. But faith was far from my mind as I moved on to university.

My father took me up to college the first weekend. Looking in my pigeonhole I found an invitation to the Sunday service at a city church. "I attended St. Aldate's when I studied here", he told me; and so the next day I breezed along to take a look.

The event took my breath away. I immediately warmed to the strangers who stood near me. Their voices and gestures seemed to indicate that they actually knew God! I don't remember what Rev. Michael Green said that day – but I do remember him suggesting I might like to attend a 'beginner's group' to explore Christianity further. I'm no beginner, I thought to myself. But on the way out I found myself drawn to join a group anyway. It was a rich beginning. It revealed the relevance of the Bible that can be both the illumination and the sustenance for my life-journey. I also began to know God personally. Reaching the end of that term, I had perhaps not put my chorister's hat away, so I sought to join St. Aldate's music group and somehow managed to persuade the music director. That group became my spiritual family – as we ate a meal and learned from the Bible together each week and rehearsed and accompanied worship on Sundays.

Ros –

I was drawn into the life of St Aldate's church in Oxford, and signed up for the student mission a couple of weeks before the start of my second year. A team of over 100 students converged on Bedford to work with the local churches, doing assemblies, coffee mornings and promoting talks given by Michael Green. It was on the bus on the way home that I sat next to Nick, and our friendship began.

I soon told Nick that I felt God had called me to work overseas. I don't think he had considered this, despite training in medicine. We resolved to explore the possibilities together. In the eighties to go overseas short term was a new idea. Africa Evangelical Fellowship sent us as their first 'Special Short Term Missionaries' to South Africa. As we were not even engaged at that time, they put Nick in a mission hospital in Kwa Zulu, and me 200 miles south in an Indian township near Durban. It was a privilege to be able to live in Phoenix, despite apartheid. I stayed in the homes of Asian believers, ate curry for breakfast, learned how to wash dishes Indian-style and bathe using a jug. For me it was significant to meet missionaries in the flesh for the first time, and to realise they were 'ordinary' people.

## Two into One

Nick –

I 'passed the test' Ros had set, and was able to assure her that I was ready to at least consider Christian mission work in the future. Delighted, and with one year left to qualify as a doctor, we were married on a hot August day in 1988.

My jobs and Rosalind's teacher training took us to York, King's Lynn and Norwich. In each place we put down roots in local churches.

Ros –

I was not used to being turned down. I was shocked to receive a letter from the Bible College of my choice refusing me a place to study for cross-cultural mission work. Their reasoning however was faultless. Their policy was to train both members of a married couple – one of the few certainties in overseas work was that we would serve together. So I dragged a reluctant Nick along with me. It proved one of the happiest years of our life.

I envied those fellow students who had had a lifelong burden for, say, Chad, and knew where they were heading. My call was vague, simply 'overseas'. Though it may not sound spiritual, Nick and I determined to carry out a 'beauty contest' of mission societies. We asked questions, met representatives from different organisations, and honed the list of contestants down to two. They had openings for doctors interested in community health, and we found their outlooks matched our own. As we proceeded in our application, one of the agencies identified an opportunity in Pakistan. We went to Bradford to buy a shalwar kameez, and borrowed slides of Kunri in the Sindh to show our churches. We started to raise financial support. Two months before we were due to leave for Pakistan, our visas were refused. By this time our jobs in England had finished, our house was rented out, and we were itching to go. The organisation set to finding us an alternative destination, and suggested Nepal. Had they initially proposed Nepal, I think we would have refused. We felt it was too well trodden. But by this time we just wanted to go anywhere.

## Friend raising

Nick –

Before leaving for Nepal we had to raise our financial support. Because our sending agency placed partners in a wide range of countries, where travel and living costs vary considerably, they calculated the average cost of supporting a given size of family (in our case three) and based the level of support needed on this figure. This was the amount we aimed to raise in the UK. It represented more than the actual cost of keeping a family such as ours in an inexpensive location like Nepal. And it meant that a proportion of our support money would be channelled to help those serving in other countries where the cost of living was high. Some might find this difficult to accept. But we valued the concept of partnership in mission, and the privilege it afforded in supporting one another as a fellowship.

The mission suggested that we should find 90% of our target figure before leaving the UK. We took a deep breath and visited churches, friends and family, explaining our future plans. We asked if they would be prepared to make a financial commitment of £12 per month. At first the process was slow, but as we neared our planned departure date, people's generosity thrilled us. While in Nepal we received a listing of our 'team support' each quarter. To read it through was an antidote to discouragement. Did we 'live by faith' for our financial needs? In a way, yes. I am sure that God heard our prayers, and prompted some to give in specific ways and at specific times. But for the most part we 'lived by fellowship' – God providing our needs through a circle of family and friends, who loved us and shared our vision.

# CHAPTER 2

# FROM KATHMANDU
# TO A REMOTE VILLAGE

## A rough landing: Illness and practicalities

Ros –

A few weeks after arriving in Nepal, I sat on the toilet, light-headed, with nauseating pains gripping my stomach. Coursing through my mind were visions of the many early missionaries who died of tropical diseases. I stumbled back into bed, and broke into a cold sweat. Cramping aches tortured my arms and legs. Re-hydration salt-sugar solution didn't help. It seemed to me that Nick would not take our family's sicknesses seriously. Besides, he assumed we would recover without drugs. After a week of painful diarrhoea, someone suggested antibiotics. We bought some over the counter at a medical hall and within 24 hours I felt better. Consequently Nick's view of antibiotics for diarrhoeal illnesses began to change. And I learned the merits of seeking the advice of a doctor outside the family.

Baby Lydia's eyes were sticky. We bathed them in boiled water but they continued to discharge. There was a dramatic improvement when we applied an inexpensive antibiotic cream that another mum had recommended.

Water problems confronted us from the outset. We arrived in Kathmandu in February, after the winter rains. The temperature rose as it became drier from March until June. Then the monsoon broke. Our guestroom had warning notices pinned permanently on the walls: 'Water shortage - please use sparingly'. So we resented the carefree attitude of the Nepali workers at the guesthouse who washed clothes under a fast flowing tap. 'If it's there, use it', was their reasoning. They did not worry about tomorrow. I felt the tension roll away when we found a spare barrel and were able to keep a reserve supply in our room.

Soon after we arrived in Kathmandu our mission representative presented us with a form entitled 'Disposal of my body in case of death in Nepal'. We giggled nervously. I remembered the sombre hush that spread through the dining hall at Bible College, when someone announced that the Wilkins family, former students, had all died in a plane crash in mountains around Kathmandu on their arrival in Nepal. Before leaving the UK we had prepared wills and, in theory at least, left our affairs in order. Practicalities, like this form, were a necessity. Some years later we mourned for a colleague who died in Nepal in a rafting accident.

## Church during our 'Language and Orientation' period

Ros –

Home-delivery pizza is a recent phenomenon in Kathmandu. The streets are not sign posted, and each week, another new building crammed in adds to the confusion. The first time you order a pizza, you have to accompany the motorcyclist to your door. A similar problem arises when you are trying to find a church - you need a guide to get you there.

At the first Nepali service we attended, on a Saturday, Nepal's weekly day-off, we had to stand up and introduce ourselves. This was scary. We soon discovered that Nepali church services begin with an hour of singing, notices, and welcoming new people. Then the children leave for separate classes, while the adults hear a sermon. After a few weeks we could join in some of the Nepali songs – helped by the fact that our church had a particularly small repertoire.

Some songs were translations from English, and so were immediately familiar. Amid the singing there was an informal 15 minutes when everyone prayed together aloud and all at once. As we got used to this, it was liberating to be able to pray in English, Nepali, tongues or a mixture of these without feeling self-conscious amid the general hubbub.

However, after an initial burst of enthusiasm, attending church became a battle. It meant sitting on a hard floor for two hours, with little understanding of what was going on around us. What's more, we had an active 18-month old to contain. We coped by leaving after the first hour of worship, and treating ourselves to a coffee and cake at the nearby German Bakery.

After church one Saturday, when I was in its tiny dark toilet, I lost an end of the drawstring that held up my baggy trousers. As I groped in the low-roofed dimness, I realised I needed some light and cautiously stepped outside. Seeing my predicament, a Nepali woman kindly helped me retrieve the lost end. I felt rather foolish. From then on I was more careful with drawstrings, and also made a habit of knotting the ends together before putting them in the wash.

## A glimpse of our future assignment

Ros –

So what were we orientating ourselves for? Three weeks into our language programme we went for work experience to Amppipal in the Gorkha district of West Nepal. This was the area to which we were likely to be assigned. We travelled by bus along the Kathmandu-to-Pokhara highway as far as Dumre. From there we caught a second bus, forded the river, and bumped along an unmade road for about half an hour to Turture. Here porters met us at the 'Hotel Beauty' teashop and accompanied us for the five hours walk up to Amppipal in the heart of Nepal's 'middle hills'.

On that first trip to Amppipal, we were determined to carry some of our belongings together with our daughter in a backpack. We wanted to disassociate ourselves from the distasteful colonial image, in our own minds, of bearers lugging wicker hampers through the jungle behind pith-helmeted Victorian ladies.

To our surprise, local people did not applaud our gallant efforts. Rather we heard a lot of muttering - "Why aren't those foreigners letting us work for them? They've got money; they should spread it around a bit... We've got families to feed and it's their duty to provide us with employment."

*Over the years, porters carried many loads for us, including our girls, in wicker baskets on their backs.*

While in Amppipal that first time we made a point of looking over the property that might become our future home. The Old Dispensary was unoccupied then, apart from rats. Downstairs was one big room with a bare concrete floor. I imagined our two-year-old falling down the steep ladder-staircase. Upstairs the torn wicker ceiling dangled down in tatters. But we could picture ourselves living here. In estate agent speak, the Old Dispensary had 'potential'. Clouds permitting, It also boasted an extraordinarily beautiful snow-peaked Himalayan view.

We wrote to Amppipal's expatriate team leader. I'm now rather embarrassed about what we asked her to do to prepare the house for us. We'd done some dreaming about how the workshop team should adapt the building – putting in partitions, rain-water tanks, curtain rails, a stair gate, fly screens, and plastic sheeting above the wicker ceiling – all time-intensive jobs. The maintenance men certainly had their work cut out, but I don't remember any grumbles.

Nick –

During that visit we met the Director of the Umbrella Organisation's health services, to discuss our future placement. After carefully considering other possible areas, such as Okhaldhunga in the Everest region, Amppipal was confirmed as our location. I was to become Health Consultant to the Community Health Programme (CHP). I can so clearly recall the Director's words: "Both of you will have strategic roles to play, although your role, Nick, will have the higher profile. You will not be in a leadership position, but you will have a vital part to play in encouraging and helping to build the team. I believe God is going to use you in that task, as well as professionally within the CHP."

## Why bother with language?

Nick –

I'm no language student. French had been an up- hill struggle at school. I never had a French friend. But learning Nepali was a completely different experience. From day one I had immediate outlets for the words and phrases that were being added to my vocabulary.

"Ek cup chiya (sweet and milky Nepali tea) and ek plate aloo tarkari (spicy potato curry)."
The shop keeper nodded and I inwardly rejoiced that it seemed my faltering words had been understood.
"How much?"
"Aat rupeea."
I recognised 'eight' so passed him one 10-rupee note and received a 2-rupee note back before returning to my solid handmade chair by a shabby blue formica-topped trestle table. Two minutes later the shop's run-around boy brought my tea and curry.

Friendships grew as communication improved. And in due course learning stories, songs and proverbs in Nepali gave my language experience spice and colour.

Ros –

When we left for Nepal, Lydia was 18 months' old. Until then I had devoted myself to being a Mum. So I was taken aback when I learned that most couples employed a Nepali teenager as a nanny for the duration of their five-month 'language and orientation programme'. Although the girl assigned to us was robust enough to hold Lydia firmly, we felt ill at ease as we separated and headed to our first language class. More painful goodbyes followed tea breaks, so for everyone's sake we decided to forgo these emotional mid-morning encounters. Lydia was just learning to talk. She picked up Nepali words from her nanny. One morning Nick asked me what the Nepali for cat was, and Lydia piped up with the answer. But new words played tricks on her too: "Shall we have samosas for supper?" "Just one osa for me please, Mummy," she replied.

Having studied German and Modern Greek at university, I looked forward with enthusiasm to the challenge of several months of intensive Nepali language learning.

Nick and I received five hours of tuition each day. The morning lessons focussed on listening and speaking. In the afternoons we were taught the Devanagiri script. The purist zeal in us meant we wanted to learn words as they were written in Nepali script, rather than in a romanized version. Nepali is unlike any European language I had learned. It was difficult to find connections with words we knew already. So learning vocabulary was hard work. We occasionally noticed a link: 'kapi' means exercise book, as in 'copy book'. 'Saboon' for soap sounds like the French 'savon'. The first word we could read in Devanagiri was 'Coca Cola'. Our language teacher had a sense of humour, so on the first day he taught us the phrase 'I'm joking'.

I found it difficult to distinguish between the four 'd's and four 't's in Nepali. Subtle differences in sound were crucial for meaning. So you had to be careful not to ask for dogs' eggs, instead of chickens' eggs. I often got the words for bangle, beaten rice and bird muddled up. The numbers 25, 50 and 85 sounded very similar at first, but getting this right was all-important when you bargained for your taxi fare. We were told the cautionary tale of a language student who went to buy an umbrella but boldly asked the shopkeeper 'show me your *chest*'. Only the final vowel distinguishes these words. Certain verbs are closely related: to learn and to teach, to eat and to feed, were easily muddled. A nurse educator laughed as she recounted telling a new mother to 'first bath the baby, and then eat it'!

Nepali surprised us with a novel tense, the unknown past. A different set of verb endings can be added to indicate that you discover your shirt is torn, or the cat has eaten the cake. You can add on a single syllable at the end of a sentence to make it reported speech - a very effective means of spreading rumours. It is also quite common to finish a sentence with 'perhaps'.

Did we need five whole months for language and orientation? Many expatriates wanted to start their 'real' jobs sooner. During language learning I was reading in my Bible from the book of Exodus. I realised for the first time that God led the Israelites the long way through the desert for a purpose. He wanted them to depend on him and to experience his faithfulness and provision. Five months was nothing compared to the forty years they waited, but I think we learned some of the same lessons.

We expected to make cultural blunders in Kathmandu, and we did. When it came to making an advance on wages, we soon recognised the need to exercise caution. Fortunately, when we moved to our village home in Amppipal we had the chance to make a fresh start. We began to know our way around Kathmandu. When we later came into the capital on brief visits, it was a real help knowing where to shop for specialist stationery items, how to get a passport photo, and which bus routes to take.

During those months of training, we greatly valued the friendships we made with other expatriates. Strong bonds were forged, which continued throughout our time in Nepal, and beyond.

## In the right place

Nick –

At the end of our language and orientation course, we sat together with our learner peers to review the lessons of the past months. "What a privilege it is to be here!" was a recurring comment. Prior to travelling to Nepal, many in our churches had said we were very brave and self-sacrificial in being prepared to 'give up so much'. But for us it was an enriching experience. We treasure the memories of the relationships we established with Nepali people; the excitement of being immersed in a completely different culture and the breathtaking rural and mountain scenery. Our minds and our eyes were opened to a whole new world. We were aliens in a foreign land, but God shows special love to aliens[1]. And come Easter, our little prayer room was lined with beautiful greeting cards, sent from the UK by a loyal and loving band of supporters. We sensed we were following the right path, and were conscious of God's guiding hand day by day.

Ros –

The swallowtail butterfly is a rare species native to North Norfolk. When we lived there, we spent hours stalking the reed beds around the Norfolk Broads, hoping to glimpse one. On our first morning in Amppipal, we set off to climb Liglig Mountain. As we paused for breath at a resting place, smiling children pleaded with us to give them a few rupees in exchange for some beautiful rhododendron flowers they'd found. At the summit two swallowtails danced together in the wind. It was a personal affirmation from God: this is your home from home; this is where I want you to be.

## Making our home in a Nepali village... five hours from the road

Ros –

"Nick and Ros tell me they walk five hours from the nearest road to reach their home in Amppipal," my Mum explained to a friend.

"Is that because they want to identify with their Nepali neighbours?"

"No, it's simply that there's no other way to get there."

*The Old Dispensary in Amppipal, made of mud and stone, has two storeys and a corrugated iron roof.*

After our language and orientation programme, we moved into the renovated Old Dispensary in Amppipal. From the bench on the shady veranda we looked down on to a patch of garden, where Nick double dug raised beds, and began to plant cauliflower, greens and garlic. Banana palms graced the far end adjoining the Community Health Programme's office.

To the left over the wall a path snaked down steeply through the wood to the hospital, a 20-minute walk. To the right ran a well-used path, the local equivalent of an A-road, along which children dawdled to school, and goats and buffalo grazed.

Our veranda was the principal meeting place in our home. It was here that we received guests, bought fruit, negotiated with sewing ladies and porters, and served lots of sweet Nepali tea. We usually propped open the heavy wooden front door, leaving the wire mesh fly-screen in place. We left shoes on the rack by the door, along with umbrellas and sun hats.

Downstairs was open-plan with a lounge-cum-dining room on the left. Beyond the dining table, a wicker partition screened off our 'bathroom' – if you can call a room with no bath, shower or toilet by that name. It did have a basin, though it was not plumbed in, as there was no mains supply. Running water came out of a tap fixed on to a plastic bucket. Underneath the basin another pail collected wastewater. We used a large plastic bowl as a bath for Lydia. Nick and I usually had a 'stand-up' wash. A private bathroom seemed essential to me - I could not face washing outside at the communal tap.

Nick –

The Old Dispensary's corrugated roof collected rainwater. Each day our washing-lady filled a water pot from the storage tanks and topped up the hand-washing container in our bathroom. Water flowed from its tap into the sink, and down into a wastewater bucket. The same lady emptied wastewater into a barrel outside our back door. A pipe led from here to the garden to water the vegetables.

Greasy kitchen water would have attracted ants in the garden, so we flushed the toilet with it. Unlike the Nepalis around us, we relied on the spring only for our drinking water.

Ros –

Our squat toilet, in a small room just outside the back door, harboured two or three resident friends. A benign spider four-inches in diameter sat on the wall, a cute three-inch-long lizard-like gecko scurried around on its suckered feet, and a toad lived behind the flush-barrel. Sometimes we hung up a bucket with a tap to make a surprisingly effective shower.

In the far corner of the kitchen by the back door, we had a sink and draining board fitted. But there were no taps over the sink. This caught me out a few times to begin with, as I went to wash my hands. We stored water in a tall barrel, and decanted it using a green bailer jug. Our plastic-ware was colour coded: green for 'clean', and red for 'dirty'. So the nappy bucket and kerosene jug were red.

Gas cylinders were expensive, as they had to be carried up the hill on a porter's back. So rather than use our two-ring gas cooker, we generally prepared our meals on a couple of fumy kerosene wick-stoves. Boiling water was a slow and tedious process, so we stored hot water in thermos flasks for drinks and washing-up.

'Cook it, peel it, wash it or forget it' was our guide for what was safe to eat. Bananas and small oranges were safe because they first had to be peeled. But before we ate any raw fruit or vegetables, like tomatoes or a cucumber, we soaked them for 20 minutes in iodine water, and then rinsed them in filtered water. Iodine water looks like iced tea, and leaves a nasty brown stain on the rim of the storage jug. Our 'ant-proof cupboard' was the nearest thing we had to a fridge. The front and sides were meshed and each leg stood in a tin of kerosene. Inside we kept fresh buffalo milk, homemade bread, cheese (brought in weekly from Kathmandu) and some vegetables.

A large brown patch marred the fresh whitewash above the ant cupboard. The walls had been re-plastered with mud and cow dung for our arrival. But it was not long before unsightly cracks began to appear. We were fortunate to have a concrete floor, rather than the traditional mud and dung floor that would have required daily maintenance.

We kept upstairs to ourselves. Our bedroom was spacious and bright – the original operating theatre in Amppipal's dispensary. The desk at the window afforded a clear view of the mountains; Nick did an hour's language study there each morning.

Nick –

From my desk the Himalaya ('Him', snow; '-alaya', house of) were stunning. At sunset the mountains took on a gold or crimson hue. But the scene before us was not always inviting. Sometimes the weather would change and the picture appeared cold and foreboding. During the monsoon season clouds hid the beautiful mountains for weeks at a time.

Ros –

Lydia's room was light and airy. She had a wooden Nepali doll's house, a little table with green wooden chairs, and a basket full of toys. On the wicker partition walls hung number and letter posters, and a notice board for postcards.

## Creatures great and small

Nick –

Among these mountains are a number of animals unique to Nepal, even yeti perhaps? Most weeks we stocked up on yak cheese, but we never saw a yak. One afternoon, a troop of monkeys raided our garden for vegetables. Jungle chicken and porcupine, as well as wild cats and bears were spoken of by our neighbours, though it was very rare indeed to see any of these animals. But one creature that did make its presence known was the common rat.

To add to our struggles during our first weeks at Amppipal, we had to contend with an army of rats. They nearly beat me. Each night they ran back and forth above our heads. I felt they were invading *our* space. But of course they must have had similar feelings about us. Over the months, my aversion to rats eased. I trapped many, but there were plenty more in the forest below, and it seemed that our mud and stone walls posed no obstacle whatsoever to their coming inside. So we reached a truce, and became co-inhabitants.

Ros –

In the lounge, a tin trunk-cum-coffee-table held our larder of packet soups, macaroni, and nuts - a stronghold against the rats. This was essential as at night we heard the scrabbling of feet, as the rodents chased one another around our attic. Nick joined in the sport. Rat trapping became a necessary hobby. One weekend a friend's cat found his way into our loft, but his 5am yowling disturbed us more than the vermin. So Nick kept setting large snap-traps - they usually killed the rat instantaneously.

But at nine o'clock one evening when Nick was away on a field trip, I heard the flailing sound of a rat caught in a trap upstairs. I listened, expecting the sounds to die away. They continued. I decided to call the night watchman. He dutifully came in with a long stick, finished off the half-dead animal, and calmly walked out of the door. I went to bed. Next morning as I went downstairs, I heard a not-quite-dead rat kicking in another trap. Once again I called the night watchman. The same man returned, killed the rat, removed it from the trap, and left without a word. No doubt stories about the cowardly expatriate circulated round the village. After that, I made sure Nick did not set any traps before he went away.

## From GP to teacher

Nick –

My role changed from general medical practitioner in the UK to health consultant in Nepal. The transformation didn't happen overnight. At Bible College I had been challenged to re-consider the value of medical institutions in mission. Looking back, many 'mission hospitals' have provided curative health services, in the name of Jesus. But, the over-burdened staff have had little energy to nurture Christian faith in their neighbours. So when we applied to mission societies we looked out for opportunities in community health.

After five months of language study, I started working at the Umbrella Organisation's Community Health Programme (CHP) in Gorkha district. I was the 'Health Consultant', the only expatriate in the Programme, with no staff management responsibilities. I worked at the Programme's office near our home and went on field trips to surrounding villages up to two days walk away. Language learning remained a key priority during the first year.

## The Community Health Programme

Nick –

I was briefed on the history of the Programme. In 1957 the local community at Amppipal invited the Umbrella Organisation to begin work in the areas of education, health and agriculture. The missionaries opened a hospital in 1969 but also recognised that preventative health activities were much needed in the community itself. So CHP started in 1971. Over the succeeding years the government assumed responsibility for health posts that had been established by CHP. While I worked for the Programme, our strategy was to identify needy villages, establish relationships and build trust. We sought to motivate people by encouraging self-development. We promoted literacy for women, skills for health workers, clean drinking water and the use of toilets. Our goal was 'to see transformed communities undertaking their own sustainable health development activities'.

I was responsible for national staff development, and for advising on health matters. One of my first tasks was to review and rearrange the Programme's library. In the process we discovered some useful volumes that helped us during the early stages of programme planning. I unearthed a range of English-medium health journals and materials that could be ordered free or at low cost[2], to resource- poor countries like Nepal. Some journals were excellent, but others were next to useless for our situation. I intended to collect and catalogue good articles for reference, but realised in practice that it was better if interested staff read them hot off the press. When they got lost, I learned not to be exasperated. I found one good way of engaging my colleagues was to ask them to present articles to one another. They had to process the material as they translated it into Nepali.

## Employing people

Ros –

The Old Dispensary boasted neither running water nor electricity. Bringing up a family in Amppipal without piped water, a freezer, microwave or electric kettle, was labour intensive. I feared that employing local people to do menial tasks in our home would humiliate them. The image of rich expatriates lording it over servants seemed offensive. I felt almost duty bound to do the daily chores myself. We soon realised, however, how impractical that was. Whether we liked it or not we were utterly dependent on the Nepalis who worked for us. Our day started at 7am. 'Water sister', a sturdy woman with a brown wrinkled face, who looked older than her years, clacked into the house in her flip-flops and sloshed spring water from a 15-litre metal water pot into our filter. Her simple wrap-a-round skirt was hitched up a little for ease of movement, and a strip of cloth swathed gracefully around her head. Water Sister then returned to the spring, ten minutes' walk below our house, to refill her pot. Later she would reappear to top up the indoor buckets, and wash the clothes. Her daily duties finished at about 9am. We gave her a well-earned cup of sweet milky tea and a bowl of beaten rice before she went home.

Meanwhile Maya came each morning at 7.30am to prepare a rice meal that we ate before Nick went to work. She was well versed in the preparation of local foods, and knew the going rate for vegetables sold at the door. She was also an expert in the many different types of banana and could tell at a glance, which were the tastiest. When hairy caterpillars caused an irritating rash on Lydia's skin, it was Maya who provided the remedy. I could not have managed the housework and cooking without the help of these two ladies. They saved me many hours of tedious chores: washing up, washing clothes, fetching water, cleaning, and baking bread. By minding Lydia for an hour or two a week, Maya also released me to do language study.

And it was through our house helps that we found our way into the community. We got to know their family members and friends and they kept us in touch with local news and events. As they shared their lives with us, we gained valuable insights into the daily struggles that they and so many others had to face. But having workers in our home took some getting used to. I learned to tidy away before Water Sister arrived. She would try and recover used milk tins, peanut butter jars, pumpkin seeds and discarded wrapping paper. On one occasion she rescued an old bra from some rubbish I had told her to burn. Nick joked with her when she asked for yet more sugar in her tea – would she like some salt and chilli powder too?

We put our foot in it sometimes. Maya was a single mother of three young children; Water Sister was an older high-caste woman and therefore had greater status in the community. Because Maya worked longer hours she was paid more. Water Sister found the perceived disparity galling. When we were out, she would beg Maya unremittingly for sugar, or a bigger portion of beaten rice. I realised I had to apportion these in advance, to avoid conflict between the two workers. But there was still tension in the air. It had been easy enough to employ water sister, but how to dismiss her honourably was another matter. We spent a lot of time pondering this issue, and eventually found a solution. We asked her daughter to work for us in her place – so that the wages would remain in the family. This arrangement worked well and there were no more grumbles from our cook. The nappies, however, turned a shade greyer in the hands of a less experienced laundress.

# CHAPTER 3

## MADE IN NEPAL

Ros –

Our second baby's due date was 4th February, exactly a year after our arrival in Kathmandu. When we announced that I was pregnant, an Australian colleague, with a stroke of creative genius, sent over the nearest thing to a bottle of champagne – at least in terms of its shape – a corn on the cob, for us to 'crack open'. Three things influenced our decision not to return to the UK for the delivery. Flight restrictions would have necessitated a long family separation; we had been in Nepal less than a year; and there were no expected complications. However our sending agency advised me to have the baby delivered where specialist help and equipment were available. So at 36 weeks', I walked the five hours out of Amppipal, accompanied by trusty porters carrying Lydia and our luggage. Rather than travel on the Nepali bus, we hired a 4-wheel drive vehicle for the remaining road journey to Kathmandu.

Friends in Kathmandu had a room on their roof, with a kettle and sink. Lydia and I slept there, but went downstairs for meals, and playtimes with the family. Other friends from our language and orientation group lived close by and invited us out for meals. A week later Nick arrived, and the next day we went to view the flat that an American couple were vacating during their home-leave. We moved in. It was in a perfect location and had a bath, a phone, and an unobtrusive cook and housekeeper.

On the 20<sup>th</sup> of January we entertained the friends who had hosted me, to say thank you. That night my waters broke. In an instant those same friends arranged transport to the maternity ward, and cared for Lydia. Elizabeth was born in a semi-public three-bedded ward, as there was no time to get to the delivery suite. A British midwife assisted me. Within four hours Elizabeth got her BCG vaccination, Nick settled the bill, and I staggered back to the flat. We phoned our families in England with the news. We spelled out her second name, 'Anandi', and explained that it meant 'joy' in Nepali. As it was a Sunday, all our churches heard the news hot off the press. In one congregation, after the vicar had prayed for Elizabeth Anandi, someone exclaimed, "I didn't know they were going to have twins!"

Elizabeth had arrived two weeks early. She caught us unprepared. At first she slept at the bottom of a chest of drawers. We were short of specific items. Matching our needs exactly, a superior brand of Scandinavian nappy liners appeared in a parcel; and we were further amazed when Norwich friends spontaneously sent the very type of plastic pants we wanted.

When we returned to Amppipal one elderly local man looked at Elizabeth in surprise. "You say she was born in Kathmandu," he said, "but her skin is white."

Nick –

A Nepali saying states: 'Let it be late, let it be a boy'.

It's good to pass around sweets to your friends to celebrate the arrival of a baby boy. But there's no need to give sweets if you've had a girl. We did anyway.

Rosalind discovered that there were also rewards to be gained in being a 'just-delivered mother', when a colleague gave her a special sweetmeat made with semolina to try.

Another common practice was for new mothers to massage their babies each day in the sunshine with mustard-seed oil. A colleague did this for Elizabeth when we visited her home. She also presented her with a swinging basket, which we hung from a beam on the veranda.

Tragically, the death rate for women around the time of childbirth in Nepal is high, as is infant mortality. Not surprisingly, a significant part of my community health work was concerned with babies.

## Facilitating Change

Nick –

"But don't make the baby scales on your own," suggested Padam. He was the new Programme Director. I'd purchased wood and 2-kg weights in Kathmandu, and was eager to experiment with my beam-scale design. I did the calculations, scratching my head to remember school-physics levers and moments. The maintenance department drilled holes at the critical points. Then we all 'played' at weighing different masses hooked on one end of the beam, by moving a 2-kg counter-balance along the other end. As we marked the scale's graduations, I was dismayed to find that even using a ruler or calculator were challenging tasks for some of my colleagues. At 1.5 metres long, our balances were rather cumbersome. The next step was to conduct a field trial with community health volunteers weighing real babies.

This trial was a moderate success. The scale was graduated in Nepali numerals and volunteers felt able to use it themselves. We went on to make ten more and sold them for half cost price to village committees for their own regular monitoring of child growth.

My work was varied. Field staff wanted visual aids to train others. Despite their glossy finish, ready-made materials rarely fitted our needs. Moreover, we often failed to retain the last copy of a poster in the office, and once that copy was lost so was our memory of it. Before going to Nepal I had attended a workshop called 'Pictures, people and power' where we prepared our own teaching aids[3]. So on monthly training days, programme staff and I explored making and using pictures, puppets and other visual aids to communicate health messages. Some years later I was able to use these skills again when making materials for teaching about tuberculosis and HIV / AIDS. After testing and modifying them, we commissioned them to be hand-painted on to cloth, or printed into manuals and flip charts.

I found our staff training days exciting and challenging. My limited Nepali meant I could never lecture for long on a topic - perish the thought that I'd try even in English - so I led training interactively. In this way I was able to share many new concepts and creative ideas with my colleagues. But the working out, the shaping, and the application of new ideas were undertaken in Nepali, where I was a learner. Others controlled the process. 'Creating an opportunity for learners to learn' became the hallmark of my approach as a trainer. And my hope was that colleagues would be motivated to make this their goal too.

Improving the literacy of women benefits family health. Several studies have demonstrated that literate mothers access health services and apply health education messages better than illiterate ones. So we used 'non-formal education' (NFE) to increase women's literacy skills. When we heard about a method of literacy teaching, called 'whole language', I took on the task of interpreting the manual with our NFE staff team. My only advantage was that the manual was written in English. I worked at understanding the concepts, and at explaining them using my inadequate Nepali. 'Whole language' leapfrogs the phonetic parroting exercises that characterise many literacy approaches and dives straight into reading and writing words and short phrases generated by the learners themselves. It was a voyage of discovery. We all had to work hard, but we learned fast. There was a positive side to my language handicap – it was impossible for me to come over as an expert, which was just as well, as I certainly wasn't one. My Nepali colleagues went on to pilot and use the whole language method effectively.

I kept just one step ahead of those I trained in computing. The United States Department of Health distributes (free of charge) a computer software package for basic epidemiology applications[4]. I experimented with the programme, and pored over the termite-eaten manual at our office. It was not easy to understand. I worked alongside the Programme Secretary to master data entry. Field staff completed a household survey in a proposed new working area. Office staff put the data into the computer. With one finger in the manual, we analysed the results for inclusion in our baseline survey report.

## Poor people

Ros –

Local people saw us as potential employers. And we needed their help as porters for journeys, and to run our house. But my heart sank each time Mr. Alli opened the gate to come and ask for work. Every day he arrived on our doorstep. I could barely understand his village Nepali, spoken without front teeth. What work could he manage anyway? I was relieved when I had a bag or a barrel for him to carry down the hill; at least then I could legitimately give him a few rupees.

I used to walk 15 minutes to the bazaar for my basic grocery shopping. Occasionally someone offered to carry the shopping home, and I willingly accepted. I realised this was something I could ask Alli to assist me with. We kept rabbits, and prepared food for them: a coarse flour of maize, rice husk and soya beans. We started to employ Alli to buy the grains, and grind them. He cared for the rabbits when we went away and did odd jobs in the garden. We paid him nearly every day, until we suggested giving him a monthly wage for about an hour's work each day. His cheerful smile showed he thrived on this arrangement.

One day when Alli was portering, he fell. He returned shaken with a gash on his leg. The wound festered and became painful. Alli could not manage even the small tasks we gave him. He went to the hospital, where he received medicines and instructions to rest and keep his leg up. He limped along the path, head bowed over, looking miserable.

"He really needs to keep his leg up. A couple of nights' in hospital will help the wound to heal," the doctor said. I talked seriously with Alli. "You must listen to the doctor's advice and stay overnight in hospital to rest. Please tell me if there is something troubling you." "I need to provide for my family, and there is no food at home," he confided.

I gave him enough rice and lentils to last a few days. Later I met him on the path struggling back from the bazaar with a small plastic bottle of cooking oil. I was upset that he had not been completely open with me about what he needed. Instead of going to hospital he was caring for his family. But I respected his dignity and sense of responsibility. He had a mentally retarded and husbandless daughter, and her two schoolboy sons to look after.

We simply could not persuade Alli to change his mind, and sadly he languished at home. For some days he failed to appear at our doorstep. We went to his house and found him recumbent on a mat in the darkness. We crouched down beside him. There were empty medicine boxes on one window ledge and full ones on another. The room was a bare square of red mud floor with a fireplace in one corner. He had only one or two cooking pots and a few clothes flung over a string line.

As we were leaving, his daughter appeared, and though a little disoriented, she picked a pumpkin from the sprawling vine, eager to give it to us. We protested vehemently. We both wondered how long Alli would live.

Alli did recover, and even started work as a part-time night watchman at the Community Health Programme. But he got a rough deal, and colleagues sometimes exploited him. One evening we were surprised to find Alli on duty at 9pm, aware that he was not due to start his night shift until 1am. The person doing the early shift was a locally influential younger man. He had retired to bed. When Nick later challenged him about not fulfilling his duty, he was quick to respond, saying, "Oh, we don't have any way of telling the time."

We had to face the question of how we should live among the poor. We were so much wealthier than those around us in Amppipal. We could afford luxury Western goods bought in Kathmandu. Many people came to our door each day selling things, asking for work, clothes, or loans. Most relied on subsistence farming for their daily food, and had little cash income.

Responding appropriately to their needs was not straightforward. An experienced missionary warned us by telling a story. When a western visitor saw a grandmother feed buffalo milk to an orphaned baby with a spoon and cup, she wanted to be helpful and gave the woman an infant's bottle. Some weeks later, the emaciated baby was admitted to hospital, where, with first aid and spoon-and-cup feeding, he recovered. The village woman had not been able to sterilise the bottle, which cultured bacteria and almost killed the child. The gift was well intentioned, but the outcome may well have been disastrous. So, how should we respond?

We were torn. We had often sung the Christian song: "Freely, freely, you have received, freely give". We wanted to demonstrate God's free and generous love in the way we gave to others. People around us were in obvious need. We felt burdened to give to those suffering and in distress, even if sometimes that meant being taken for a ride. Of course we realised that if we expatriates were not living in Amppipal, those seeking help would have to find another way to live. By giving, we made people become more dependent on us, and we risked damaging their self-esteem. It was a dilemma about which we thought long and hard.

Two sewing ladies kept on coming to ask for work. Once they'd done all our mending, we had little to offer them. So Nick got some sewing projects underway. This involved a huge amount of work on our part. We bought cloth, Velcro and zips, and measured and cut out the fabric. Improving and maintaining quality was a constant challenge. However many peg aprons the seamstress made, she still somehow managed to produce unacceptable variations. It took half a dozen alternative versions, and a 'sewing class' on our dining table, before the ladies understood the assembly method for a new Bible cover design.

## A step back in time

Ros –

For the first six months in Amppipal we lived by candlelight. In the precious evenings, once Lydia was asleep I strained my eyes to read, or sometimes wrote letters. We washed by candlelight, and went to bed at nine. It was a great step forward when Nick fixed a solar panel on our roof, and wired low wattage bulbs in each room.

Nick –

When we arrived in the village, Amppipal had no mains electricity. It was our friends from the UK who bought us the solar panel. The battery fed our computer and tape player (at 12 volts) and fluorescent lights (at 240 volts, produced by an 'inverter'). But when the inverter was on, a hum interfered with music listening. Remembering my school physics, I eased the problem by fitting a capacitor across the supply to the tape player, made from two sheets of tin foil rolled together, but electrically insulated from each other by sheets of paper.

Ros –

An average day's sunlight kept two bulbs alight for 2-3 hours. Writing letters by solar light was much less tiring, so we stayed up later to finish jobs. But this made it all the harder to get up for the early morning callers at the door.

The loud greeting of a banana seller roused us at 7am on one of our days off. We decided to stay in bed and ignore him. He continued to call out. Fifteen minutes later, he was still there. So Nick sneaked out of the back door, over the wall and, as if returning home, marched up to the front door. He bought some bananas to make the vendor leave us in peace. I'm not at my best at seven; but village Nepalis get up with the dawn to fetch water, to mud the veranda and to see to their buffaloes.

To live in our rural location was to step back in time. There were no take-aways. All our food had to be cooked from basic ingredients. We prepared what we needed for the day. Mr Alli often ate the "finish ups". I boiled milk morning and night to keep it 'fresh', or preserved it by making yogurt. I learned to crack eggs one by one into a separate bowl. One bad egg would ruin a whole cake mixture.

Nepalis thrive on rice and curry twice a day, but we needed more variety. In Amppipal we ate a rice meal each morning. But we had bread-and-cheese for lunch, and a western-style evening meal.

I improvised when ingredients weren't available: spaghetti 'mungalaise' (with mung-beans instead of mince) was a family favourite. To make a packet crème caramel set, I remembered my girl guide camping days, and covered the bowl with a wet tea towel. I then placed this in a larger bowl of cold water, on the windowsill. My make-shift fridge came up trumps, setting the pudding in just 90 minutes - exactly in line with the instructions on the packet.

## Living in a goldfish bowl.

Ros –

Children peeped through our windows on their way to and from school. Strangers at our door casually stepped inside to take a closer look. Once we gave 50 rupees to a poor man to buy shoes. The next day our cooking helper knew all about it. Our 'private' lives were anything but private.

We admired a Scandinavian family whose home was usually full of people. A deaf and dumb man sat on a cushion eating some spare curry, while the Finnish hostess chatted to the gardening lady over a cup of tea. The children and their Nepali friends ran out into the garden, laughing and playing happily together. This family exemplified love in action. They received anyone into their home: the rich and the poor; the revered and the despised.

Our home was not as open. Anyone was welcome to sit on the bench on our veranda – and everyone did. But only those invited came inside. We insisted that our daily workers announced themselves before entering. This may sound over-protective, but when visiting a Nepali home it is the cultural practice not to progress beyond the veranda. The host invites visitors inside only for the intimate occasion of eating a rice meal together.

I battled to preserve my personal space. It was almost impossible to sit in the garden to read our long-awaited post. The garden wall ran along the edge of a well-used path, and any passer-by seeing us 'doing nothing' would inevitably start up a conversation. It was even difficult going for a walk on our own, without a trail of ragged children shadowing us. Our lives were constantly on show.

Glucose biscuits, made in Nepal, were available in the village shops. Made with white flour, they stuck to the teeth in a way dentists would abhor. Coke and Fanta were also on sale. These products had a high prestige value among Nepalis. At a tea shop you could choose between a traditional Nepali snack, like rolled beaten rice with vegetable curry, or a packet of biscuits to accompany your sweet Nepali tea.

We grew up in England thinking that it was entirely our own affair how we spent our hard-earned cash. Life in a Nepali village was hard enough for us, and we felt we deserved some little luxuries. But the fact remained that our shopping habits in the village made an impression. People knew what we bought – they saw us purchasing the goods, consuming them, and disposing of the packaging. So we aimed to set a good example by buying healthy foods. At the teashop two hard-boiled eggs cost the same as a packet of biscuits.

It was only when we were on holiday, away from the penetrating gaze of inquisitive neighbours, that we felt we could legitimately break these habits. As we revelled in the shady restaurant gardens of Pokhara lakeside, sipping chilled drinks at inflated prices, we sometimes wondered if we were being hypocritical. I suppose it was only natural to react in this way. The stark contrast between two worlds stared us in the face.

## What the weather had in store

While others were looking at us, we were looking at them and learning about our surroundings. Seasonal changes often surprised us.

Nick –

On warm spring evenings, points of green light, bright enough to illuminate nearby leaves, filled the air, flicking on and off every two or three seconds. If we moved in with a torch to inspect these flying ant-like insects they switched off completely, and were difficult to find.

Unlike our European spring, March-April in Nepal is generally dry. Hidden underground, or inside the mud-and-stone walls of buildings, termites prepare for their annual exodus. One evening each year, all the colonies in our neighbourhood would emerge simultaneously with a rustling of wings. The insects streamed out like great clouds of smoke. Toads and chickens had a feast snapping up any that delayed their take off. In the morning you could pick up handfuls of abandoned wings, the surviving insects having found new hideouts.

*The first spring rain turned our landscape pink.*
*The grassy bank 'risers' between each terraced field*
*near the Old Dispensary were full of crocus-like*
*flowers that leapt into bloom once a year.*

Ros –

Vegetables were only available in season. So we ate nothing but aubergines for several weeks, disguised in moussaka, ratatouille or curry. We learned techniques for bottling, pickling and making jam. It became a hobby: I chopped and prepared green tomatoes, cucumbers, or peaches; while Nick sterilised the jars. I crystallized some ginger when we had a bumper crop. We diluted the ginger syrup by-product for a spicy hot drink.

## Monsoon

Nick –

Winters are dry in Nepal. After one dry spell when our rainwater tanks were virtually empty, I remember lying in bed one night undergoing the 'Nepalese water torture'. Rain hammered on our tin roof. But our guttering was under repair, so none of the blue gold was going into the tank. The following day I searched for a ladder to sort out the guttering. We harvested the next rain shower.

From July to September, the monsoon brought unbelievable volumes of rain. For hours and hours it drummed deafeningly on the tin roof above our heads. Paths became cascading watercourses. And the downpour continued on and on relentlessly. 'How can there be any more up there?' I asked myself. Roof water could fill our two thousand-litre water tanks in 12 hours.

Ros –

Though the monsoon rains eased the annual pre-monsoon water shortage, they brought other anxieties. Bugs of all shapes and sizes proliferated. I stored dried beans in powdered milk tins. One day they looked fine, the next I found the beans crawling with tiny black bugs. I learned to store only small quantities of flour, as weevils had the capacity to multiply out of nowhere.

Nick –

What is that squealing noise? Is it a car wheel's defunct bearing, or a neighbour drilling through the party wall? I'm sure someone must be using a chainsaw in the forest. Could it be a newfangled phone, with a shrill electronic tone? Tropical insects, sometimes at a stunning volume, mimicked familiar noises from home.

Ros –

Nick hurriedly removed the nightshirt he had just put on. He said he felt an intensely sharp pricking. Tiny red ants, barely visible, clung to the fabric. Other wily ants breached the defences of our ant-proof cupboard by balancing along a saucepan handle that just touched the wall.

During the monsoon, clothes in cupboards grew mouldy unless we aired them on the sunny days between downpours. We draped wet washing around the house for weeks. When the sun appeared we opened all the windows and took out mattresses, washing, floor cushions and clothes to dry in the brief spells of blazing heat. The hard disc of our computer jammed during our first monsoon. The following year we kept it dry in a waterproof cover with sachets of silica gel. Other expatriate friends kept a light on inside the cupboard where they stored audiocassettes and photographs. The monsoon reminded us not to store up treasure on earth where termites and mould destroy.

# CHAPTER 4

# A DOCTOR... OR WHAT?

Nick –

From time to time during our years at Amppipal, I spent a week as a general physician at Amppipal's mission hospital. Nestled between terraced fields and woods, beside a small bazaar lay its array of buildings. The hospital provided medical services to some fifty inpatients and a hundred outpatients each day. Six mornings a week, crowds of villagers squeezed on to the waiting room benches or queued at the pharmacy or cashier's office. The facilities were basic but somehow the medical, nursing and administration teams managed to care compassionately for the sick. Each time I went to the hospital I felt somewhat apprehensive because my community work rarely required clinical skills. However, the stints were thrilling, and my memories of them rich. They brought me face to face with both inspiring and depressing aspects of rural Nepali life. But the notes in my diaries seem to focus on the bloodiest events.

A 5-year-old lad walked two days with his grandfather and 8-months-pregnant mother to reach the hospital. He'd had a nosebleed for a week. He was anaemic and had a low platelet count. Unfortunately the grandfather's blood group did not match the boy's. "So can anyone else give a unit of blood to this A rhesus-positive lad?" I asked. The medical superintendent, Dr John, offered himself as a donor, and I proceeded to transfuse his blood to the boy.

One evening I stood beside Dr John as he leant over a man's abdomen and conducted an examination. A single, dim 3-amp car bulb above the bed was the room's only illumination. But that was sufficient to lure in a large, loudly buzzing black beetle. It swung about, batting the walls, and then landed on the patient's umbilicus. Later, as I left, I drove a stray dog out of the ward.

I assessed a baby that had been born on the path en route to hospital. Her mother seemed fine but the tiny infant was 4-6 weeks premature. She was cold and covered in leaves. We had no special-care baby facilities, so we taught the woman 'kangaroo nursing' (skin-to-skin, cocooned against the mother's chest). We augmented suckled milk with expressed milk delivered through a fine plastic tube. I was disappointed when, after only three or four days' progress, the family insisted on going home. The chances for that baby girl were slim.

I was out of my depth when another pregnant woman arrived. She had bled for two weeks and been semi-conscious for four days. The baby was dead. Her condition seemed stable, but before we could arrange her transfusion, she suddenly deteriorated and died. We learned afterwards that she was a third wife. Her husband had not come to hospital with her. His first wife had also died in childbirth.

Sometimes I had the chance to take on a patient's whole care. A young woman had miscarried some two months before but was still bleeding. She looked anaemic and had a racing pulse. Being out of hours, no laboratory services were available. So I did the blood grouping for her, and her brother and husband. The husband matched. I took a unit from him for her. Three hours later I undertook a D&C. The next day I discharged the patient.

During one week, I listened to heart murmurs and diagnosed rheumatic fever; I treated cases of intestinal worms and other parasites; and I started a couple off on the road to treating infertility. I struggled to understand what patients said to me. I reviewed TB and leprosy sufferers attending for their monthly supply of drugs, and met those staying as in-patients for their first two months of intensive therapy. I did a quiet night on call. I dug into my formulary for doses of even the most basic drugs. I taught the junior outpatient examiners, and was entertained for coffee and meals at the homes of those who lived near the hospital.

## What exactly is a 'health' worker?

Nick –

Those hospital weeks aside, I worked primarily at the Community Health Programme (CHP). What was my job there? Was I an advisor? a teacher? a supervisor? ...or what? I was confused. My boss, Padam, pointed out that although this was a problem for me, no one else seemed concerned. (I'll say more about Padam and some of the things he taught me in another chapter.)

What did however become clear was that my new role at the CHP was leading me further and further away from clinical medicine. At one village health post we opened a tuberculosis workshop. As Nepali health workers and I sat in a circle, the participants introduced themselves. I heard that many had started out as teachers, and later trained in health. My career path was moving in the opposite direction.

One night I dreamed vividly about a job interview in London. At it I met peers from medical school. They presented themselves with panache. I was wearing the wrong clothes, and felt like a country mouse in town. I came nowhere near getting the job. The following day I walked for five hours to a riverside village, where I talked with local leaders about formulating a new training programme for female community health volunteers. I was entertained at a wedding, and had an opportunity to do some Bible study with a friend. We drank lots of sweet Nepali tea and I found myself baffled by a mix of different tribal languages. The next day as I trekked home, I began to reflect on that dream. I found it a struggle trying to set aside my aspirations to pursue a medical career. But clearly God was leading me along new avenues.

Before I began work at the CHP, a colleague had investigated the link between adult literacy and health. He interviewed groups of women who had completed our three-year NFE programme. This quote embodies what many said: "I have learnt so much from being involved in this class – the importance of cleanliness and good hygiene; how to care for my children when they have fever or diarrhoea; and why immunisations are necessary. I have learned to read and write, and now enjoy reading just for fun. I can speak more confidently in front of other people. When I compare my life now with three years ago, I see that my family is more healthy. When I go shopping I can add up the bill and I know what the correct change should be. Before NFE, I had to rely on others to do this for me."

Each spring, groups of medical students visited the Programme to observe our activities. One year I set them the task of asking health workers what motivates them. A local female community health volunteer, explained, "I had many children. I knew nothing about health. I got an opportunity to be trained as a Community Health Volunteer. I learned a lot. My children and I had intestinal worms then, but after the training, and by following the things that I had learned, my family has become healthy. I want the other villagers to be the same, so I try to teach them what I know – washing of hands and food, salt sugar solution for diarrhoea, the use of pit toilets. It costs a lot to go to hospital, and even for paracetamol you have to pay 100 rupees [about a day's wages]. Nowadays I have a medicine kit, and it costs almost nothing. I want the pregnant women to be healthy. Though we are not rich, I want my neighbours' children to get proper food and not be malnourished. I went through so many trials myself, that's why I want to help."

I like these two quotes. They demonstrate what a programme such as CHP can achieve.

Two vicar friends came to visit us in Amppipal. They commented on how 'non-medical' the Programme was. I wondered if this was because they had not seen a stethoscope or a medicine bottle. The CHP sought to equip local people with skills for promoting health. Our emphasis was not curative care. But I was still a 'health' worker. Although my clinical skills were becoming a little rusty, I was convinced that I was harnessing my professional training to perform a useful role in a deprived and needy location.

My ongoing learning was primarily achieved through the invaluable school of experience - 'learning by doing'. In the middle of our nine years in Nepal we returned to the UK for 12 months and I was able to study for a master's degree in 'public health for developing countries'. During that time an academic foundation was laid to under-gird the community health themes I'd started exploring on the field. Although (as a missionary) I was isolated from mainstream medicine, I was able to attend a number of conferences and short courses. I recognised how important it was to try and keep up to date with developments, as best I could. We did not have easy access to the Internet in the locations where we lived, but various professional bodies regularly sent me their journals[5]. These proved useful, although pressure of work often meant that I had insufficient time for reading. But one thing I made a point of doing during our years in Amppipal was to keep a diary and to review it frequently.

## Storytelling and life in the paddy fields

Nick –

Setting out from Amppipal I walked with colleagues for about six hours to reach villages in the north of our working area. Our aim was to help train local Non Formal Education facilitators.

Over the next three days a chicken with chicks, a skipping kid-goat, and a lazy dog joined us in class. At an evening event, I was cajoled into playing pass-the-parcel, with forfeits. I had to sing a song, so I chose my favourite one, 'Khushi, khushi manaou...' - 'Rejoice, and give honour to Jesus.'

Throughout our time in Nepal field visits were highlights for me. They were opportunities to get to know my colleagues better. And they also allowed time for story telling – an integral part of Nepali culture. I paid a return visit to the home of a local health worker. "Tell us a story again," said his landlord, "one about your religion this time." I told the story of Abraham and how during his test of faith he had even been prepared to sacrifice his son[6]. "Tell us a story about Jesus," he asked, so I told one of Jesus' own stories about a son who squandered everything, but whose father still loved him[7]. I don't know that I'm much of a storyteller, but people seemed keen to listen and kept asking for more.

I tried adapting Bible stories to the Nepali context: 'Near Amppipal there's a dangerous path that runs through dense rhododendron woodland. In winter the treetops are clothed in glorious red blooms. Half way along the path thugs attacked a traveller, robbed him of everything and left him for dead. An hour later a wealthy warrior-class Nepali saw his body by the path, but did not stop. A high-caste gentleman also came across the man. Thinking him dead, and fearing for his own life, he also hurried on. Finally a low-caste menial arrived. He went over to the semi-conscious man and gave him a drink. Assisting him to his feet, the helper clasped him around the waist and they staggered together to a lodge, an hour down the steep hillside path. The helper left enough money for curry and rice for three days and promised to return to pay any further expenses.

...So who was the neighbour to the injured man?'[8]

I attended a seminar on story telling. I learned that it was essential to let a story have its own meaning for the listener, and not attempt to impose one's own interpretation. The workshop leader explained: "It's no problem if stories raise unanswered questions. Ultimately we teach people in three ways: firstly, by our example; secondly, by our example; and thirdly, by our example"[9]. I collected stories from my colleagues too. 'A Hindu priest returned from a distant town on a big festival day. He was tired, hot and dirty from the long road, and arrived at the feast just as he was. An attendant met him at the gate, directed him to a long queue, and assigned him a place in the corner of the temple courtyard in the scorching sun. "It'll be three hours before I get near the food," he thought to himself, so he decided to have a wash and change his clothes. He returned to the temple with a fine robe flowing behind him. On seeing the priest's elaborate apparel, the steward hurried forward to welcome him, and everyone moved aside to make way for him. Seated in the cool shade of a sal-tree he was quickly offered a plate of tasty curried meat and chutneys. He took the meat pieces and began to smear them over his robes. Wide-eyed at the spectacle, those around the priest sought an explanation for his strange behaviour. "My coat got me this meal, so I guess it deserves its share," he replied.'

'A large group of guests arrived at a poor man's house. "How can my wife possibly cook rice for so many people?" he asked himself. So he went next door to his shopkeeper-neighbour and borrowed a large saucepan. The next day the man placed a small pan inside the big one and took them to the shop. "What's this other pan doing inside," said the shopkeeper rather sternly. Peering in, the poor man exclaimed, "Aah, how sweet, it's had a baby!" With a conceited expression and not the slightest hint of gratitude, the shopkeeper took both saucepans. Another day a distinguished guest arrived at the poor man's house. He slipped around to his neighbour once more, and this time asked to borrow a plate that would be suitable for his honoured guest. The shopkeeper selected his very best brassware. Over the next few days the poor man kept out of sight. After a week there was a loud hammering on his door. "Where's my plate?" demanded his irate neighbour. "Oh, didn't you hear?" he solemnly replied, "It died!'"

My second Nepal work assignment gave me as many hours travelling in buses as I'd spent walking the hills when we lived at Amppipal. As we bumped along a boulder-strewn track together, I mentioned to the man in the next seat that I was looking forward to celebrating Christmas. An hour or so later another man asked me to explain to him the essentials of the Christian faith. I told Jesus' story of the prodigal son. News travels, so as we walked around the town the following afternoon a young man stopped me and invited me to his home, saying he too was a Christian. During the evening I met with the five new believers that made up the tiny six-month-old church in the town. We read our Bibles, prayed and praised God together.

Another bus journey I often made was the six-hour trip from Pokhara to Kathmandu. One day, a Buddhist monk and Tibetan language teacher, named Thup-ten Lama, sat beside me. He prayed using his beads, while I silently worded the phrases of the Lord's Prayer. We chatted in a mixture of English and Nepali, and I learned how to say hello in Tibetan. By the end of the journey we were friends. He invited me to his home, so I joined his family for their Tibetan New Year celebrations the next day. There were piles of sweet breads that we washed down with salty butter-tea. Thup-ten pronounced a Tibetan blessing and we ate rice and mushroom soup with croutons. I was also offered homemade rice beer, served warm with inedible floating bits in it. After the meal they gave me a place to rest. There was some Tibetan singing, and Thup-ten's elderly father recited a story. I felt welcomed and warmly accepted there.

A year later I searched the monasteries of Pokhara, in the hope of finding and renewing friendship with Thup-ten

Lama. At the first monastery, I was ushered into an upper chamber where elderly gentlemen were engaged in a meeting. I greeted them, but quickly apologised and retreated – I was looking for a younger man. At the second one, bystanders directed me to the end of a row of small houses where Thup-ten Lama's wife welcomed me in. Strange, I thought, I didn't know he was married. And the photo on the wall was not the man I knew. At the third monastery, I came upon yet another Thup-ten Lama – a young primary school teacher – but he certainly bore no resemblance to my friend. It amazed me that I had met up with three Thup-tens that afternoon, but not the one I'd been looking for. I had no idea that it was such a common name.

Field visits and journeys were rewarding times, when I built close relationships with my Nepali colleagues and with people from the community. We lived together as a team and shared our thoughts with one another.

I used to find a corner to sit and read my Bible and drink my early morning cup of tea. How encouraged I was when colleagues showed an interest in what I was reading, or asked what the Bible teaches.

Ten years previously, in the UK, we had led an enquirers' course in Christian belief. It comprised six sessions of New Testament study that tackled basic questions like: 'Who was Jesus?' 'Why did he die?' and 'What are the costs of being a Christian?'[10] I was challenged by the course, so we decided to adapt it into Nepali and use it for teaching both singles and couples within the team.

## Subsistence farming

Nick –

Field visits also gave me insights into how local people lived. Most village Nepalis are farmers. It is a stunning sight to see the beautiful bright green paddy fields that are so cleverly constructed on the steep hillsides of Nepal. Not a square metre is wasted. On the six-inch wide terrace-edges, lentil plants utilise the soil still above water while their roots add strength to the terrace structure.

Subsistence farmers are wholly dependent on the weather. One spring the rains failed and the maize was ruined. On a festival day in that dry season we met a group of people making their way down to the river to pray for rain; they were carrying leaf plates loaded with flowers as offerings to appease Hindu gods.

It is not until June that the monsoon rains come as a deluge. Water cascades from terrace to terrace, and paths are turned to watercourses, aiding irrigation. Access becomes impossible, unless you are prepared to walk on top of the stone walls that lie alongside the paths. During the monsoon tending the rice fields becomes an all-absorbing occupation.

One day some colleagues and I found a buffalo wading in the paddy, eating rice plants. Scouting along terrace edges, shouting and beating the air with our sticks, we set about driving it back to the path. As we reached the bazaar, there was a heated debate in progress. "What's the issue?" I asked, "Rice irrigation."

Early one morning, Rosalind and I set out on an hour's walk to the village where a work colleague lived. We wanted to 'help' him in the enormous task he faced in preparing his fields. He first feasted us on rice, chicken and yogurt drink made by his wife, using the milk of their two buffalo. The meal over, he armed me with the tool I needed for the day's labour. We followed the party down a narrow slippery path to the family's land.

In the nursery bed Rosalind uprooted rice seedlings and tied them into bundles. I began to learn how to maintain the narrow, steeply terraced, water-filled fields. I trimmed the old retaining edges, and rebuilt them with clods of fresh weed-free mud. As I dug, by hand, corner sections that the bull-drawn plough had missed, I was plastered in mud. It reminded me of my boyhood days spent in Cornwall with my cousins, when we larked about constructing dams and watercourses. I attempted driving a yoked pair of bulls to plough and level the mud, but discovered that I couldn't speak 'bull', so they went their way, not mine.

When farmers plough with a pair of bulls, an experienced animal is often made to work with a younger one. The older one takes the lead and sets the pace. Jesus said, "Take my yoke upon you and learn from me"[11]. I realised that Jesus' invitation is to walk close with him, side-by-side in fellowship – like those two bulls yoked together. There's work to do, but He leads and sets the pace for our lives.

The women planted the ploughed fields with seedling rice up to the very edges, with precision spacing, and at top speed. Ros stooped to work alongside them, shin-deep in mud that oozed between her toes. We worked much more slowly than our companions, but felt we earned our mid-afternoon snack of rice, curry, deep-fried breads and sweet Nepali tea. As we walked home to take a bucket-shower, neighbours laughed with us at our appearance, saying we must have been 'playing in the mud'. We ached all over for the next week.

Some months later, when we hoped to conduct a community meeting at a nearby village, again everyone was too busy. The village chairman and his wife were threshing millet in the front yard of their home by beating it with long canes. While we waited for the health volunteer to return from an errand, we watched her sister re-mud the veranda. Another lady spoke with us while she worked at weaving a rice-straw mat. Her husband meanwhile was winnowing rice in the light breeze.

*Subsistence farming in the Himalayas.*

I will always remember the time when we stopped at a stone resting-place in the mid-morning sun, and a visiting expatriate colleague from Kathmandu read from Psalm 129. This song includes several rural images: ploughmen making long straight furrows; grass that struggles to grow on a thatched roof; reaping the harvest; and binding sheaves. The Bible came alive for us in its vivid depiction of the daily activities we witnessed around us. Now I can picture someone broadcasting seed, or labourers at a threshing floor.

## A new Director for CHP

Nick –

Amid the frantic after-tea bustle in our home, settling Lydia and dealing with the night watchman at the door, Padam sat cross-legged but upright on the cushions on the floor. In his gentle arms Elizabeth dropped off to sleep. His warm round face and kindly manner were immediately attractive. He wore the Community Health Programme uniform: black trousers and a white shirt.

My colleagues and friends described Padam Parajuli as 'a brother', 'a father', 'like Jesus among us'. In a song he wrote, he described 'yielding his life as a gift'. We were delighted when we learned that he was to be appointed as our new Director, for we recognised the privilege of working under the leadership of such a godly man.

*Padam Parajuli.*

During the evening, he told his story. Born in Pokhara, he came from a Hindu family. As a boy he was devoted to the goddess Kalika. Before class he would go to her temple and pay her homage, firmly believing that she would help him in his studies.

Padam was studious and he would often test himself with general knowledge questions. There was one question that had him baffled -"Which is the largest book of scripture in the world?" He began to think about the Hindu epics he had read, such as the Ramayana and the Mahabharata, which are about six inches thick. But he was surprised to learn from his textbook that the Bible was the correct answer. "It must be at least a foot thick," he thought to himself. "I must see if I can find one somewhere."

Padam was only the third student in his village to obtain the School Leavers' Certificate. He shared books with an educated woman in the community, who, though not a Christian believer, offered him a Bible one day. Padam was astonished how easily he could handle it, for it was not the enormous volume he had been expecting. He began reading from the New Testament, but the names of places and people were a mystery to him. His friend explained some of them. She also invited him to church. He had not heard the word 'church' before, so although he agreed, he had no idea where he was going.

What impressed him about the church was that people shook his hand: "I was used to shaking hands with my friends but not with my seniors." In caste-conscious Nepal this was a gesture of equality. He continued to go to church, but more out of admiration for the pastor's skill in translating the preaching from English to Nepali, than anything else.

Padam got the chance to train in laboratory work and stayed with a Christian family. But his heart was still unmoved:

"I am a Hindu. Whatever I do, I will remain Hindu; and I will not eat buffalo meat or drink alcohol." As he worked at a mission hospital, he learned more about Christianity, and was again impressed that his seniors treated him, a junior, on equal terms. Gradually he became disillusioned with Hinduism, and his Christian landlord helped him on the road to faith in Jesus. Some time later, a group of new believers were being baptised, and he asked to go and watch. By this point he felt that he was neither a Hindu nor yet a Christian. It was clear, however, that the Holy Spirit was at work in his heart, as he decided to put some spare clothes in his bag, before making his way to the river. As the baptisms took place, he felt compelled to publicly confess the Lord Jesus as his Saviour, and asked if he too could be baptised. The leaders talked and prayed with him, warning him of the cost of becoming a Christian: "You may well be imprisoned for taking a stand for Christ." But he was undeterred. That was August 1974.

Although he did not face physical persecution, Padam frequently experienced the pain of isolation. He found it very difficult relating to his family during Hindu festivals. At first he 'escaped', saying he had to work at the hospital and could not get leave. Both he and his parents were unhappy about this. Thankfully his father showed him some sympathy, and did not insist on him having to wear a tika (the red powder mark on the forehead that shows someone has taken part in Hindu worship), and he was not prevented from eating with the family. But when visitors came for worship he would leave the house and kill time at the local bazaar. From that time on it was possible for Padam to go home for Hindu festivals. Neither side was compromised. Padam worked for 19 years in Tansen. He developed skills in community health work as a team leader and gained competence in many disciplines, including how to perform simple dental procedures. He also matured into a quiet but forthright leader in the local Christian church. He met and married Shanti. They reared two children. Then, in January 1996, became Director of Gorkha Community Health Programme at Amppipal. This was a whole day's journey from the family home in Tansen, resulting in long periods of separation from his wife and two student-age children – a sacrifice he was willing to make for the work he believed God had for him to do in Gorkha.

One thing that Padam had a passionate longing for was unity and harmony among God's people. When asked how he viewed the church in Nepal, he expressed concern about the rivalry between Nepali leaders of different denominations. "Forty-five years ago there were only three or four Christians in Nepal. Now the Church is widespread. But with growth has come division."

"And what are your dreams for the future?"
He revealed a heartfelt yearning to help needy Christian communities. He spoke confidently of God's providential care encompassing every aspect of a believer's life. His two favourite scripture verses were – "My grace is sufficient for you" and "I can do everything through him who gives me strength"[12].

Although of high caste, he lorded it over no one. He was the most unassuming man I have ever met. Shortly after he arrived at CHP, Padam set to and cleaned the very grimy office toilet. At his final staff annual picnic he served everyone and ate last.

He displayed unusual wisdom in dealing with day-to-day situations, and never rushed into making decisions. He suffered from a stiff foot, which reduced his pace of walking. He once said to me, on a day when I was pacing out ahead of him, "If you want to learn from me, you must first learn to walk slowly."

We all relished his delightful sense of humour. He always kept a level head and was never known to get angry. He was a man of vision and had the amazing gift of being able to re-focus hearts and minds, to enable others to see things from his perspective.

There was not much you could teach Padam about inter-personal skills. Three of us were hard at it, planning a workshop, when two new faces arrived at the door. Padam immediately made strangers feel at ease, warmly welcoming them as he would friends. "Hello, do come in and sit down." With a genuine sense of interest and concern, he asked who they were, where they lived and what they did. Aware that we needed to continue our workshop discussion, Padam, with the utmost courtesy and tact, gently suggested that they may like to relax for a little while in the next-door room, reading our newspapers. This was so typical of the man who had such a heart for people.

Early one morning, Padam came to our door with a problem. Our half-time office cleaner had requested money to support her daughter through a two-year course. She had passed the school leavers' exams and attained a training place. Over the next few days we discussed and formulated ground-rules for a 'Local Peoples' Training Fund'. The fund supported one trainee at a time, encouraging family members to help contribute towards the expenses. Over a number of years, expatriate and Nepali donors gave anonymously to the fund, which assisted half a dozen or so trainees.

Padam was an active member of the church committee. He always let others contribute their views before offering his own. When he preached, he usually began with a light-hearted story. He always applied his sermons to his own life. One Nepali church member said that she hadn't seen a good role model for the Christian life until Padam came and lived among them.

To avoid being alone, Padam brought his young nephew, Mohan, to live with him in Amppipal. We began to get to know him. One afternoon, as we arrived home from a weekend away, we met members of the church returning from a Christian burial. Mohan and I went back to the graveside and stood silently under the trees, looking at the crudely lashed cross. We prayed together, asking God to bless and comfort the widow. And we placed our own lives in God's hands. I knew, from that short prayer time together, that Mohan, like his uncle, was a believer in the Lord Jesus.

On Saturday June 28th 1997, Padam left Amppipal for three weeks' annual leave with his wife and family at Tansen. Late in the evening on the following Monday, his son heard him singing a song "I'll be at Jesus' side." In the morning his wife found him dead. He had died peacefully but unexpectedly, aged only 43.

The week that followed was one of the most exhausting of our whole time in Nepal. In my morning devotions, I read Genesis chapter 39, recording how God gave Joseph added responsibility. We are told the Lord was with Joseph and that his work prospered. I opened my diary and felt compelled to pen a simple question to God: "And so with me?" I had an inkling that God had something in store for me, but was quite unprepared for what was to follow. Within two hours of making my diary entry, I learned of Padam's death and was asked to become the interim Director of CHP. My emotions went up and down like a yo-yo. Sometimes I was able to think and plan; at other times I was consumed with tears.

Padam had been a gentle, humble and just man. He had given such wise counsel and had always been available when we needed him. It was he who had guided our programme's work and had stood by us in times of crisis. The church felt his loss very keenly, as he had been a fatherly figure, providing much-needed mature leadership. What's more, he'd played board games with us and made us laugh as well.

His simple and transparent faith was matched by a simple lifestyle. He had no designs on wealth or prestige. He was a man with a grateful heart, who was satisfied with very little. For him, a basic meal of rice and lentils was as good as a feast. I can think of no Nepali we respected more. And now he was gone. My rational thinking was punctuated with spasms of grief over the loss of one whom I loved and who had given me so much.

A night watchman and the part-time cleaner came weeping to our door on hearing about his death. Padam had cared for ordinary people and helped in so many practical ways.

Rosalind travelled to Tansen with a programme colleague and our baby Elizabeth to express our sympathy to his widow. She showed great courage and faith. Tears filled her eyes, as Rosalind handed her Padam's Bible and some personal photographs from his Amppipal flat.

His departure changed my role. I juggled my work as Director with ongoing report writing. At the time of Padam's death, we thought the event might create spiritual openness among my colleagues. But that didn't seem to happen, and we wondered where we had failed, or what we should have done differently. I was, however, aware of an upsurge of support from the Programme staff. Understanding the financial accounts was not the black hole I had feared. Being in a position of responsibility highlighted yet again the need for me to improve my language skills.

The situation faced by Mohan, Padam's nephew, gave us cause for concern. He was eager to remain at school in Amppipal but had no home, or guardian figure there any more. He was a keen leader of the church youth fellowship. It would have been all too easy for us foreigners to say that this was the Nepali church's problem, but our Nepali friends rightly pointed out that we could share with them the responsibility of finding the solution. Mohan stayed on in the village, supported by the church that paid him a small youth-leader 'honorarium'. We tried to encourage him in his studies and his Christian walk by meeting with him over a meal once a week.

Mohan, however, failed the School Leavers' Certificate examination. We knew he was quite weak academically, but we had hoped he would overcome this hurdle. At twenty-two, he was fed up with repeating school years again and again. As I left for a short period of leave in the UK, I suggested to some of my colleagues that they might consider offering Mohan a short-term post in the CHP.

In my absence, a vacancy did arise which could not be filled with a qualified candidate, and they appointed him on a three-month contract. We were so heartened that they had not discriminated against him because he was a follower of Jesus. He was pleased to have this chance to prove himself, but sadly owing to lack of qualifications, it was not possible to make his position permanent.

## Preparing for change...

Nick –

I had left general practice in the UK and had found a new role in Nepal. My first appointment had been as the Community Programme's 'Health Consultant' with occasional stints of medical practice at a mission hospital. I was a learner, an encourager, and coach of others. I did some creative tasks too. I moved on to become a trainer in healthcare, and developed many new skills. My basic language proficiency forced me to adopt participatory methods of teaching. Padam had modelled a style of servant leadership that I tried to emulate. When I took over his role, I found that I was faced with many new responsibilities - so I had to go through the cycle of being a learner once again.

Nepalis take a keen interest in foreigners. It's easy to strike up a conversation in the street. But while language learning in Kathmamdu, I found myself deliberately trying to avoid making contact with some of those I saw day-by-day. I would accelerate my walking pace, and put on a veneer of 'I'm too busy now.' I realise that Western Christian missionaries worldwide are often criticised for being 'so busy with their work, their meetings, and driving around in 4-wheel-drive jeeps, that they never have time to stop and talk.' Thankfully there were no motor vehicles in Amppipal. So I promised myself that I would not pretend to be busy, but give time to those I met along the way.

Thankfully, I generally did keep to my promise, and as a result made many acquaintances. When occasionally I was silly enough to play the game of looking busy, I'm sure everyone could see through my pretence.

During our years at Amppipal, my roles and motivation shifted and evolved. As far as work was concerned, I tried to keep two priorities central in my life – my desire to see the health of local communities improve, and my hope that those around me might know Jesus more. Very often my activities seemed to be focused almost exclusively on one or the other. Highlights of my life were when I managed to combine these priorities.

# CHAPTER 5

# BLENDING AND BLUNDERING

## Roles for Rosalind and language progress

Ros –

We were proud of our progress in language learning during the five months of orientation. However when we arrived in Amppipal the language teacher there soon cut us down to size. He leafed through my vocabulary book and covered it in red pen. We had been told not to be concerned about long and short 'e's which are written as a loop over the letter, either forwards or backwards. But our new teacher, who had studied Sanskrit in Varanasi, was a strict traditionalist. Orthography was important. He proved an excellent instructor, adept at the art of language practice through sustained conversation. He gave us dictation most lessons, read books and articles with us and listened to us read aloud. The 'Amppipal Nepali' he taught was the equivalent of Oxford English, with all the correct verb endings. It stood us in good stead.

I enjoyed language learning and it added to my appreciation of the culture. There are at least three different words for 'rice' in Nepali, depending on whether it's cooked, uncooked or grain-with-the-husk. To 'eat potato', however, means to fail, so a 'potato watch' is un-repairable.

I never managed to master the precise terms used for the myriad of different family members. Relations have different names depending whether they are on the mother's or the father's side of the family, and according to their seniority. Similarly there were words designating the birth order of children in a family. I found I had a bond with other first-born daughters, and Nick related easily with last-born sons. The names for 1st, 2nd, 3rd and 4th daughters rhymed attractively: maili, kaili, saili, taili.

On a slippery path a Nepali might say, 'don't catch fish'. When river fishing in Nepal, you launch your whole body forward to cast your net. We joked about frying the fish we'd caught for our tea as we skidded in the mud.

Some of the most confusing words were ones that have been borrowed from English. A 'der-rum' is a barrel; a 'muffler' is a scarf. I searched all over town for a plug for our sink until I realised I needed to ask for a 'chain plug'.

## At our home

Ros –

I had three priorities during our first year in Amppipal: Lydia, language and letters. I cared for our two-year-old daughter, learned Nepali and corresponded with family and friends. The next year, our second daughter's arrival re-shaped my priorities. But whatever my own ideas, it was often the callers at the door who demanded my attention.

One day, in a steady stream from 7am, I counted no less than nineteen visitors to our home. These included two sewing ladies, a porter, three church friends, a fruit vendor, two short-term expatriates, our three regular workers and the milk seller.

*Our milk lady called each day. Sometimes*
*we checked it with a lactometer...*
*and paid less for diluted milk.*

A village woman came to the door, but I had no idea why. She unwrapped part of the long strip of cloth bound round her waist, to reveal a small chicken's egg and a few beans, which she wanted to sell me. "Would you like to buy a chicken?" asked another woman on the doorstep. "What chicken?" I thought. Casually she uncovered the unfortunate creature tucked under her shawl. I went shopping about once a week. This entertained Lydia, exercised my language skills, and got me out of the house. With baby Elizabeth safely in the backpack, Lydia and I would set out down some steep stone steps, and along the edge of a terraced field where the maize had just been planted. I held Lydia's hand and coaxed her along. She often watched her shadow as it 'walked' along a lower terrace. "Look where you're going," I warned her. She could easily have lost her balance and fallen on to the next level below, a drop of some 6 to 8 feet. Buffalo grazed nearby, munching the leaves on a tree. Lydia liked climbing the stone steps on all fours and I would help her up and over a wall to join another path. She ran through the dry leaves, blissfully unaware of the hidden stones that might trip her up. A hundred yards further on, we passed a neighbour using ash to scrub pots blackened from cooking her morning rice. We greeted one another. Her chicks cheeped under an upturned wicker basket. Lydia stopped to count them. Children on their way to school giggled or tried out their English on us. I pointed out 'our' buffalo as we passed the neat courtyard of the home our milk came from.

The tailors' off-cuts strewn on the path indicated we had nearly reached the bazaar. The first shop we came to sold bangles and trinkets. Then there were a couple of tailors, a goldsmith, a grocer and some rather dingy teashops. A couple of places sold cloth and some ready-made garments. Women and schoolchildren hung around the wooden shuttered doorway of the grocery store we entered.

Inside people leaned all along the wooden counter. A harassed-looking middle-aged man, with quick eyes and a patient smile fielded requests from all quarters. I was never quite sure how the queuing system worked. Someone sorted through a tin of pins. A woman received a packet of cigarettes, and then rejected them for another brand. A young man paid five rupees for what locals referred to as 'chocolate' - a handful of cheap toffee sweets.

I stood and studied the merchandise. It was amazing what was stacked away. One side of the shop was piled high with flip-flops in plastic bags. The shelves on the other side bulged with T-shirts, cloth shoulder bags, wrap-around skirts and Nepali men's caps. Behind the counter were jars of sweets, squares of washing soap, green packets of 'Quality Dust Tea', packets of instant noodles, glucose biscuits, lighters, bottles of ink, piles of exercise books, torches, hair clips, Horlicks, and Red Tooth Powder.

I caught the shopkeeper's eye and asked for a kilo of onions.

"Sorry, not today, Madam."
"Never mind, tomorrow will do. Any garlic?"
"Yes."
"Good, I'll have half a kilo."
He disappeared through a side door, and returned with a bag of bulbs. To check the weight he hooked two metal pans to the weighing scale's crossbar. They balanced.
"Tea?"
"Only the small packets."
"I'll wait."
"And sugar?"

From somewhere below the counter he measured sugar into a plastic bag. Sugar was sold by volume rather than weight - I needed five manas (a mana is about half a litre). I handed my box over for some eggs, and a schoolboy helped fill it. Other schoolchildren pressed in all around - some left once they'd been given a sweet; one peered over to read my shopping list. While the shopkeeper totted up the bill, I looked at a smudgy wall calendar, and a poster of the large blue elephant god, Ganesh, surrounded by a jumbled assortment of other Hindu figures in gaudy colours.

I recognised Nepali numbers, but still found it quicker to convert them into English to check the addition. I waited for my change, loaded up the rucksack, and headed out into the sunlight with Lydia to make our homeward journey. The contrast with my weekly shop in an English supermarket couldn't have been more stark.

The pattern of life changed in many other ways too. During a typical week I ate rice and lentils at half past eight on six mornings. I frequently entertained groups of Nepali colleagues to snacks of beaten rice, vegetable curry, and tea. We lived a simple life style. I watched no television. Instead, I gazed at the stars in all their brilliance and identified Leo for the first time. Rather than give money to a charity, I bought cloth to make school uniforms for our cook's children. I ate papaya and mulberries in place of blackberry and apple. And I listened to sermons in Nepali rather than in English.

Some things, however, remained the same. It was important for me to keep my spiritual life fresh. I read a portion of John's gospel with one of Nick's colleagues; prayed regularly with an expatriate friend, and participated in communion once a month on a Wednesday evening. I organised an Easter egg hunt. We made a point of celebrating festivals.

Small children the world over restrict what their mothers can do. In Amppipal it was hard to get out of the house – I needed to plan ahead and hire a porter to carry Elizabeth. When Nick was available to help with the children, we would go on longer walks. These reminded me there was a wider world. Every two to three months I needed to travel out of Amppipal to prevent the onset of cabin fever. I needed the stimulation of a new environment to widen my horizons again.

I gradually took on other roles too. I became Nepal 'correspondent' for our mission agency - encouraging others to write articles for publication. I chaired the tutorial group committee to support the expatriate school and teacher. I started a correspondence course on prophecy, and this led on to a degree course with the Open Theological College. It was good to exercise my brain.

## Playgroup and school

Ros –

Without libraries, parks and swimming pools, it was difficult to keep young children occupied. Sometimes I drew inspiration from books of craft ideas for toddlers. Our playgroup was a lifeline. In Amppipal, another Mum and I set this up together. The sessions started with play dough modelling. We Mums joined in with this with this – I love the feel of play dough.

Sometimes a story developed out of the figures we formed, or we used them to bring events back home in the UK to life…

"Let's say this is your cousin" (play dough figure balanced on a stubby horse torso).
"She was out riding last week – dum-de-dum - happily riding along, when her horse stumbled and she fell off" (figure drops to the ground).
"O dear she has hurt her arm. She has to go to hospital. Now her arm's in a sling (dough arm quickly attached) but she's feeling much better".

Each week, our theme, such as transport, or farm animals inspired a craft activity. After a snack we read a story and sang, finishing with 'Jack-in-the-box'. We had a large cardboard box, big enough for a pre-schooler to stand in. During the song each child had the chance to be 'Jack'.

On other weekdays, for my own sanity and sense of routine, I followed a guide for pre-school years that suggested thematic activities day by day. However there was not so much rubbish packaging available for 'crafts' as there is in the West. So when we were doing a series on nursery rhymes I remember it was a small triumph when I realised we could make 'candlesticks' from the sturdy local washing up bottles. I cut the tops off, the girls coloured in flames, and then we jumped over our creations to illustrate 'Jack be nimble'.

In the afternoons we often went for a walk. Although the children set a frustratingly slow pace, we had time to take a closer look at interesting leaves or bugs along the path. We saw chickens, goats, pigs and buffalo. One day we stopped to watch a nanny goat that had just given birth and was licking the tiny kid clean.

It was customary for the Umbrella Organisation to set up a small primary school for missionary children in each of their projects. In Amppipal the expatriate team roped me in as the non-parent representative on the Tutorial Group's management committee. (At that time, Lydia was still pre-school age). I became the chairperson. I observed how crucial an issue children's education is for parents. The committee's role was to support the teacher. We also established term dates, and dealt with matters relating to the school premises: repairing the roof, or coping with damp in the library. Up until then I had been so wrapped up in my own family, that I had little idea of the difficulties faced by the one and only resident teacher. It made me appreciate her level of commitment over three difficult years of service.

In the following year staff shortages resulted in a lack of continuity in the teaching. This became very apparent when Lydia joined the school. During her first year, there were several months when there was no teacher; and the following year we had a succession of five short-termers, who stayed between eight days and three months.

At such times, we were forced to experiment with home schooling. A little Irish girl and Lydia were both in first year primary. Her mother and I tried to teach the two of them, but I found educating Lydia at home almost impossible. We clashed, and she refused to co-operate. So we combined forces with the other mothers and children, even though it meant walking half an hour down the hill to the Tutorial Group's room. I taught the 7 to 9 year olds, while their mothers worked with Lydia and her friend. We found it helped to use the classroom. I ran a project on the Tudors, resourced from a materials' bank in Kathmandu headquarters. We acted Shakespeare and voyaged round the world with Drake. A Tudor banquet marked the finale of the project. We feasted on peas pottage and eggs; we played 'trump' with cards and 'hazard' with dice.

## Angels unaware?

"I will lift up my eyes to the hills –
where does my help come from?
My help comes from the Lord,
the Maker of Heaven and earth…
The Lord will watch over your coming and going
both now and for evermore"[13].

Ros –

In England we took easy journeys for granted. We planned them to the second and grumbled when the train was a minute late. In Nepal journeys are risky and unpredictable. They made us conscious of our dependence on God, and we saw His faithfulness first-hand.

The girls and I travelled from Amppipal to meet Nick in Anandaban, south of Kathmandu. The journey to the capital usually took a day: five hours' walk and five hours by road, and Anandaban was a good hour further on. I only attempted the marathon in one day because another expatriate family had offered me a seat in their hired vehicle. We set out on foot together, encouraging the children with promises of cold Coke when we reached the road, and chips for lunch. We chatted about how relaxed we felt knowing there would be a jeep to pick us up. But when we got there, there was no vehicle in sight. Humph! Did anyone know about a hired jeep? No. We ended up squashed into the lavishly over-decorated cab of a Tata truck. After jolting 13 kilometres to the main road, we clambered out, and stood in a huddle, wondering what the next step might be. Within half an hour my friends had negotiated seats on a tourist bus, and we set off again. It proved an excruciatingly slow ride. As we approached the capital, I noticed a rainbow against the black clouds. It was above an advertising hoarding for a watch. 'Yes, Lord, you know about the timings of our comings and goings,' I reflected. Having reached the ring road, I stepped off the bus and landed in some foul black grime on the ground. We took a short taxi ride for the next leg of the journey to Patan. My plan to catch a bus from Patan to Anandaban fell through, as the last bus had long since left. I didn't want to be faced with an exorbitant taxi fare, but as the light was fading I began to wonder what other options were left. I was reluctant to spend the night in Kathmandu.

Quite unexpectedly a polite dark-skinned gentleman appeared and asked in immaculate English, "Can I help?" I explained my plight. "Just wait a moment, I have a vehicle going to Anandaban in ten minutes. You're lucky my meeting finished late – I wouldn't normally be returning at this time." Our Father was looking after us.

I have already told about a trip to the shops. Just getting out of the house in Amppipal with two young children was an effort. One day I planned to go down the hill for a coffee morning, leaving home at half past nine. At a quarter to ten my porter had not yet arrived, so I set off with Elizabeth screaming in the backpack, wondering how I would cope. I'd just recovered from diarrhoea and still felt weak. The steep winding path through the wood was unusually slippery, strewn with loose leaves ankle-deep, as our neighbours had been cutting firewood. I felt apprehensive. Lydia, aged two, toddled ahead and fell headlong. Feeling unsteady with the unaccustomed load on my back, I blundered forward as fast as I could to comfort her. It was at this point I sent up a hasty prayer for help to get us down the hill. We went on gingerly. Less than five minutes later, a friend appeared. He was a man of few words, but a believer. In a flash, he confidently swept Lydia up in his arms, and delivered her safely to the main path. I was convinced he was an angel. We continued along that path, until my tardy porter appeared. I gratefully handed Elizabeth over to her.

## Energised vermin

Ros –

Eighteen months after our arrival at Amppipal we noticed tall straight tree trunks lying at regular intervals along the nearby paths. A month later, a single light bulb glowed enticingly in the bazaar to prove that electricity would soon be available to everyone. Nick had wired up our home so that the lights could run either on mains electricity, or from the solar panel. We used a large red switch to transfer from one power source to the other. We bought a fridge. We no longer boiled the milk twice a day. And I was able to make ice cream for the first time.

But one day, as our helper wiped down our spanking new fridge, sparks flew out at the back. Rats had gnawed the plastic-coated cables, leaving bare wire. Rats also ate the office mouse (well, its cable anyway). We wondered if they felt energized after nibbling the wire to our battery charger.

Shrews, with their narrow pointed noses, were much more difficult to trap than rats. The oily food odour coming from the bucket under our kitchen sink seemed to attract them. One morning we found a shrew paddling around in the dirty water. A couple of days later, a trail of pink baby shrews (each holding its sibling's tail in its mouth) proceeded across the kitchen floor. Hidden among our pots and pans in the back of a cupboard, we discovered a shrew's larder of old potatoes.

## Discovering the local church... worse than a language lesson

Ros –

At Amppipal attending church was no easier than it had been in Kathmandu. We wondered whether other families faced the same struggles as we did in trying to arrive on time. Just before leaving for church, minor family crises would arise: we would discover a dirty nappy; or Nick would be busy chasing up a watchman who was late for duty. Leeches found ways to crawl between our toes, or under the straps of our sandals as we walked down to church. We pulled them off as we removed our shoes at the church door. Occasionally, in the middle of the service a bloated black leech would drop off on to the carpet. Leeches inject an anticoagulant, so a leech bite continues to bleed for several minutes. I found the bite marks itched for days.

Everyone sat on mats on the floor - men on one side of the room, women on the other. Children seemed to gravitate to the women's side. I sat cross-legged but it was hard to keep my legs modestly covered in my wrap-around skirt, with small children clambering over my knees. As soon as one child settled comfortably, the other would press her claim to a portion of Mum's lap. At those conspicuously quiet moments in a service that mothers dread, I resorted to breastfeeding. This was such a useful tactic that I continued breastfeeding Elizabeth until she was two. I looked enviously at Nepali mothers with their quiet, submissive children, sitting peacefully in church; but I was also pleased that my active and inquisitive children thrived on stimulation.

After the notices, the service leader chose someone to give thanks for the offering and pray for the children's class and the preacher. I learned to avoid making eye contact, for fear of being 'volunteered'. Sitting through an hour-long Nepali sermon I couldn't understand proved something of a challenge. I decided it was best to use the time to read my Bible quietly, or pray for those around me.

Another thing I did, when the children were not distracting me, was to mark new words in the hymnbook in pencil for subsequent translation. This enabled me to compile a transliteration and rough translation of the songs we sang most frequently. Short-term expatriate visitors, my parents and later my children found the book made it possible for them to participate in Nepali singing.

And how did we cater for our children? In Amppipal we organised a toddlers' Bible story for the expatriate under-fives at the same time as the regular class for Nepali speaking children. Parents took it in turn to lead this so that the others could remain in church to hear the sermon.

For me, building relationships with Nepali believers at church was painstakingly slow, particularly at Amppipal. This was partly due to the fact that expatriates tended to come and go, and so Nepalis were reluctant to make deep friendships.

I noted triumphantly in my diary the first time I was bold enough to share a request at the prayer meeting – two years after arriving in Nepal. But I couldn't understand why the young people found it so amusing. I discovered afterwards that I had mispronounced one of the four types of 'd' in Nepali, and asked prayer for Nick's 'passing wind' instead of his 'study'! I blush as I remember it.

## Adopting a Nepali brother

Nick –

I was somewhat calculating as I looked around the small hall where the Amppipal church met. I prayed: "Who could I approach and ask to be my prayer partner?" I noticed Syam, an older Christian who had no interest in learning English.

The half hour spent with Syam became a weekly highlight. I prayed hesitantly, and attempted to read from a simplified Bible version, but we both knew the bond of being Christian brothers.

One day I met Syam in his fields. He was guarding newly planted maize from his neighbours' goats. In our Bible reading that day we looked at the fruits of God's Spirit in our lives. Another day, after reading about sharing one another's burdens, I met some neighbours on my way home, and helped them carry their load of wood up the hill.

Have you ever got someone into trouble simply by showing friendship to them? Syam was not a man of means. But his neighbours harshly criticised him, as they were under the mistaken impression that he received money from me. I wondered what my response should be. After I prayed, I felt at peace and we continued to meet.

Ros –

When our girls were small, the most stressful time of day was around 5pm. The children were crotchety; Nick was still at work; and the evening meal was burning because I'd left a pan on the stove, to answer the door. I'm sure it was another tactic of God's enemy that on Tuesday evenings things always seemed to go wrong. Nick dashed in from work, collected his Bible, and headed off down the hill to meet Syam. Instead of admiring Nick's dedication and godliness, I found it a struggle to let him go. "Why should I have to hold the fort?" I thought to myself. It took some time to recognise that we had a joint ministry, and we relied on one another. Nick had the more external, visible role, but he appreciated that I was freeing him up for that. I remember how encouraged I was when he acknowledged this to his friends. We came to an amicable arrangement: one afternoon a week on his day off, he would take responsibility for the girls, and that gave me time for study.

## Festivals and rites of passage the Nepali way

Ros –

At that time Christmas day was not recognised as a national holiday in Nepal but Christians took the day off to participate in church celebrations. In Amppipal the Christmas service was supposed to begin at ten, but long after then groups of women continued busily peeling garlic, chopping onions and grinding spices. They cooked a meal over big wood fires. Three hours later we queued for rice and curries, and ate, squatting on the ground outside. The afternoon continued with a 'programme' of songs, skits, and homemade entertainment. For our children, and for us too, this marathon event was an ordeal. We usually slipped away after the meal to take pre-arranged phone calls from our families in England. Turkey and Christmas pudding were amply made up for by an expatriate team meal on another day, when we shared our stockpiled supplies of tinned ham and chocolate.

On December evenings, a group of Amppipal believers would make their way along the dark winding paths around the village, visiting homes. I can still sense the thrill and joy of being with them. We sang a carol, and one person told the story of Jesus' birth, explaining how He left the riches of heaven to be born in an ordinary stable. A nearby buffalo shed served as a suitable visual aid. We then prayed for the family. The few Nepali carols we learned are imprinted on my memory, and it is these hymns I miss most of all.

On various special occasions during the year, our Hindu friends presented us with leaf plates filled with festival specialities - deep-fried ring-shaped bread, and spicy chutneys. We decided to prepare some extra festival food at Christmas and Easter to give our neighbours: homemade biscuits cut in the shape of stars; hot cross buns; and hard-boiled eggs painted red, after the Greek orthodox tradition. Sharing in this way gave us opportunities to explain the significance of our festivals. I remember one neighbour's amazement, "You certainly know what you are celebrating," she exclaimed.

The one time in the year when even the poorest of our village neighbours feasted on meat was at Dasai, the biggest Hindu festival in Nepal. It was the traditional practice to offer meat to guests. So at Dasai, our workers, colleagues and neighbours eagerly invited us to their homes. Nepalis are warm, generous and lavishly hospitable. They piled our plates high and garnished the food with fermented radish chutney. I was thankful that Nick had a big appetite and readily accepted second and third helpings, a tangible sign of appreciation. I learned how to eat slowly, and declined further helpings by putting my hands over my plate. But as my food got cold it became less appetising. The hardest part for me was chewing through the 'meat'. It seemed that village butchery ensured every piece contained bone, flesh, gristle and skin. I even picked out bits with hairs on. It was sad and ironic that I didn't enjoy the meat our hosts could ill afford to give us.

When a parent dies, sons are expected to perform the prescribed Hindu rituals. Neighbours and family put pressure on Christians to follow these customs. When we went out walking, people frequently analysed the make up of our family. "You have no son?" they would ask incredulously. For Hindus a son is deemed necessary to ensure a safe passage in the journey beyond death. We explained that the son we relied on for salvation was Jesus, the Son of God.

When a Nepali Christian girl gets married there is debate about the style and colour of her wedding outfit. Should she wear a red sari (as Hindu brides do), or a white wedding gown (seen as Western and therefore 'Christian', but the colour of mourning in Nepal), or something different? At the first Nepali Christian wedding I attended, the bride wore a white sari topped with a fluorescent green shawl.

After a village Christian wedding I asked Elizabeth's porter what she had made of the ceremony. She thought back wistfully to her own brief and sad Hindu marriage, quickly arranged and quickly shattered when her husband abandoned her to look after their disabled daughter on her own. "Today everyone gave their public consent," she said, "that was a pukka wedding."

At five months, a Nepali girl is fed her 'first rice' amid much Hindu ceremony. Family and friends smear red powder on to her forehead, pronounce a blessing, and give her new clothes and money. When Elizabeth was five months old, we wanted to show our gratitude to God for her life, and invited our friends, neighbours and colleagues to celebrate with us in church.

Maya and Alli set off at 10am and only returned at 8pm, dragging a reluctant goat. A constant barrage of questions had obviously exhausted them. "Where did you get the goat? How much does it weigh? What did you pay for it? What is it for?" I know exactly what it's like; my patience has often been worn thin by such questions. The next morning we tethered the animal on the veranda, while Elizabeth sat happily in her bouncy chair nearby.

It was a big day for us. We got up at six, and started to arrange our room downstairs to make space for guests. Two women prepared garlic and onions on the veranda; Nick and the watchman put up bunting. Someone delivered a large sack of rice, and decanted it into our red plastic bath-tub. Lydia played with it. We stacked up firewood. A colleague boiled water and sharpened knives before deftly dispatching the unfortunate goat.

A Nepali friend helped me put on my sari, and taking tiny steps I walked down to church. It was moving to hear Nepali and expatriate friends offering prayer for us all, and giving special thanks for Elizabeth. A Scottish family sang a song of blessing. After the service, the entire congregation, including a bevy of children, walked up the hill. At our home, one by one, they came forward to pray for Elizabeth, and thrust rupee notes and packets of glucose biscuits into her hands. We served rice, goat curry and tea. My parents phoned us on the public solar phone five-minutes walk from our home. Village neighbours started to arrive at three in the afternoon: sewing ladies, local shopkeepers, and our language teacher with his family. They, too, brought various presents, all wrapped in newspaper: little waistcoats, baby suits, money, and pieces of cloth. At half past five, Nick's CHP colleagues came en masse. They dressed Elizabeth up in a bright spotty outfit, complete with hat, bangles, pearl necklace, and flip-flops. The man employed at the phone kiosk came at twilight after finishing work. We had fed and entertained 80 people that day, for the equivalent of about £60.

## It's costly to be a Christian

Ros –

The young Nepali church rejects certain traditional cultural practices and adapts others. Before democracy came to Nepal in 1991, being baptised as a Christian meant a year in prison; baptising someone else meant six years. It takes a great deal of courage to publicly affirm uncompromising allegiance to Christ. Persecution follows.

So even in 1997, there was an air of secrecy one Saturday in Amppipal after the church service. We gathered for a snack lunch together outside a church member's home. Sitting on rice-straw mats, we ate dried beaten rice, peanuts, popcorn, and crunchy fried lentils. The plate was a sheet of paper torn from a magazine. We finished with a glass of hot milky tea.

Then we took off our shoes and went inside. All the furniture had been cleared out. The floor was bare except for a large plastic barrel filled with water. We sang a Nepali song, and an elder invited one woman forward. After confessing Jesus as Lord and Saviour of her life, she climbed into the barrel and was ducked under the water. As each candidate came up, we sang and prayed. The largest lady waited till last. Then water splashed over the sides of the barrel, and we all got wet. It was a deeply moving occasion, and I felt privileged to be there.

Following Christ cost two teenagers their friendship. Mohan and Hari had acted together in the youth Easter drama. A week later I saw Mohan alone – "How's Hari?" I asked. Eyes downcast, he shrugged his shoulders. Hari's uncle had forbidden him to see his Christian friend again.

For one husband and wife it meant running away from home. A Christian family told them about Jesus. It became obvious in the close-knit community that they were no longer doing the required ritual Hindu worship. Neighbours avoided them, and refused to eat with them. One morning the wife went out to fetch water from the communal tap. Other women blocked her path, and refused her access. She went home frightened, with her empty pot, and told her husband what had happened. That day they gathered their few possessions and fled. They sought refuge in Amppipal, where they were welcomed by the church and started a new life.

"Go ahead, look in my bag. Kill me if you like." On the lonely wooded path, near a steep gorge, his body might never have been discovered. The four tipsy 'security officials' drilled Mohan for half an hour. When they found a Bible in his bag they had an easy target. "You've been preaching. Where have you been? Who were you with?" Mohan could only recall a few villagers' names. He'd been doing a temporary job at the Community Health Programme - but had no identity card. Eventually they let him go with a warning: "Don't dare carry a Bible with you again." A few weeks later I met Mohan setting off on another field trip. With a smile he assured me, "Nothing is going to stop me from carrying my Bible on every trip".

A Nepali friend who worked at Amppipal hospital had sought an educational grant from the Umbrella Organisation to study to become a health assistant. When his application failed, he felt anger towards God and the Organisation. He subsequently came second in the entrance exams, and received a scholarship from the government. When he attended his mother's Christian funeral a few months later the police arrested him for being a Christian. Officials accused him of believing in order to get financial help from the missionaries.

He was able to stand his ground, and thanked God that the Umbrella Organisation had not given him a grant.

Despite suffering and opposition the church has advanced in Nepal. Believers bear simple testimony to their friends and neighbours of what Christ means to them, and they see the reality of their faith in God through answered prayer for protection or healing. It is significant that it is Nepalis themselves who play the major role in fostering church growth. By contrast, expatriate missionaries can, quite unconsciously, be a hindrance to the development of a mature church. Sadly, many see Western missionary 'wealth' as the panacea to poverty. And this often leads Christians to cultivate a dependency on the westerner, rather than on God.

We visited a village where, many years before, two missionary women had lived and served at a clinic and nearby school. "How many Christian families are there here now?" I asked. "When our sisters lived here every family believed, but now there are Christians in only four homes."

We and other missionaries were glad to be part of the local church in Amppipal. Among other things, it served to illustrate unity and diversity. Although expatriates were members of the church, they did not assume leadership roles. But, even so, our presence created a feeling of imbalance. This was partly because we had incomparably more wealth than village Nepalis.

Most of the expatriate team worked hospital hours. Nick's community health job, however, was more flexible. This allowed us to explore the possibility of forging a link with a church in another village. One of the most accessible local fellowships was 3 to 4 hours' walk away. We began to go there once a month. Our aim was to widen the horizons of the church in Amppipal, and we went with their blessing. Sometimes a group of us from Amppipal walked together to that neighbouring village early on a Saturday morning. Over the course of the next year our friendship grew and the small Christian fellowship at Maidan led by Ram its pastor, became our extended family.

## Blending and Blundering

Ros –

No doubt we made more cultural blunders than we realised. One is etched on my memory.

At our request, hospital workmen cut back three large trees inside the perimeter wall of the 'Old Dispensary' where we lived. However, it turned out that the wall was not the official boundary. Those were not our trees to cut, and we should not have given away the firewood to our workers. The tree owners' family began to pull boulders off the stone wall. They threatened our workers. We were out of our depth. We sought the help of a respected, older friend, and he took a mediating role. The issue was resolved, leaving a battered wall around the disputed trees. It served as a constant reminder of how little we understood the local social norms.

One Christmas, Nick presented me with a cardboard cutout bead necklace with a gold centrepiece. This was an advance gift – a promise that he was going to have a pukka necklace made for me in the new year. It was the Nepali equivalent of a wedding ring. We found out how much gold was required for the centrepiece. It was important that the weight fitted my status as a doctor's wife.

So we bought half a tola of gold (1 tola = 11.7 grams). The Kathmandu merchant cut a small piece from a tablet and weighed it carefully. We also chose the string of beads.

'Every tailor takes a little cloth for himself, and every goldsmith, a little gold' so the Nepali proverb goes. So on the appointed day, Nick, our cook, and I each took two one-hour-long shifts to watch over the goldsmith in Amppipal bazaar. For six hours of skilful work he charged only a fraction of the price of the gold he handled. He beat the gold, heated it, beat it out again, wrapped it into a cylinder around a rod, joined it with solder, and hammered it into shape. The goldsmith worked sitting on the floor, with tongs, hammer, fire and bellows - a machine that looked like a hair-dryer with a turn handle. Nick used the goldsmith's own scales to re-weigh the finished centrepiece. A friend strung the beads either side of it. Since then I have worn the necklace every day. I am pleased that we researched the appropriate weight of gold, because Nepali village women have often unashamedly approached me to lift the 'tilary' between their fingers and judge how heavy it is.

It became one of my most treasured possessions, and helped create a bond between Nepali women and me. As I walked along the path, I often heard positive comments about my necklace. Later I found out that local people had difficulty in pronouncing 'Rosalind', so I was affectionately known as 'Necklace Sister'.

I was able to identify, in one sense, with the Nepali women around me, by wearing Nepali dress and a wedding necklace. But it was quite a different matter trying to identify at a deeper level.

However, common human experiences, like being married, giving birth, bringing up children and celebrating festivals drew us closer together. Expatriates – singles and families, were able to contribute varying and complementary skills to the church and community. Inevitably, we changed our life patterns, and adapted some Nepali customs. Our thanksgiving for Elizabeth mirrored the local rice-feeding ceremony. And like cutting those trees, there were plenty of occasions when we made mistakes too.

# CHAPTER 6

## GOD CAN USE US

### Mobilising churches in the UK...
### Home Assignments

Ros –

Three years after our arrival in Nepal, we received a letter from our sending agency asking when we were planning to return to England. It came as somewhat of a shock. We were aware that home assignment was looming, but we had put it to the back of our minds. Both of us felt settled and were reluctant to leave. We negotiated to extend our stay in Nepal until May – so we could escape the Nepali monsoon, and enjoy a cool summer in Britain.

Before leaving Nepal we gathered a box load of resources. We were ready for anything from services to Sunday schools, from toddlers' groups to men's breakfasts. We enlarged and mounted photos, wrote case studies, prepared multiple-choice quizzes, and pictures for children to colour. We devised a prayer cube for people to make. A picture on each face prompted supporters to pray for health, safe travel, spiritual life, colleagues, finance and the local church.

We arrived back from Nepal exhausted. The whole family fell ill with chesty coughs and fevers, and had to stay in bed. Our parents, who had come to visit, ended up nursing us. Soon after our return to England on that first home assignment one of the family expelled a 20 cm worm in the toilet. We were glad we had taken the wise advice of fellow missionaries to de-lice and de-worm as we left Nepal.

In the past 'missionaries' came back to their sending countries on 'furlough'; nowadays 'cross-cultural workers' come for 'home assignment'. We visited supporting churches (did deputation), caught up with family and friends, spent time on professional update, were spiritually refreshed and rushed around doing countless jobs.

It was good to experience the warm hospitality of family and friends. We enjoyed the crunch of a Cox apple, a good cup of tea, and cow's milk on bran flakes. I luxuriated in hot bubble baths.

That first home assignment proved to be a rapid refresher course in British culture. Garish supermarket displays provoked reverse culture shock. My eyes glazed over. I didn't know where to begin to choose from 50 varieties of cereal. Products like Marmite and Golden Syrup, which we had bought at exorbitant prices in Kathmandu, were surprisingly cheap in Croydon.

It was difficult to grasp that the two worlds of the UK and Nepal existed simultaneously. If we were finding it hard to relate to Nepal from Britain, how much more difficult was it for our supporters? Seeing photos and meeting people who'd been to Nepal brought the two worlds together again.

We had lived in various places when Nick was training as a GP. So we had a ready-made network of friends in seven churches where we'd been members. Seeing familiar faces at our supporting churches meant a great deal to us. Sometimes we had the opportunity to share our experiences with new groups.

The aim of our presentations was to capture an interest in world mission. We promoted support of God's work worldwide, through prayer and giving. It was also our hope that some would hear God's call to go. We spoke candidly about the highs and lows of living and working in another culture, and of our godly Nepali friends whose faith challenged our own.

During that first home assignment we perfected the 'Nepali experience evening'. We started at 'Heathrow' with some tips about looking and listening. Nick urged participants to have big ears and eyes, but to watch their big feet. Then we sent groups to visit a Himalayan village home, and a Nepali church. I dressed up as a village woman in a wrap-around skirt, crossover blouse, and flip-flops. I demonstrated to my guests how to use different household utensils, and showed a video of a woman cooking over a fireplace inside a mud and thatch dwelling. Those visiting the Nepali church left their shoes by the door and sat cross-legged on the floor, men on one side and women on the other. Nick taught them a Nepali song. Later in the evening we all ate a typical Nepali rice meal, some with spoons and some with their hands. One man said afterwards he had expected a talk with slides, but now felt that he had 'been there'.

We encouraged friends to keep on sending packages to us in Nepal, by telling how God had provided gifts at just the right time. I recounted how the very week Lydia complained that the elastic on her pants was loose, a parcel of knickers arrived. Alphabet and number posters reached us as we were decorating Lydia's bedroom. We loved getting packages of chocolate and craft materials, or books for the girls. But we groaned when we received a chicken casserole mix, to which we 'just had to add chicken'.

We warned friends not to put enticing descriptions on customs declarations – to write 'educational materials' rather than 'children's books', or 'confectionery' rather than 'chocolate and angel delight'. Generous friends sent nearly new children's shoes and included some chocolate. The customs label simply read 'second-hand clothing and bits and bobs'.

We were interviewed on London's leading Christian radio station. We led the programme at church weekends-away. Nick preached. He illustrated his talks from Nepal and tried to remain relevant to the UK. We discovered we had different, but complementary styles of working. To keep his presentations fresh, Nick liked to plan every meeting from scratch. I was happier to use familiar material, as repetition improved my fluency. Working together at church events was the highlight of deputation for us.

We made mistakes and people frowned. We arrived late at a house group because we'd spent too long at the park; in one church Nick spoke for longer than the 12 minutes allocated for the sermon. And travel with two young children was demanding. I remember Lydia asking plaintively, "How many nights are we staying here?" We warned our hosts that for our sanity we should stay at only one home in each place, and that we needed to keep 5-7pm free to feed, bath and put our daughters to bed. When we were on the move, I found it helped to keep up some semblance of routine. Only one of us led daytime meetings, so the other could stay with the girls.

## Multi Media Communication

Ros –

A mature looking lady I didn't recognise, approached me during the coffee break at a mission conference that summer. She was eager to find out about one of our Nepali colleagues. She wanted news on the recent strikes, and details of our children's progress. What a privilege it was to meet someone who prayed for us daily, even though we'd not actually met before.

Doug prayed. He kept letters and notes close at hand. They were annotated and highlighted. He used them to pray through the specific needs of Christian workers abroad, including us. He badgered us for more detail; he asked awkward questions about my role and how I was using my gifts. Our survival and effectiveness depended on prayer supporters like Doug.

A colleague claimed that deputation was less of a necessity if we kept up with our correspondence while we were abroad. I saw communication as a vital part of my role, and I loved doing it. Though I was struggling to converse with Nepalis I could pour my heart out in letters home. During daylight hours in Nepal I could never settle to writing letters; the girls demanded my attention. But I remember evenings when I sat facing Nick across the dining table, catching up on correspondence, with a row of five candles between us. The mailman, reputedly a fast walker, journeyed from Amppipal to Kathmandu and back every week, to take and collect the Project's post. Mail reached us on a Friday, and we had to post our letters by the following Monday morning. We found that this weekly deadline acted as a helpful spur.

Nick typed his 'impressions' on the computer each week. We printed them out on to A5 sheets, and I wrote personal replies by hand on the blank side. I think my relationship with my parents deepened, as we shared more in writing a weekly letter than we might have done over the phone.

People warned us that letters might go astray. To begin with, we carefully numbered and dated our missives - so that it was obvious if one got lost. After a while we tired of this pernickety system. During Dasai, the ten-day national holiday, post piled up in sorting offices. It may sound apocryphal, but we heard that one year, defeated by the sheer volume of unsorted mail, the post office burned the lot.

Important letters did get lost. A close friend gave birth to a baby boy before we heard she was pregnant. And when post did get through, sometimes we still failed to communicate effectively. Soon after we arrived in Kathmandu we saw people digging with hand tools, and described it as 'small-scale farming'. A month later, we received the newsletter from the UK, with an illustration of a 'small' English tractor.

It was next to impossible to email from Amppipal. There was only one phone in the village, and it was solar-powered. This forced us to make a clean break from the life we had left behind in England, and gave us time to build new relationships. In Amppipal we were frequently cut off from the outside world. Once the mail runner had left, we relied on the public phone. When that was out of order, we had no easy way to send a message. The only other option was a courier. Thankfully, we never had reason to resort to this.

I generally find missionary newsletters pretty boring. A solid block of text is daunting. I can't remember who so-and-so is, and get very confused with the names of local places. We wrote our newsletters about four times a year. We wanted our supporters to read them immediately they were received. Someone suggested that we should include only *one* theme per newsletter. Topics included: a day in my life, a tour round our home, and an interview with a Nepali friend.

Initially, publishing newsletters was a complex process. We wrote the text by hand, and posted it, with suggestions for illustrations, to a friend in York. She typed it, finalised the layout, and printed it onto headed paper. A copy of the finished newsletter eventually reached us in Nepal some time after our supporters had received it.

We insisted that newsletters be distributed personally, fearing that sensitive information might get into the wrong hands. Later we discovered that people often put our newsletters up on notice boards, or printed excerpts in parish magazines. So we made sure we didn't write anything that might incriminate

Nepali friends. Sometimes this meant changing their names. Indiscreet disclosures could have made life difficult for the Christians we knew. Association with Western Christians occasionally resulted in suffering for national believers.

Certain items were too valuable to entrust to the postal service. Once we recorded a cassette for a mission event; and on another occasion we borrowed a friends' camcorder to make a video of the girls for their longsuffering grandparents. A friend who had come to visit us delivered these in person.

## Friend raising continued...

Nick –

Churches, friends, and family supported us financially for the nine years we spent in Nepal. But could we show them value for their money? Probably not!

Soon after arriving in Nepal I was shopping in Kathmandu. I spied 'real' European chocolate for sale. It was four times more expensive than its Indian counterpart. As I reached for my wallet I felt a pang of guilt. Some of our financial supporters gave beyond their means, and I did not think that I was making good use of what they had sacrificed. Was it right to buy *any* kind of chocolate, let alone the expensive brand?

I must admit that I did buy Swiss chocolate occasionally. We knew our supporters trusted us, and that they would not want us to be denied occasional treats. When it came to bigger things, like holidays, we did have to weigh up carefully whether our funding was being used in a wise way.

Part of my job in Amppipal was relating to donors. I compiled plans and reports for the three organisations that funded us. In one plan, I described our intention to hand over the supervision of mother and child health clinics to government health workers, so we could focus on different activities in a new area. One donor said this sounded rather drastic. I was pleased that they'd commented. It forced us to review our proposals and clarify our rationale.

I had the chance to video our work for a funder's annual harvest appeal. We presented the stories of people who had benefited from a water system and a mother and child health clinic.

I set out alone for the 4-day trek with borrowed video camera, new tapes and a spare fully-charged battery in my rucksack. I sought to capture footage that showed the rural context and told about our activities. Standing on a high point on the path I panned round the partly terraced, partly wooded landscape and focussed on a woman filling her metal water pot from the village stand pipe. When I asked her to tell how her life has changed she explained: "Since piped water came to this village, we can stay in our beds until it gets light." At another village a mother sat with a lively baby on her lap. She described how the clinic had transformed her son's health.

In keeping with the harvest theme, I filmed ripening wheat and farmers digging potatoes by hand. The funder's UK office edited my footage and produced a slick eight-minute video. This gave weight to their appeal, and also proved a useful tool for our deputation meetings that year.

## Visitors to Nepal

Ros –

Though we tried hard to transport people to Nepal, metaphorically speaking, at our Nepali experience evenings, there was no substitute for people actually visiting us.

Before going overseas, our mission agency advised us that we should not think of returning to England, or indeed of entertaining family visitors, until we had completed the first year. I could see the wisdom in such counsel. It gave us time to become accustomed to Nepal. But I am conscious that such advice, these days, might sound overbearing.

Friends working in Kathmandu came to stay for our first Christmas in Amppipal. We asked them to tell us honestly how they found our home. "We had a great time, but there is a lack of privacy, it's rather cold, and the toilet's a bit smelly," they responded. Though we knew my parents were fit and adaptable, someone wisely advised us to allow them to adjust gently. On their first night we booked them into a hotel, rather than the mission guesthouse. We travelled by hired jeep, rather than local bus. We took supplies from the German bakery, rather than expecting Mum and Dad to eat rice at a teashop en route.

The Royal Nepal Airlines plane that brought Nick's parents to Kathmandu, was only forty minutes late. Before setting off into the city, we warned them of the things we had found hard to accept when we arrived two years earlier: Kathmandu is dirty, and the traffic is chaotic. The truth was that we had become so accustomed to these that we hardly noticed them any more.

When our girls were small, it was hard for their grandparents to communicate with them from a distance. They needed to spend time together and get to know one another – so that was the focus of the various visits they paid us. We have happy memories of trips to Chitwan National Park, riding elephants and walking through the jungle together in search of tigers. Our parents also helped out with practical tasks in the home and garden. Mum taught our cook to make lemon meringue pie; Dad painted, weeded and helped build a rabbit hutch. We laid lino together in our attic. Mum and Dad even taught English to Nick's colleagues one training day.

It helped our Nepali friends to see that we had wider families. Writing letters home became much easier too, because we knew our parents had some idea of what we were talking about. We cherish the invaluable support our parents gave us, and the role they played as our ambassadors in their churches.

We share a special bond with all those who have visited us in Nepal. One visitor inspired Lydia's interest in all kinds of bugs. She also spent a day photographing each of us every half an hour, for a slide show on 'a day in our lives'. Others accompanied us on a local trek and camping expedition, which prompted us to explore our surroundings more widely. Some encouraged us with thoughtful gifts. One visitor joined in a Bible study with Nick's Nepali brother Syam; Nick translated alternately from English into Nepali and then from Nepali into English. Another was almost blind. But it was culturally acceptable for Nick to hold his hand for the five-hour walk along very uneven paths to reach the road. We were pleased to have the services of a gap-year student, who was adept at computers and able to solve several niggling problems we were having with our office PCs. "But you won't get me soldering the motherboard, or anything like that," he forewarned us. Later Nick found him trying to solder a socket in to place using a screwdriver and a candle flame. Nick bought a soldering iron, and he completed the job. Although guests encroached on our 'routine', we were delighted to see them. Visits were a wonderful way of cementing friendships. But as the security situation in Nepal deteriorated during our second term, with frequent strikes and roadblocks, we needed to discourage all but the keenest travellers.

## God can use us here

Ros –

After Padam's death, there was no obvious Nepali candidate to fill the post of Director of the Community Health

Programme. The person with the greatest potential for the job was the Co-ordinator of the Programme. He was a capable man, but needed to gain some extra experience. So, in consultation with headquarters, we made new plans. Nick delayed a proposed study-leave block for a year to give the Co-ordinator the opportunity to work as a manager in another project. So after three months' home-assignment we returned to Amppipal for a final year. Nick continued as Director. Following that the Nepali Co-ordinator would relieve Nick of his responsibility.

As we landed for this second term in Nepal, Kathmandu airport felt familiar. When an official spotted Nick wearing a Nepali cap in the 'all other foreigners' queue, he beckoned us over. When he saw our residents' visas, he said we were entitled to go through the 'official and diplomatic' passport channel in future. We steered our strong-willed trolley purposefully through the swarm of taxi drivers buzzing around 'arrivals', and negotiated a ride at the cheaper, metered rate. As we jolted along the pitted ring road, amid the sprawl and jumble of Kathmandu, we looked at each other and grinned. We were home again. The room prepared for us at the guesthouse happened to be the same one where we had spent our first five months of language study, three and a half years previously. The familiar barking of stray dogs prevented us from sleeping off the jet lag.

We travelled to Amppipal the next day. The team's thoughtful preparations meant we were able to sleep in our own home on the first night. Rat and monsoon damage had been made good. The 'Old Dispensary' had been swept and aired; flasks had been filled with hot water, and there was freshly baked bread on the sideboard.

During our first three years in Nepal, I often found it difficult to distinguish Nepali faces. I remember the significant occasion when I looked at an old Nepali man's face, and saw how similar it was to that of an English friend's. I think Nepalis had the same problem with Westerners. We were mistaken, one for another. In spite of being out of Nepal for three months, we felt warmly welcomed by our colleagues and neighbours. The fact that we had come back seemed to reap dividends. We were showing our commitment to the place and people, and this served to cement friendships. Each time I walked to the bazaar I met people I knew. And they knew me. I felt I belonged. Even when nothing was planned, the days seemed to be full because of the contacts I had. I focussed my attention on people I wanted to encourage: the wife of a Nepali doctor, who came for English lessons and Bible study; Nick's colleagues; Padam's nephew Mohan, who needed coaching for his exams; and Ram, the pastor of Maidan church. Sharing child-care with our Irish neighbours made looking after the girls easier. During that year I was able to contribute more effectively than before. This gave me a sense of fulfilment and purpose.

## Leading. Engaging with people's lives

Nick –

I sensed that I was growing in my skills as a health programme leader. But more importantly, I began to understand what it meant to 'walk the talk'. Padam had taught me that there was no substitute for having a servant heart. The legacy that he left was the foundation on which I sought to build. So during my time as Director of the Community Health Programme (CHP) I aimed to be aware of my colleagues' needs, and did everything I could to cultivate team spirit.

In the Nepali language 'Namaste' means both hello and goodbye, but it's more than just a word. To greet someone, normally requires not only the use of your voice, but also your hands, your eyes and your head. The palms are held together (as if praying), the eyes glance down, and the head is given a gentle, but definite, nod – a mark of respect. Friends of equal rank, however, meet one another more casually; they often shake hands – men with men, women with women.

As I reached the office each day, I made a point of greeting every member of the team with a "Namaste" *and* a handshake. Although this broke accepted convention, I wanted to show that I valued each of them equally, regardless of their status. Some found my manner awkward at first, but in due course everyone seemed pleased to shake my hand. Although they respected me as their leader, they also began to trust me as a friend.

Our middle-aged office cleaner died of rheumatic heart disease and was due to be cremated. Her home was near ours, so I joined some local men as they carried her body, at breakneck speed, to the nearest river. Other men carried firewood. Women took no part in the ceremony, I discovered. While the platform of boulders (a 'ghat') was being made to support the pyre, the woman's body lay partly submerged in the water. I empathised with her two sons as they sat weeping beside me. An experienced man prepared the body using red vermilion powder. The sons then wet their heads and a helper shaved each one bare, except for a small tuft at the back. Then they washed their mother's mouth with river water. Wading through the water, they lit the pyre - one with a flaming torch and the other with a simple wick-lamp.

For the next two hours the primary issue was a practical one. Burning an adult human corpse needs a lot of wood. Looking on was not for the faint hearted. The body was crudely reduced to small charred fragments. Finally, the ashes, the remaining wood, and the stones of the platform were all pushed into the river. The men then moved a few yards upstream and washed. Her sons changed into the simple white garments that mark out mourners for a period of thirteen days. In memory of the dead woman, everyone stood in the shallows and splashed water on a boulder 36 times with their hands. Then we returned up the hill to Amppipal.

It was through becoming involved in people's lives and identifying with them in their trials, that we built meaningful relationships. The bonds deepened as I spent time in colleagues' homes. Rosalind and I sought to extend our friendships beyond the boundaries of CHP and Amppipal. We were especially glad when we started working with the church at Maidan, 3-hours walk away, and began to support Ram, their pastor.

## Ram and the 'Amppipal Bible School'

Ros –

We walked the three hours to Ram's village about once a month. Lydia walked and Elizabeth rode in a specially adapted basket with a seat, on a porter's back. We stayed overnight in the tiny mud and stone church building. At half past five in the morning I heard Ram singing and praying aloud from his room. Bleary eyed after a night on the hard mud floor, I was only just up and dressed at eight, when Ram's wife came to sweep the floor and rearrange the rice straw mats in readiness for the morning service. A simple white cloth, with a cross in red fabric sewn on it, was draped over a table. The brown, mudded walls were bare. Ram, a slight, unassuming man in his thirties, with deep-brown shining eyes, a moustache and a broad smile was the pastor of this church. Our friendship deepened during our final year in Amppipal.

He walked closely with his Lord. One day he recalled the occasion when he climbed on to a bus and found a seat; but he had no peace. He alighted and waited for another vehicle. Later he heard that eighteen people had died that day when the first bus had crashed.

A neighbour who poured scorn on Ram's work, and shouted abuse at the believers, was struck deaf. Ram recounted this to us as if it were quite unremarkable. When inquisitive police gathered outside the church building, Ram simply prayed and carried on with the service. Afterwards he engaged them in conversation. He was never ashamed to acknowledge his Saviour, even though it put him in danger.

"Why are the apples on your trees so good?" a passer-by called out to Ram.

"Because God blesses us," he replied.

"God's with me too," countered the neighbour.

"Yes, you're right, but the bad things we put a barrier between God and us, so we don't receive his blessing. Come to the church fellowship and find forgiveness, then your apples will be better," was his unabashed reply.

Ram's family had an abundance of productive fruit trees.

Unlike many Nepali husbands, Ram appreciated his wife and the chores she did around their labour-intensive village home. He milked the buffaloes. Beehives made from hollowed tree trunks hung on their veranda. Ram was the acknowledged local expert on honey production. He could hold a mass of writhing bees in his bare hands without being stung. He caressed and calmed them with his gentleness.

For those not familiar with the culture, it may seem a little strange that Ram facilitated matchmaking among believers - a significant but risky role for a pastor. He arranged the marriage of two young people from nearby villages. The bride's family however were not Christians at the time of the wedding, and I watched as, with winsome courtesy and bold conviction, Ram reasoned with a group of male relatives after the service. He radiated a passionate faith, aware of his freedom from the empty rituals of his Hindu background. He spoke of the release from worshipping created things, and of the joy he had in serving the Creator God.

One day when we were staying at his home, Ram's daughter went out herding their goats. When she returned, one was missing. Her father questioned her. Where exactly had she been? What had she done? Though it was getting dark, he set out to search in the woodland, and at other homesteads, thinking the missing goat might have joined another flock. An hour later he returned, with the lost animal bleating at his side. Relief and happiness shone on his wife's face. It called to mind the parable Jesus told of the lost sheep.

No one had been able to cure a sick local girl. She writhed and shook, and her eyes rolled round in their sockets so that only the whites showed. She ate huge platefuls of rice, enough for three people. The witch doctors had chanted, puffed breaths over her, and demanded numerous chickens for sacrifice. But her condition only grew worse. As a final resort, friends took her to Ram at the local Christian church. He and others there prayed for her, and over some weeks she gradually recovered and came to believe in Jesus the healer. Despite the miraculous change in their daughter, her parents put pressure on her because of her new faith. They prevented her going to church services by hiding her shoes or clothes. They did not allow her to eat with believers. But there was no turning back. She bravely went on to be baptised. Although her family continued to make life difficult for her, she coped with God's help, by taking opportunities to leave the village for training in Christian service, and by prayer and fasting. That local girl became a radiant and mature leader in the church.

Ram's concern for his lost neighbours prompted him to walk for miles up and down the steep paths, to reach those in isolated village areas. He had a monthly schedule of visits. On entering a village, he would call at a believer's house - to sing, tell stories, or explain a Bible text. People passing by would often stop to hear him speak. Ram's ministry was marked by selfless service, and he was an inspiration and encouragement to many.

Ram had read the entire Nepali Bible, but there was much he did not understand. He was so committed to his local community, that, unlike many, he had no ambition to go overseas for Bible college training, or even to Kathmandu. During our last year in Amppipal we decided to meet with Ram twice a month, to study the Bible together.

We used notes from our own Bible college days as the basis for what we grandly called, 'Amppipal Bible School'. We wanted Ram to grasp the overarching story of the Bible, and appreciate the different types of literature contained in it. Usually I prepared a topic and a passage to read, and Nick implemented my lesson plan with Ram. They read and discussed together. It was clear that the Holy Spirit had already conveyed to Ram much of what we had learned at Bible College. I recall one evening when we read some pithy wise sayings from the book of Proverbs. We had fun working out what we thought they meant, and then compared them with modern English and Nepali proverbs.

On the evening of our ninth wedding anniversary the girls were asleep in bed. I had changed into a dress, and had prepared a fondue to celebrate. We had decided not to go to the prayer meeting, but to have a romantic candlelit dinner for two. As I was about to serve up the meal, we heard coughing outside the door. It was a surprise to see Ram. He had no way of telling us in advance of his intended visit, and it was too late for him to consider walking home. We had to invite him in. Nepalis rarely celebrated birthdays, let alone wedding anniversaries. The look of incomprehension on his face as we tried to explain why we were celebrating, was matched only by his incredulity at the strange Western meal we shared with him. After eating, he and Nick walked down to the Nepali church meeting together.

## Praise and joy and Jyoti

Nick –

One Saturday we managed to set off from home at half past six, just as it was getting light. After only two and a quarter hours, we arrived at Ram's village.

The church room measured a mere seven-foot by fifteen. Taking off our shoes, we stepped inside to a chorus of warm greetings, and squeezed on to straw mats on the floor to join the morning service. Ram sat on my left and smiled as he prayed and sang. That day he gave a clear message about Jesus the good shepherd, from John chapter 10.

The singing at that church was tuneless. But it was a joy to worship with our friends there because the hearts behind the singers' voices rejoiced in God. The open prayer times seemed chaotic. They were opportunities for everyone to pray aloud together, exclaiming praise to God and the victory of Jesus. No one left a service without having made a personal contribution to the worship.

On each occasion we went, I was able to give a short Bible message. After my faltering delivery, Ram would summarise it in clearer language. He always seemed to grasp what I was trying to get across. After the service, we sat a little longer, chatting, or looking at a Bible verse. One Saturday I spoke with a newcomer whose Hindu family had sent him to the Christian church for healing from painful joints. They'd heard about Jesus the healer.

Ram's family entertained us to curry and rice at their home. Over the months, he made us feel very much at home. Before we ate or drank, even a cup of tea, he paused to give thanks to God.

Another Saturday I felt privileged when Ram asked me to lead a 'baby blessing' for their two-week old daughter. We gave thanks for her safe arrival, asked God to watch over the child, and prayed for her parents. As I went to sit down, Ram looked across to me, exclaiming, "but you haven't given her a name." "Aahh…" I thought. We paused and prayed again, asking what to call the little girl. In my mind's eye I saw a coloured beam of light, so I suggested the name Jyoti, which means 'light'. Others agreed. So we prayed once more for the babe, this time by her new name.

# CHAPTER 7

# A GOOD-ENOUGH ADMINISTRATOR

Nick –

As part of a voyage of self-discovery, Ros and I completed a Myers Briggs personality-type indicator test. The test explores four axes that define personality preferences. My type is INFP - I'm an idealist.

'I' I am an introvert;
'N' I am intuitive (I tend to emphasise insight rather than more tangible reality);
'F' I prefer to make decisions on the basis of personal feelings and values, rather than objective logic; and
'P' I organise my life in a flexible way, discovering it as I go along, rather than making decisions in advance. (P stands for perceiving.)[14]

It was interesting to discover that, in the case of three of the four axes, Ros and I are opposites. She's a realist. I hope this means that we complement one another. She organises me, but I have occasional brilliant ideas.

INFPs are said to be quiet and adaptable – but when their values are violated, the normally sedate INFP can surprise people with their strong stance. It began to click. This characteristic of my personality type helped me to understand my occasional impassioned reactions to my work colleagues. I found it helpful to know about my own personality, and to realise that what seemed reasonable to me might not be to someone else.

It is also true, in line with other INFPs that I thrive on uncertainty, and like to keep my options open. In the first weeks after I became Director of Gorkha Community Health Programme (CHP) my desk overflowed with papers and leadership team meetings that I chaired lasted for hours but reached few concrete conclusions. Confronting the tendencies of my personality, I realised that it was simply unworkable to leave every decision open and flexible. I learned the need to make decisions within an acceptable time frame and to exercise decisiveness in processing the paperwork on my desk.

I like the concept of 'good enough' parenting, or a 'good enough' gardener. It depends, of course, on what one means by 'good enough'. It is unrealistic to strive to be perfect. But was my management style 'good enough'? When I worked as Programme Director in Amppipal, it was only occasionally that I reviewed our spending line-accounts. A year into my job, the business office staff drew my attention to a questionable materials order that had been charged to the programme. As I followed it up, the staff member concerned dug himself into a hole and eventually admitted that he'd used the suspect items (some cement and expensive pipe fittings) in his own home. When I offered him an alternative lower level job, he handed me his resignation. It was not only he who was a loser. I regretted having been lax in the way I checked the programme accounts. If I had been more rigorous, he might not have been tempted to cheat.

## Developing leadership skills

Nick –

There were times when my principle-led style clashed with my colleagues. I did not know it at the time, but the working area of Gorkha CHP extended only as far as the Marsyandi River. Three staff and I conducted a short feasibility survey at a riverside village. "Should we cross the river and spend the night in the town, or stay here?" they asked me. I didn't mind. In the end we waded through the shallow water and lodged for a few rupees in the town, returning the next day to Amppipal. At the end of the month, when I scanned the monthly allowance claims, I saw a much higher rate than I expected for that night we'd lodged together. "Our rules state that we can claim more when we stay outside the working area," the team leader affirmed. My blood boiled. "But we're claiming far more than it cost us!" I retorted, downsizing her tally sheet. I nearly had a strike on my hands. I was in the wrong. The rules were clear. I backed down, and made a mental note to be wiser next time.

Another day at Amppipal, when I returned home for lunch, Ros asked me what I'd been up to. "Well," I replied, "I attended a meeting looking at how different sections of our programme could relate to one another more effectively in their day to day work..." But could I remember anything about the meeting other than the things I had said myself? I wondered if I was the only one who had such a self-centred memory… I realised that, as a leader and facilitator, I needed to encourage individuals to think and speak for themselves. So I tried out some group discussion methods. The preparation for one session involved collecting pebbles.

"I could have said more, but I ran out of stones" one colleague complained afterwards. I had explained the topic for our debate and had given three pebbles to each person in the circle. Each time someone contributed a point, they had to offer up a stone. I thought carefully before I spoke, and listened well to the things others said, recognising the value of each contribution. Everyone spent their three pebbles, and no one dominated.

I had the chance to learn more about leadership when I observed the activities of other Umbrella projects. In Palpa district, a community health and development project undertook work that was similar to ours in Gorkha. I reached a field-office on a cramped and bumpy bus. During my two-day visit, I was able to shadow four field staff. I saw kitchen garden demonstrations. I attended non-formal adult literacy classes, where I witnessed the dramatic change that this type of training can bring in the lives of those participating. The women of a newly formed class hid behind their shawls and hardly dared to utter their names. By contrast, participants of an established group spoke with remarkable self-confidence.

My 'lesson of the trip' sprung from hearing the story of a woman staff member. She had worked with the project for some years, but like many others, felt tempted to leave. "Why?" I asked. The wages were not as high as those offered by other development agencies, but that was not her only concern. More importantly, she had become disillusioned and discouraged because she received little feedback on her performance as a development worker. Rarely was anything said by way of encouragement, and she was never made aware of her shortcomings.

I recognized that this problem was not limited to Palpa. In Gorkha, we found it was essential to train supervisors to motivate their teams. This improved staff members' job satisfaction and effectiveness. As Director, I tried to make a point of thanking colleagues for the work they accomplished. When explaining our programme and strategy, I would speak with enthusiasm. And when discussing planned activities, I always remained optimistic that they would succeed.

At the beginning of a five-day training programme for health post staff I decided to say a few words of introduction. Before opening my mouth, I moved to the centre of the circle of chairs and sat cross legged on the floor.

"Who is greater, a mother or her son?" I asked.

After a pause I suggested the answer:
"When he is small she cares for him, but when she is old he cares for her."
"Who is greater, a guru or his disciples?"... "Without their guru the disciples are nothing, but without his disciples, the guru is nothing."
"Who is greater, a teacher or a pupil?"... "Today's student could be tomorrow's prime minister."

I once attended a seminar where Robert Chambers began by lying down on the floor[15]. As he adopted a position devoid of power and authority, he asked us about the relationship between facilitators and participants, and between teachers and learners. I firmly believe that trainers are not greater than those they train; nor are leaders greater than those they lead. So I endeavoured to instil this sense of equality in the staff team.

As my extra year of service in Amppipal drew to a close, I thought about the staff teams, aware that they would inevitably change. I prayed that, in the short-term, my Nepali colleagues would continue to function well under their new leader; and that they would retain the skills and life values I'd seen them express. Our programme co-ordinator had now completed his year's on-the-job leadership training at an Umbrella programme in Pokhara. He and I spent two short weeks 'handing over'. I was looking forward to taking study leave in London. The year would give me opportunities to build on my experiences in Nepal and to learn more about health and development.

## Development in practice

Nick –

In preparation for my Masters course, I conducted a study to look at community people's views about development[16]. Two themes emerged. Although some individuals admitted a pitiful dependence on outside agencies, the majority of respondents asserted that their village had the potential for self-development. Moreover they said they were prepared to take active roles in implementing change. However many respondents were convinced that lack of community harmony was the principal barrier to progress.

This made me think. If community relations was such a key issue in the development process, were we right to concentrate our efforts on health training, clean water and education? Should we not focus more specifically on community cohesion? Many writers affirm that effective development strategies should include social regeneration and network enhancement[17].

Goulet[18] said "Development keeps confronting societies with a cruel choice between bread and dignity." He argued that we should distinguish between *fullness of good* and the *abundance of goods*. People (or communities) can *have much* but *be poor*, or *have little* but *be rich*. Some have said that when 'development' reaches the proportions of the West, it runs the risk of defeating the initial aim – the enhancement of wellbeing. We may be freed *from* wants... but we are freed *to* want... which easily leads to jealousy and greed. We either find ourselves manipulating others to satisfy our self-indulgence, or being manipulated.

In the middle of a community meeting an exasperated development worker shouted at the participants. "Tut, tut," we muttered, as we looked on shame faced. "Of course I can shout at them," she retorted afterwards, "they're my family!"

If we don't love the people we aim to serve, how can we ever hope to be agents of change? That was the big challenge facing the leadership of community programmes, such as ours. We were acutely aware that unless commitment and love could be nurtured among the programme staff, they would not be motivated to put their heart and soul into promoting community development.

So I was left where I started, asking myself "what is development?" I'm still not sure, but I have discovered signposts that mark part of the trail. (I have included some further discussion about development in the appendix to this book.)

## Where had we got to?

Ros –

I had struggled to build meaningful relationships in Amppipal. It was not easy to identify with the village women. Those I had most association with were the ladies who came to our door and were dependent on me for work. They saw me as an employer, which created a social divide I found hard to bridge. However, during our final year there, things changed, and I was able to develop a meaningful role in providing hospitality and teaching English to Nick's co-workers.

Nick grew into his work responsibility, and sharpened his understanding of development issues. We both found fulfilment and joy in our growing relationship with Ram and his church.

Bible study whetted my appetite for taking a theological course. Soon after Elizabeth's birth, I realised I needed to stimulate my brain. So I started a correspondence module on prophecy, and relished the time away from the demands of the children. Nick's working hours were flexible enough for him to care for the girls one afternoon a week, so that I could study. However as he got busier at work, I developed a new strategy. Each morning, I disappeared with my study books to a quiet room at the office, and would take an hour for language learning or course reading, while our cook-cum-helper looked after the girls. I returned refreshed and able to face a day of nappies and play dough.

Though the days caring for young children seemed long, I had glimpses of my usefulness. I was certainly involved in the development of my daughters. I had time to teach them informally at home, to do crafts, cook and to spend time talking together. I employed a porter regularly to carry Elizabeth down to the hospital, and at that young woman's request started to teach her to read and write too.

A more experienced expatriate friend had a heart for meeting believers one-to-one, reading the Bible with them and praying. She called this 'discipling', and encouraged us to develop similar relationships. While we were in Amppipal, I attempted to follow this model with a colleague of Nick's, and with a Nepali doctor's wife.

Family holidays spent in Nepal's national parks at Chitwan and Bardia, and in some of the Umbrella Organisation's projects, including Tansen, broadened our understanding of Nepal's geography and culture. We took our tent for one-night camp-overs and for two-to-three day treks. We felt increasingly at home in Nepal.

I considered it a major achievement to be able to stay as a family overnight in a village home. This was a challenge with young children. It involved negotiating squat toilets by torchlight, coping with mosquitoes and bed bugs, trying to sleep together with two wriggly girls in a narrow double bed, and eating spicy food at unusual times. By telling long, involved stories, we encouraged the girls to walk for hours on end – they heard Cinderella from the perspective of the sisters, the mice, and the pumpkin. Receiving hospitality strengthened friendships with Nick's colleagues. These visits helped combat the feeling of claustrophobia I otherwise felt, stuck in our own home. What's more, the girls loved the chance to pet goat kids and chicks belonging to our hosts.

Despite the fact that we had no television, no car, no sit-down toilet, no telephone, and no piped water, we thrived in Amppipal. We discovered the skills of making chutney and bottling tomatoes. Home grown rabbit meat enhanced our diet. Our peers in the UK had bought larger homes and progressed up career ladders. We had found fulfilment in a simpler lifestyle.

For Nepalis, saying goodbye is no casual affair. At the end of our four years in Amppipal, Ram's church fare-welled us in style. The believers festooned us with garlands made from fresh bougainvilleas and marigolds. An enormous ugli-fruit was carved up for everyone to share. We were presented with Nepali New Testaments, and hand-woven shoulder bags. Then they commissioned us for our missionary journey back to the UK. They prayed fervently for our journey, down to the last engine on the plane. We could not have wished for a warmer parting.

## From Nepal to N5... a Pit Stop in London

Ros –

A year before our projected stay in London, we had spent just one day looking for accommodation and schools. We started at the college office. With a sigh of relief we learned that Nick's place on a Master's course in public health *had* been deferred a year, as we had requested. The letter confirming this had simply failed to reach us.

We'd heard about housing accommodation in North London earmarked for missionaries. The manager graciously showed us round a lofty flat. He thought there'd be somewhere available for us the following August.

A vicar and his family, friends from Norwich days, happened to live a few minutes' walk away. We rang them, and went to share our sandwiches around their kitchen table.

After lunch, Nick was curious to see our friend's church. So we wandered through the park to find it. Not only did we locate the church, but also the church school. It was August, and the building looked as if it was shut up for the holidays. We peered in through the glass doors, and were startled when someone came to greet us. He was wearing shorts and a sleeveless waistcoat. He invited us in, saying he was there because of the builders. "I expect you're going to tell us you're the headmaster," Nick dared to suggest. "Yes, I am." He showed us round, and enthused about the Christian ethos of the school. We were impressed, and took an application form.

We had only a hazy idea about plans for the year we were later to spend in London. But it was clear that God's hand was in all the detail. Although neither the accommodation, nor the place in school had been confirmed, we felt at peace about the arrangements.

Our time in London was a pit stop. We had a chance for repair and refuelling, ready for the next stage of our journey.

## All we needed...

Ros –

When we returned to England we initially stayed with Nick's parents, as our flat in Highbury was not yet available. Though this was a bit frustrating, it gave us a welcome rest. We had not realised how tired we would be after the farewells and strain of packing up to leave Nepal. It was great to enjoy the good food and comfortable beds our parents provided, before moving to an unfamiliar corner of north London. That summer we also attended an inspiring Christian conference. The provision of a flat, a car, a place for Lydia in the church school, and for Elizabeth in a local playgroup, were little short of miraculous. The government department responsible for international development provided the remainder of the academic funding for Nick's course, with no strings attached. Our mission agency gave us a living allowance and paid the rent. Again, we felt sure we were in the right place.

We valued the fellowship of our vicar friend's multi-cultural church, where I joined a mums' daytime Bible study group, and did odd jobs at the asylum seekers' project a few hours each week. Nick got involved with church music and worship, and an evening house-group. When we returned to Nepal, we found ourselves involved in similar activities to those we'd pursued in the UK.

## Developing my public health thinking

Nick –

At the public health college in London where I studied, my class had 40 students, with almost as many nationalities. Everyone had experience of working in health in the developing world. We gelled together well. The highlight of each week was a seminar in which students presented a health topic of personal interest. We heard about control of malaria in sub-Saharan Africa, arsenic in ground water in Bangladesh, and the problem of escalating drug abuse in former Soviet Union republics.

Other courses I attended included epidemiology and statistics, politics and health policy, family planning, health promotion, and management. With four years of work in Nepal behind me, it was a great time to take a master's degree. I built an academic foundation to under-gird the practical experience I had gained in community health. Some aspects of the teaching seemed akin to a sausage factory – courses were intensive, and their content too prescribed. I wanted a little more flexibility. But overall, I benefited immensely from the year.

I, along with two fellow students, was elected as a class representative. We sat in on teaching committees that were ready to hear students' views. Towards the end of the year, as we approached final exams, we organised revision seminars where we worked through past papers together. We set our sights high. Many in the class contributed to our team-based teaching and learning.

Acquiring head knowledge on academic courses is one thing. Being able to apply that knowledge in real life situations is something quite different. However, I did feel that in subsequent years I was able to put into practice much that I learned in my master's degree.

## Jumla or Tansen? The Umbrella or the French?

Ros –

We fully expected that as soon as Nick had completed his course, we would return to Nepal for a further term of service with the Umbrella Organisation - this time to a different rural location. But we were yet to discover what was in store for us.

Just before leaving Nepal, we had been on a reconnaissance trip to Jumla, in the remote north west of the country. The travel alone had opened our eyes to its inaccessibility. Though we had plane tickets in our hands, we waited three days beyond our scheduled flight in the sweltering humidity of Nepalgunj, uncertain whether we would be able to fly or not. Several planes were under repair, and it baffled us newcomers that Royal Nepal gave priority to other flights. Nick patiently took our luggage to the check-in desk each morning, only to hump it back to the guesthouse later when he was convinced that our flight would not leave that day. Just to remain bearably cool, I showered at least three times a day in the makeshift hut outside the guesthouse. When the electricity failed at night, and the fan stopped, I found myself wide-awake and bathed in sweat. We could not remain in Nepalgunj beyond a certain date, and just as we were considering alternative plans we received news that our flight was ready for departure. After a hasty 30 minutes of bag checking and loading up, we lifted off from the all too familiar airport.

The steep green hillsides around Jumla, with coniferous forests capped by a ragged snowline, made us think of Switzerland. We trekked into the hills, and the children rode on ponies for the first time. Opportunities for training young people there in practical health topics appealed to us. We looked forward to expanding our survival skills: drying meat, and bottling fruit and vegetables were essential in a place where potatoes were the only fresh produce available for much of the year. And the needs were great. I saw children with dirty faces, too helpless to brush the flies off their cheeks. Human faeces fouled the paths.

Our girls cried when we went to look round the Buddhist shrine in the town centre. We felt a spiritual oppression hanging over the place. Our visit highlighted the need for a strong sense of calling to work in Jumla.

A few months into our study leave in London, the Umbrella Organisation offered Nick the post of Project Director for Jumla. Although our reaction was enthusiastic, we realised that we needed God's guidance. So we sent out a newsletter, asking our supporters to pray and provide feedback. They responded as never before: some were concerned for the children; others feared for us in such a remote location. I remember the day we set aside to evaluate the pros and cons of working there. We each wrote down what we thought were the key features of the job and location. We combined our lists. We then gave a score to each feature based on a scale of one to ten. After carefully analysing the results, we concluded that our overall outlook was more positive than negative about going to Jumla. We informed the Umbrella Organisation and our mission agency that we would be prepared to accept the position, on condition that there was another family there with primary school age children, with whom our girls could learn. At the mission agency conference a few months later, we explained how God had led us, and we were encouraged to put out a wanted notice for another family to come and work in Jumla. The following week a family applied. It was beginning to look as if this was to be our destination. We waited for further news, and then in August we heard that the family had decided to withdraw. Although it came as a bit of a surprise, we took it as a clear sign that God wanted us to work somewhere else. But where?

The Umbrella Organisation flagged up the possibility of work in Tansen, in community health. About the same time a French aid agency, who had kept our address from a careers' fair earlier in the year, contacted Nick, asking if he would like to be considered for a post in Tansen as Coordinator of a new TB / HIV programme. We weighed up the pros and cons of working for a secular organisation. Christian agencies in Nepal were finding it increasingly difficult to obtain visas, and so our mission encouraged its personnel to pursue alternative avenues for service there. Nick was invited to attend interviews in Paris and Grenoble. The French aid agency job was much bigger than we had imagined. They wanted someone to set up a programme from scratch. It would be based in Tansen but also operate in surrounding districts. To our surprise they offered Nick the job. That weekend we prayed and agonised over whether to accept it. On the Monday he went to talk over the possibilities at our mission agency's London office. After further consultation with the Umbrella Organisation in Nepal, it was agreed that Nick should accept the French appointment.

We realised that the decision represented a great challenge, as much of the work would be pioneering. It was a consolation to know that we were going to live in a familiar place, where we would have the support of Umbrella Organisation friends. When we wrote our letter of acceptance, we asked that the project's funding be guaranteed for a year, and that Nick could be involved in the appointment of the other expatriate, an administrator. From then on the French agency paid for our maintenance, flights and accommodation. But we retained the link with our mission agency, who provided us with pastoral support.

With less than two months remaining before departure, we hurriedly arranged visits to our supporting churches. We spoke of how God had led us, and of the challenge of TB and HIV / AIDS work. We asked unashamedly for continued commitment both to pray for us and to send us chocolate.

It was only after we began our new assignment, that we realised the extent of the difficulties we would have to face.

# CHAPTER 8

# RED TAPE

Nick –

We arrived back in Nepal expecting to launch the French agency's tuberculosis and HIV / AIDS programme. I was shocked to discover that the organisation did not have government permission to commence the work, or visas for expatriate staff. Far from opening the new programme, I spent months negotiating agreements with the government.

A French colleague worked as our administrator during the first five months. He was an unforgettable guy: tall, with long, thick, tightly plaited hair, and a great sense of humour.

## Getting by without logistical back-up

Nick –

The agreement process ground on at a snail's pace. We also had practical jobs to complete. Some of them were no less frustrating.

The first time we entered Nepal, the Umbrella Organisation had arranged for an experienced Nepali staff member to escort us through airport customs, to retrieve our unaccompanied luggage. He skilfully negotiated his way through the complex process, with us in tow.

Six years later, I found myself up against the same 'system' when I went to the airport with my French colleague to pick up his belongings. As we approached the airline office a

*A French colleague and I set up a new office and battled together to seek government agreements and funding.*

'helper' hooked us, and before we knew it we found ourselves immersed in a jungle of red tape. With an air of confidence, our helper waved my colleague's papers at every official he came across. Our progress, however, soon ground to a halt. One thing was lacking: a letter from our French organisation requesting release of the luggage. In haste I set off to our temporary Kathmandu office and prepared a letter on headed paper, imprinted with impressive purple stamps.

On my return to the airport we received a handful of documents for processing at the customs office. At this point, another helper - a more senior man - appeared on the scene and took control, enthusiastically filling in an array of paperwork and liaising with various officials. In a hushed tone he advised us not to reveal the value of our belongings to the customs inspector. We looked at each other, rather bemused, as there was nothing of value to declare. My friend was finally permitted to enter the warehouse and identify his trunk. The men who lugged it out demanded payment for their efforts. Once we had displayed the trunk's contents, an official confirmed that no customs duty was due. We breathed a sigh of relief, but were not allowed to leave until all the details had been entered on their computer. After two frustrating hours, we headed for the exit, carrying the well-earned trophy.

The financial side of this affair was fraught with difficulty. The first helper accepted what we considered a reasonable fee, but it was hard work trying to satisfy the second. He claimed that his assistance had saved us a large import tax bill, and felt that it was only fair that he receive a good slice of the benefit. We were not impressed by his story, and sought to get to the truth. It turned out that he had to pay the officials at the airport a monthly sum to be allowed to work as an agent there, and so he wanted to prise the money out of us. We eventually agreed a figure for his services, and parted, apparently on good terms.

For the first few days we based ourselves in Kathmandu, but over the following month, house and office hunting in Tansen became a primary goal. It was quite an adventure. Ros and I viewed a huge flat with all its rooms opening off a draughty, central corridor. Even though we said it did not meet our needs, the landlord feasted us on sour grapefruit laced with salt and chilli.

When Ros took me to look over a possible new house, the 'long room' with its breathtaking view won us over. "We like it, but is there anywhere to plant a few vegetables," we said to the landlady. Pointing down to a terrace the size of three tennis courts, she replied, "You can have the whole field." It was not difficult to reach a decision. So we managed to find a suitable home, and also an office. The sticking point was negotiating monthly rents. As foreigners, new to Tansen, and looking for property, we were a landlord's dream. In consequence, we ended up paying inflated amounts.

I had my eyes opened as I began to do some of the tiresome practical jobs. I bought a gas stove. After preparing the full price receipt, the shopkeeper gave me the 10% discount that I'd previously requested. The money I paid and the amount on the receipt did not correspond. Cooking the books in this way appeared to be common practice. I realised that this would have implications when national staff undertook purchasing for the programme. I spent an afternoon in Kathmandu learning the rudiments of the workings of our photocopier, as there was no repair centre near Tansen.

During our first few weeks in Nepal with the French organisation I tracked down Mohan. Since our days together in Gorkha, he'd married Nirmala. But he was out of favour with both families, as he had refused to follow the Hindu marriage customs her parents had demanded. Moreover, Mohan's Christian relatives in Tansen did not approve, because he'd married a Hindu girl.

When I met him in Kathmandu he was working for a meagre daily wage. He and his wife lived with relatives in a tiny, damp downstairs room. A disabled, but radiant, aunt had prayed for Nirmala, and told her about Jesus. She had become a Christian.

Mohan's position at a local hospital had been made permanent. By contrast, we were still awaiting official agreement from the government to commence work. In the eyes of the immigration office, my French colleague and I were regarded as tourists. I asked Mohan if he would consider working with us. It would be more varied and interesting than the labouring and odd jobs he did at the hospital. I explained that I could promise him no job security, and that he and Nirmala would have to move to Tansen. After considering the implications, they decided to join the new project.

Mohan was intent on purchasing metal-topped kitchen cupboards at the best possible price, and was prepared to bargain tooth and nail right down to the last 25 rupees (approx. 20p.). That same afternoon, a solid looking chest-of-drawers caught my eye in another shop, but the vendor would not budge below 3,000 rupees. With Mohan present, I couldn't bring myself to entertain such extravagance.

The next week we moved our office from Kathmandu to Tansen. At five in the morning, as my French colleague and I waited for the lorry, a small boy appeared, carrying a leaf plate. He placed it in the middle of the road. I noticed that it contained an egg and a simple oil wick-lamp. His duty complete, he walked away. I had no idea what he was doing. When the hired vehicle arrived we first loaded Mohan and Nirmala's few possessions. We then juggled and re-juggled steel cupboards, desks, chairs, and boxes containing files and computers - the office equipment of our organisation's previous project - until the load was stacked high. Five of us crammed into the small cab and we set off. A cat crossed the road. Our driver stopped the lorry and waited for another vehicle to be the first to traverse the animal's track. Then we moved on again. After he explained the superstition he laughed at himself. These days, I too notice if a cat crosses the road in front of me… but I don't draw over.

After dark we reached Tansen and unloaded. I rashly ordered rice for everyone. I subsequently paid for the rice I never ate and headed home to see Rosalind and the girls. Unknown to me, they had prepared a special welcome-home meal.

Over the next month Mohan and I sorted the new office. After working on the first room together, Mohan was able to carry out the wiring and plumbing jobs independently. He whitewashed everywhere, and undertook to purchase and arrange new furniture. Subsequently, he was formally employed as store man cum caretaker. He and Nirmala moved into the top-floor rooms. Although we could not commence programme field-activities until we had government approval, there was plenty to keep him occupied in preparation for our future work.

## Tansen and Kathmandu… Sticky sweets and spicy samosas

Nick –

With a population of 17,000, Tansen is the administrative centre of Palpa district. The landscape is hilly - like that around Amppipal - but the Himalayas are more distant.

*Local craftsmen had fashioned the beautiful carved wooden doors, windows and roof eaves of many of Tasen's older buildings.*

Tansen is the home of two traditional industries. In one quarter of the town, metal workers cast, turn, and polish elegant brass-spouted drinking water pots with tall peacock-shaped lids. As you walk by, you can see different stages of the work in progress. The distinctive smell of small-scale foundries fills the air, and there is no mistaking the rasping sound of lathes and polishers. In another area, cotton fabric production is the principal industry. Here the sound is very different: a rhythmic tap-tee-tap, tap-tee-tap. In under-lit rooms, pairs of women sit at large handlooms weaving elaborate designs. This is the fabric used to make expensive shawls and Nepali men's caps. I was the proud owner of several of these caps. It made me look a bit Nepali and prompted approving smiles.

Tansen's streets are lined with the assortment of shops you find in any Nepali town. There are innumerable teashops, displaying sticky deep-fried sweets and piles of spicy samosas. Outside brightly coloured fabric shops, tailors can be seen working their pedal-powered sewing machines. One steep paved street is home to twelve goldsmiths. To keep their charcoal fires roaring, they operate mechanical 'hair-dryer' air pumps by hand. The craftsmen soften gold in furnaces, and, with minute hammers and punches, work it into intricate designs.

The Umbrella Organisation's hospital stands on the outskirts of town. A sign announced, "We serve - Jesus heals". Our home was five minutes from the hospital.

## Support for Nick in Kathmandu

Nick –

Although we were setting up our future office in Tansen, and Rosalind and the girls were based there, most of the government officials responsible for registering the programme were based in Kathmandu. So for several months I travelled to the capital for work each week.

I have a love-hate relationship with Kathmandu. It's a grimy and dilapidated place, but at the same time brightly coloured, lively and exciting. My work was frustrating, but a tapestry of Nepali and expatriate friends supported me wonderfully.

In my first days back in Nepal I tracked down Nepali friends from Amppipal's Community Health Programme. Staying in their new Kathmandu home was a delight: they fed me with huge quantities of delicious Nepali food and gave me plenty of my own space. Syam, my old prayer partner, and his wife had also moved to Kathmandu. We laughed together, sang Nepali hymns and read our Bibles. I arrived for a planned visit to their home on the wrong day, but they were not in the least upset. They insisted I stay the night, but as their whole family were crammed into two small rooms, I managed to excuse myself politely.

One Sunday, an English couple entertained me after International Church. They were particularly hospitable and encouraging people, always ready to open their home to newcomers to Nepal... and to a fellow from the hills who had to come to Kathmandu for his work... I needed transport to get between government offices, and it was this kind couple that let me use their moped. As I was rarely seen without it, it became my mascot.

I generally stayed overnight in a block of flats where three families linked to our mission agency lived. It was a home from home. The family in the upper flat had been trying to set up a computer business and were encountering similar problems to the ones we faced. Both our ventures were dependent on the goodwill of the Nepali government, and the only way forward was to gently push on the doors that appeared to be opening. Needless to say, we followed each other's progress with interest. It was so useful having access to our friend's office after-hours, as this enabled me to prepare many of the letters and documents that formed the basis of the acceptance process. In office hours, if I was not out on the moped, my friend's Nepali staff and I kept each other supplied with mugs of sweet milky tea.

During those long months of negotiation, I bought office supplies from a tiny shop called 'Popular Stationery'. I soon discovered that the brothers who ran the business were from Palpa district, and a friendship sprang up. It was difficult to pass the shop without stopping for a chat. Going behind the counter, I would squeeze between piles of exercise books and files, and perch on a stool. They invited me to their home, and, although they are Hindus, were very happy when I asked if I could pray for the needs of their family in Jesus' name. It was great to share in their lives.

## The new programme's nine month gestation period

Ros –

We returned to Nepal in November. The next month we moved into our own house in Tansen, Palpa. I thanked God for a home, a school, and for our newly employed house workers. Within two days of moving in, local people delivered milk and honey to the door – a sign that we were in the land God promised to give us. Psalm 16, verse 5, rang true - 'the boundary lines have fallen for me in pleasant places'.

Nick –

Alice the camel has 9 humps,
Alice the camel has 9 humps,
Alice the camel has 9 humps,
So go, Alice, go, turum tum tum...

Oh no, an interminable song…

Nepal's Health Services Department shares an unkempt site with the National Health Laboratory and Health Training Centre. Whenever I arrived at the high front gate on foot or bicycle, the uniformed guards asked me to sign their book. When I came by private car or motorbike, they saluted me through without question. Inside was a labyrinth of corridors. Each was lined with battered steel cupboards piled to the ceiling with tatty paper files.

One dusty afternoon in December I negotiated the maze to the Health Services' Planning Division. From behind his empty desk, the Director's secretary told me she was out at a meeting. "I don't expect she'll be in the office again today," he added. But he was able to locate our file, and found the letters from the National Tuberculosis and AIDS Centres recommending our proposed programme. He assured me that the Director would review these and write to the Health Department's chief, who in turn would write to the Health Ministry.

Later that day I visited the AIDS and Sexually Transmitted Diseases' Centre. Its director had changed since I was last in Kathmandu. Her personal assistant immediately arranged a short meeting. The new director interrogated me about our programme and whether I was qualified to lead it. She left me feeling that I was not wanted as an HIV / AIDS service provider in Nepal.

I proceeded to the Health Ministry, to enquire if my family might receive temporary non-tourist visas. These would bridge the time between the expiry of our tourist visas, and the granting of long-term non-tourist visas once the project had formally been agreed. The Under Secretary smiled as he reclined in his large comfortable chair, but did nothing to help us. He suggested we should leave the country for six months, during which time a Nepali representative of the organisation could secure our agreements.

Alice the camel has 8 humps,
Alice the camel has 8 humps,
Alice the camel has 8 humps,
So go, Alice, go, turum tum tum.

While still pondering his response, my French colleague and I set out to visit the four district centres of our proposed working area. This would be our first contact with local officials and community leaders. Within ten minutes of leaving Butwal by bus, we found ourselves stuck in a traffic jam. Had we had our wits about us, we would not have paid our fares so willingly at the very start of a long journey. Some hours previously a bus had knocked down two students. Rumour had it that on realising what he had done, the driver reversed over the victims, to be sure that they were dead. "How could he do such a thing?" I asked in utter disbelief. What I learned was that compensation claims made against bus owners frequently resulted in large payouts. And it was deemed cheaper to pay funeral expenses than hospital bills. Family and peers of the dead youths blocked the highway.

So we sat on the roadside, drank sweet Nepali tea, chatted, wrote our diaries, and waited. As we watched, farmers nearby worked their fields by hand. I felt envious. No hold ups plagued their lives. But as I reflected more, I realised that life for them was a constant struggle to produce sufficient crops to make ends meet.

Two and a half hours later our bus crept forward 200 metres and stopped again. We abandoned it and walked up the 1 km queue of waiting traffic. An animated crowd milled around the site of the accident. With raised voices, the bus operator argued with the friends and families of the students. Police attempted to mediate.

Ahead lay 5 km of empty road. One hour of walking in the hot sun brought us to a police barrier at the head of a second queue of traffic. Another bus took us on our way. After midnight we finally reached Sandhi-kharka, situated at the end of an un-tarred road. We were glad to be accommodated in a cramped lodge that the bus crew patronised, and collapsed into our beds.

In Sandhi-kharka we made fruitful visits to the District Development Committee, Red Cross office, local hospital and a European-Union-funded project. The District Health Officer said he would write a letter recommending our new programme to the Health Ministry. We chatted to the local MP who happened to be walking down the main street. Those we met welcomed us to start TB and HIV work in their district.

In the meantime, the dispute over the dead students had escalated. Further rumours reported that an angry mob had killed the bus owner, only to find out afterwards that they had singled out the wrong man. An out-and-out regional bus strike ensued. It was to last a week; but there were only three days to go before Christmas. I had to get back home to Ros and the girls. What should we do? We debated the options into the night. At 5am the next morning we set out to walk home across country.

Taking an unknown path with no map is foolish, unless you believe in angels. One joined us as we left Sandhi-kharka bazaar. He was a young man on his way home to a village halfway along our route. As we crossed and re-crossed a shallow river, I sensed that he had been specially sent to help us. Arriving at his house, we had a glass of water and met his father. The father insisted on sending his son to guide us to the motor-road. In seven hours we reached it. A jeep's grinding engine was like music to our ears. We bade our angel goodbye and squeezed aboard, along with ten other travellers and a broken-down motorbike. When we arrived at Ridi bazaar for the next leg of our journey, we found the bus station empty. That meant that no vehicles would be going to Tansen that evening. It was a great relief to find an army recruit pacing up and down the line of teashops, hoping to find company for the 4-hour walk. He knew the path and was anxious to leave as soon as possible.

We bought torches and batteries and set off into the night up a winding river valley. As we followed our guide in the dark, we imagined how spectacular the scene would have been in daylight. At a quarter to one in the morning on Christmas Eve we arrived home, completely shattered.

Alice the camel has 7 humps... So go, Alice, go, turum tum tum.

We began to find a path through the jungle of Nepal's bureaucracy. In the summer of 2000 the Nepali government drafted a foreign aid policy. It had broad inter-party support, and was likely to be passed if parliament ever resumed normal activities. The paper set out the government's criticism of foreign-aided development work in Nepal. According to them, project spending was not being documented in government budgets, and many projects were never registered. Too many programmes employed expatriate workers who were weak at transferring skills to Nepalis. Foreign aid was being driven by donors' priorities, and these priorities differed from those of the government. Furthermore, many projects were small and used resources inefficiently.

Frankly, I felt that most of these criticisms were fully justified.

To overcome the difficulties, a number of important proposals were made. International aid would be channelled through a single window (the Social Welfare Council), enabling the government to have more control over incoming funds. Development work would focus on the *government's* priority areas, and District officials and Nepali non-governmental organisations (NGOs) would oversee management of programmes. Where possible, qualified Nepalis would be employed in preference to expatriates.

## Agreements and visas

Nick –

All aid organisations working in Nepal require both general and project agreements. Once the basic responsibilities of the agency have been outlined and agreed, the first expatriate visa is granted. Following this, any number of individual project agreements may be filed. And it is in these more defined agreements that the case has to be made for additional visas.

I was not an experienced government negotiator; I was a learner again. At the Health Ministry I formally presented our programme, and sought to begin the general agreement process. "How should I proceed?" I asked. "You've lived in Nepal, so you know what is needed," an under secretary assured me. I didn't know what was needed. Was he fishing for something? I asked myself. "And what about the role of a private consultant to assist us?" I enquired. "No need to bother about that," he replied, smiling broadly, "just give me the fees instead!"

Alice the camel has 6 humps... So go, Alice, go, turum tum tum.

## The long road to Kathmandu

Nick –

Our family home was in Tansen, but central government offices are all in Kathmandu. So I got to know the Tansen to Kathmandu road very well. The journey was not for the faint hearted.

The best public bus left the bazaar around dawn. One morning I headed for this service, greeting students as they made their way to early morning classes. The conductor stored my rucksack in a side compartment and I climbed aboard. Promptly at six the bus departed. During the first hour and a half we twisted and turned along the road to Butwal. Three people leaned out of the windows to vomit. My ears popped as we finally descended into the town. We stopped at a place where wayside vendors were serving sweet Nepali tea. Twenty minutes later the bus driver revved the engine, tooted his horn, and we set off again. Along the flat road to Narayanghat we halted in a huge forest. Most passengers alighted. Women squatted behind trees; men were less discreet.

The rivers that cross the road are virtually dry between December and May. But torrential currents during the previous year's monsoon had washed away many of the bridges. At these points the road took a diversion down and across the riverbeds. I wondered if the bridges would be repaired before the next monsoon.

Alice the camel has 5 humps… So go, Alice, go, turum tum tum.

From Narayanghat the road turns north, following a steep-sided gorge. We reached Mugling at midday. Here you could buy curry and rice 24 hours a day. I got a helping for 40 rupees (about 30p). The remaining journey to Kathmandu took three more hours. We passed Manakamana, an ancient Hindu temple that has become a popular destination since the advent of a cable car. It is a stiff two-hour climb to the shrine on foot, or a 10-minute cable ride. Among the visitors are couples that desire sons. They pray and worship Hindu gods at the temple. At Naubise I drank another cup of Nepali tea, but resisted buying pungent dried fish and stale-looking popadums from roving traders. Just beyond the village I glimpsed the landmark I always looked out for – a white tower situated near the outer rim of the Kathmandu valley. "We're getting there at last," I sighed. We ascended the zigzag road for 40 minutes, in first and second gears, with clouds of blue exhaust spewing from every vehicle. As we proceeded over the pass and down into the valley my heart sank. It did every time. The lush fertile landscape was littered with new residential developments, grimy lorry-repair workshops and smoke-discharging brick factories. A grey haze hung over the whole of Kathmandu valley.

When we reached the ring road I thanked the bus driver and squeezed aboard a 'micro-bus'. These private vehicles ply for custom along numbered routes all over the city. Ten minutes later I called out for it to stop, and walked the last two hundred yards to the flat where I was staying. The cup of tea I made for myself tasted particularly good, mercifully unsweetened.

These long journeys to and from Kathmandu gave me lots of time to sit and think, and pray. It was Robert Warren, in his book 'An Affair of the Heart'[19], who first gave me the idea of focusing on a particular issue when saying the Lord's Prayer – be it Nepal's security situation, my family, or a forthcoming meeting - and then giving lots of time to mull over each phrase. I've especially grown to appreciate the three lines: "give us bread", "forgive our sins", "as we forgive others." These phrases embrace the physical, spiritual and social issues we face every day. I've found it is also possible to pray in the same manner when saying the 'Grace'[20].

## Learning the ropes

Nick –

From December 2000 to March 2001 I worked to obtain general and project agreements through Nepal's Health Ministry. I visited many offices in Kathmandu and Western Nepal to obtain letters of recommendation. At the end of

March an under secretary casually informed me of the Ministry's decision to reject our application. He advised us to submit our papers to the Social Welfare Council (SWC) – a subsidiary of the Women, Children and Social Welfare Ministry. I gave a long groan. Five months into my assignment, I re-started the negotiations, with a second government office on the other side of town.

Alice the camel has 4 humps... So go, Alice, go, turum tum tum.

In Nepal government offices, senior staff cannot make a move without the support of junior staff, and junior staff are unable to take decisions without their seniors. More often than not, the absence of a staff member was the reason given for bureaucratic delay. If I could get a dollar for every time I've been told to "Come back tomorrow" or "Come back next week", I would be a rich man. I learned not to telephone for an appointment, as a secretary would inevitably advise me to come another day. It was far better to go in person (with a good book to read while waiting) and negotiate with officials face to face.

All civil service employees had excellent job security, or so it seemed. One official pointed out that junior staff could refuse to follow a directive without fear of being penalised. The 'go slow' tactic was popular. When I was desperate to process Rosalind's visa application, the same man taunted me, "You can't proceed to type the letter of confirmation on the same day that authority has been granted – that's just not done." Only later did I realise that if I had been prepared to pay a small bribe, that official might have acted very differently.

Coping with endemic corruption was very wearing and frustrating.

The quickest way to obtain a letter from a ministry office required six steps, and could take several weeks. The SWC had prepared an introductory letter about our French organisation for submission to the Ministry of Women. I offered to be the 'postman' to carry it across town. First, it was registered at the Ministry's front desk (step 1). Then it was handed to a senior ranking official, who assigned our case to a lower officer (step 2). He hole-punched the letter, tied it into a new brown cardboard file, read it and prepared a suggested action plan (step 3). The file then rose through three tiers of officials to reach someone of sufficient seniority to authorise the plan: in this case, the Ministry's Secretary (step 4). She gave me a few moments to introduce our proposal, and suggested we appoint a retired under secretary to assist us with the complexities of government negotiations. In what appeared to be a gesture of goodwill, she said she could recommend someone.

I suspected, however, that she might well have had a member of her own family in mind, so tried to steer her back to the project plans. We didn't want another 'helper'; we just wanted her department to process our paperwork speedily. Knowing I had to keep on her right side, I kept smiling, but avoided making any promises.

Then I returned to the person who had prepared our file in the first place. He dictated and later signed letters to the Finance Ministry, the National Planning Office and the Home Ministry, requesting them to recommend the new programme (step 5). Once these letters had been logged at the front desk, and the appropriate official stamps applied (step 6), I was permitted to take them on to their respective recipients.

We discovered that the Finance Ministry could not take our papers forward without the National Planning Office's approval, and the Home Ministry needed the go-ahead from the Finance Ministry. With such little trust between both departments and officials, it was little wonder that no single person was authorised to make a decision independently.

At 5pm that evening I raced towards the bus station to catch a 'night bus' that I hoped would get me home to Tansen around one in the morning.

Alice the camel has 3 humps... So go, Alice, go, turum tum tum.

During the final twists and turns of our negotiations, I was finally granted a 2-month non-tourist visa. At the eleventh hour we needed an answer to a crucial question – could Ros (and the girls) be provided with similar visas? Despite having received approval from a senior official, a junior took it upon himself to write a letter recommending that approval should not be extended to the rest of my family. Nothing I said would persuade this man to back down. In the end we had no option but to abandon the process and make a fresh application for a temporary visa for Ros. Junior staff seemed to love flexing their muscles and proving their influence.

In spite of these protracted negotiations, the concluding agreements did not permit more than one expatriate to work for our organisation in Nepal. In line with foreign aid policy, the Social Welfare Council argued that we should appoint a Nepali to the post of administrator, rather than an expatriate. The French organisation persuaded me to apply pressure for a second visa, as it was their custom to place two expatriates together in a location, and funding for Nepal had been sought with this in mind. My efforts were in vain, and this meant we had to face the problems associated with a succession of short-term tourist-status appointments.

Alice the camel has 2 humps... So go, Alice, go, turum tum tum.

Disaster struck. I lost my passport. Had I left it at the Immigration Office the previous day? When I enquired, an official sympathised with me – but also made a special point of reminding me of all the hassle and expense that would be entailed in getting a new passport through the British Embassy. He said it was more than likely that an Immigration Officer had found it and was keeping it safe. He also hinted that a gift might be in order to secure its return. Clearly he knew exactly where it was. I felt relieved, but I also knew that I had been trapped. What should my response be?

It had been my own foolishness to leave my passport there, I reasoned, so I did give the man a 'thank you payment' as he returned my documents.

## Separation and Uncertainty

Ros –

Though it was Nick who was running around negotiating agreements, we both had to endure repeated separation and uncertainty. Each week Nick set out for Kathmandu unable to predict when he would return. Our weekends were Friday-to-Saturday. One Wednesday evening, Nick phoned to say he had an appointment with a government official on Friday morning. I cried. As it was a day's journey from Kathmandu to Tansen, and buses left early in the morning, Nick would spend our days off on the road. The whim of a bureaucrat had ruined my hopes for a weekend together.

After this we resolved to establish a new pattern. From then on Nick travelled to Kathmandu on a Sunday (the start of the school week) and returned the following Thursday. He made a point of telling me the maximum time he would be away, rather than his optimistic minimum. It was easier to cope with planned time apart, than to expect him home and be disappointed.

Keeping in contact by phone each day was essential. After some frustrating evenings when I repeatedly disturbed Nick's Kathmandu hosts, we fixed 9pm as the time for our daily chat. Those were the days before mobile phones.

## Leaning on God

Ros –

By January it was becoming obvious that things were not progressing as expected. I wanted to know what we should do if the negotiation process failed. We talked with our UK sending-agency about contingency arrangements, and this helped to ease my anxiety.

By February I felt weary; the process of gaining an agreement was painstakingly slow. In March a hymn we sang at our fortnightly English service moved me to tears: 'Peace, perfect peace, our future all unknown? Jesus we know, and He is on the throne'[21].

How did I keep going? I leaned on God and on his clear call to Tansen. "Go 'north'," one prayerful supporter had said; it was only later we discovered that Tansen means 'northern town'. As we planned our return to Nepal, Nick had been offered two jobs - both of them in Tansen. The French option gave us an opportunity to work with a humanitarian aid agency, and broaden our experience. As well as the challenge of pioneering a new programme, the posting would enable us to enjoy the friendship of the team at the mission hospital in Tansen. There was no doubt in our minds that God wanted us to serve him there.

The Nepali New Year, which occurs in April, always took me by surprise. That year Mohan's wife, Nirmala made a New Year's resolution. She asked me to be her prayer partner. "We could meet once a week to pray and read the Bible together," I suggested. "I was hoping it would be every day," Nirmala replied, with a wistful smile. We started to meet three times a week. Nick had taken on Mohan to help him with the practical jobs of setting up the office. His assignment was initially on a temporary basis, and the lack of job security was a cause for concern. So Nirmala and I started to pray together about the practicalities of establishing the French organisation's work. Nick had become discouraged when a government ministry kept procrastinating over the provision of letters of recommendation. Nirmala and I prayed specifically about this. That evening, at 5pm the officer agreed to write the letters – though putting pen to paper had to wait until the following day. On another occasion, Nick told me on the phone that he had been unable to get an appointment with the man responsible for VAT. Nirmala and I prayed over this issue too. The next day Nick had a useful meeting. We began to witness the profound value of focused and persistent prayer. At each small stage in the process we saw God answer. It was a week-by-week lesson in trust, better than any discipleship course I might have devised for a young believer.

As the months slipped by, our situation became more fragile. We could not renew our tourist visas that were due to expire at the end of May. Without a valid visa you are stymied: you can neither stay in Nepal legally, nor leave. We provisionally booked a flight to the UK for the end of May. It had to be confirmed two weeks beforehand. Only then, if the process looked likely to fail, would we pack up our house and go. 'Expect the best, prepare for the worst, and be ready for anything', was good advice from veteran missionary Carl Friedricks[22].

I like to plan ahead. To leave Nepal at short notice, without adequate preparation, frightened me. And yet I found myself unable to pack. Could this have been God's hand? Things continued very much as normal. The children followed their weekly routine of going to school; and on Saturdays we still enjoyed locally made 'croissants' for breakfast.

"Does God get sore ears?" asked one of our prayer supporters. We urged them to pray, and to keep on praying for the process with the government. Each Thursday at our

Nepali house-group, I reported on the latest chapter of the saga, and our Nepali brothers and sisters also brought our needs to the Lord. At the eleventh hour, in mid-May, Nick finally secured temporary non-tourist visas for us. The agreement process was moving forward, and we trusted it would soon reach completion. We thanked God that there was no need to confirm the air tickets.

A phone call at 6am on June 1st 2001 roused us from our bed. The local British Embassy warden rang to inform us that King Birendra, Queen Aishwarya and other members of the royal family had been murdered at the palace. The usual broadcast of news in English on Radio Nepal was replaced, without explanation, with continuous nondescript music. News filtered to us through the BBC world service, and Indian television. Apparently a drunken Crown Prince Dipendra had gone on a shooting spree, before turning the gun on himself. Nepal was in stunned shock. After a subdued hour of prayer at the Nepali church, the mission hospital expatriate team discussed emergency evacuation plans. This precautionary measure did not shake me, as I'd been living on the edge of my seat, ready to get up and go, for the last eight months.

I woke up in a cold sweat. In my dream officials signed the elusive agreement in pencil; Nick's visa lasted eight years and mine, two weeks.

Nick –

When the day came for us to sign our general and project agreements, it should have signalled a strengthening of our partnership with the Social Welfare Council. But sadly, this did not turn out to be the case. Last-minute delays postponed the meetings that had been planned. When eventually we met, it was obvious that the SWC were keen to get publicity in the national press, and even had a photographer present for the occasion. But the whole thing left me feeling flat.

The slog of obtaining agreements and visas had taken its toll, and had dented my enthusiasm. It certainly was not the way of making us feel welcome to work in Nepal.

*We signed our general agreement. On the outside I smiled, but inside I sighed with relief.*

Alice the camel has 1 hump... So go, Alice, go, turum tum tum.

Alice the camel has no humps,
Alice the camel has no humps,
Alice the camel has no humps,
'Cos Alice is a horse!

Like children, gleefully torturing their parents with a song that never ends, the bureaucratic process to establish the legal status of our organisation in Nepal seemed to grind on endlessly. And some of the high hopes we had at the outset were never realised.

Ros –

Confirmation of the agreement between our organisation and the Nepali government was announced on Radio Nepal's English news at 8pm on August 16th. I could hardly believe my ears. It was an enormous relief when I saw the actual document signed in ink. At last our visas were secured. Unlike my pregnancy with Elizabeth, this gestation period had been intensely difficult. After a painful 9 months and 12 days, our second Nepali 'baby' was born.

# CHAPTER 9

# LAUNCH OF THE TB AND HIV / AIDS PROGRAMME

Nick –

The Programme I set up covered four districts in western Nepal: Gulmi, Arghakhanchi, Syangja and Palpa. The office base was at Tansen. The aim of the Programme was to combat the continuing high prevalence of tuberculosis, to prevent the escalation of the HIV epidemic, and address needs among an increasing number of AIDS sufferers. Some 40% of adults in Nepal are infected with TB bacteria. Each year approximately 1 in 500 Nepalis develops active TB. UNAIDS estimates that 1 in 200 adults are HIV positive.

The Programme sought to motivate and educate Government Health Workers, to make them competent trainers. With so much stigma attached to both diseases, community awareness formed a crucial part of the work.

Our intention was not to act independently of government health strategy, but rather to complement, or 'add value' to the national TB and HIV programmes. This meant working with the staff of existing TB and HIV / AIDS screening and treatment clinics. Operating in conjunction with national programmes was never easy, but we strove to do all we could to maintain a healthy relationship.

## Can a dog befriend a cat? Relationships with government staff

Nick –

The difficulty between cats and dogs is their mutual lack of trust. Sometimes it seemed impossible to build trust between government and international non-governmental organisations. I contemplated this as I sat through the long-winded speeches at a local government meeting.

"Honourable Chairman Sir, Chief District Officer Sir, District Health Office Chief Sir, French Organisation Co-ordinator Sir, senior representatives from other district offices, programme staff, local journalists, District Health Office colleagues, gentlemen, ladies." We had no option but to endure the endless courtesies at the beginning of the opening speech. Turning to the wall, the speaker read from a painted cloth banner – "Today, the 3$^{rd}$ of Baisakh, 2059 (Nepal does not use the Gregorian calendar), I welcome you to this annual co-ordination meeting for TB and HIV control and prevention." It seemed to be a carefully choreographed performance: the next six speakers opened their contributions with virtually identical recitals.

I, too, learned my rank in the order of district level actors. Before a meeting's formal opening ceremony, I would hurriedly consult my little notebook and revise the Nepali vocabulary for 'chairman', 'honoured guests' and 'office chief'. However, it seemed to me that this very artificial practice was a waste of time and only served to prop up an unhealthy hierarchy. Seniors all too often exploited this hierarchy when they belittled the capabilities of their juniors.

At an informal introduction to a week's course conducted by my colleagues, I picked up a card with half a fish drawn on it. Everyone else had a bisected picture too. Each of us walked around the room looking for our match. In pairs we swapped introductions – our names and where we lived, the make up of our family, something we liked, and something we didn't. "Tell me something you don't like," I asked, "I don't like when people undermine what others say," my fellow participant replied. He was a mid-level government worker. Social structure in many government offices appeared to be built on power relationships in which criticism of one another's actions maintains the status quo. We sought to conduct our training events in a non-hierarchical way.

Another government worker confronted me:
"Your organisation used to work in Myagdi district, didn't it?"
"Yes", I replied.
"I seem to remember that your co-ordination with government was poor, wasn't it?"
"I can't comment on the old programme, as I wasn't even in the country at that point," was my defensive response.
"Well, make sure your new programme makes a much better go of it this time."

It was strange how government staff found time to criticise our work, but rarely to give any praise. They also found fault with the methods we used for training.

Two colleagues and I, in collaboration with a district health office, commenced a week of training for government health supervisors. With energy and skill, one of our team led an informal opening programme in which we exchanged introductions in pairs and then presented one another to the whole group. Later in the day I spoke enthusiastically to the district doctor about the high calibre of my colleagues: "Many of them don't have advanced formal qualifications, but they facilitate learning very well, don't they?" Immediately I regretted my casual remark. I had admitted to breaking a sacrosanct rule of the government health sector. When it came to teaching, it simply was not acceptable to receive training from a less qualified person. Over the next few days, my 'undergraduate' was only allowed to assist with peripheral aspects of training. As a result, the participants lost out.

Senior qualified staff may be ineffective trainers. Conversely, junior personnel who grasp a subject well can make first-rate teachers. Problems arise when senior staff feel threatened by competent juniors, so they insist on a rigid hierarchy for training. It serves to protect them, and keeps juniors subordinate.

## Grab what you can

Nick –

Why do people keep on pressing for ever higher personal benefits? I guess that's human nature. Our neighbours' children played for hours and hours on the swing in our garden. While there, they took the opportunity to feast on the cucumbers and carrots growing in my vegetable patch. It seemed to me that some district health staff were like those children. They received assistance, but were always on the lookout for any extra benefits they could gain from our programme.

Two colleagues were having some difficulty with a local health worker, so I attended the last day of a training course to help them. When I arrived, participants were learning how to prevent HIV transmission. To my dismay, the health worker saw my visit as a golden opportunity to complain about the allowances that he and the second government trainer received. He lectured me for an hour. In some areas, district health workers had been pushing our staff to stretch the rules on allowances, to such an extent that our regulations had become meaningless.

When co-ordination at the district level worked well, all parties benefited - government staff, our organisation, and the community. But that rarely happened. We were suspicious of the motives of government staff; and they, no doubt, were critical of us. It was akin to the cat and dog relationship – understanding each other was almost impossible; both parties tried to get one up on the other.

## Visionaries make all the difference

Nick –

Nepalis are resourceful. But government systems of working tend to stifle creativity. At one health post I observed that some basic services were lacking.

"We haven't a single sterile needle," a nurse complained.

Pointing to a brand new pressure-cooker unit, still wrapped in plastic, she said, "What good is this, if we don't have paraffin for the stove?" Later we were told that they no longer weighed infants, because the cloth baby-trousers used to hang babies on the scales needed re-sewing.

At the National TB Centre I demonstrated our locally made flip charts. Health volunteers used them to teach their neighbours about tuberculosis. "They look great" enthused a staff member.

"Could the government distribute these for use across Western Nepal?" I asked.

"Of course, that would make sense."

"How many do you need?"

"We'll let you know."

They never did.

There was keen interest when I suggested that we could provide microscopes to Western Nepal through the national TB programme.

"Please tell us which models of microscopes you are using in Nepal, so that those we give match your existing ones."

"Yes, of course."
We heard nothing more.

"Can you give us training and test-kits so we can set up our own local HIV-testing service?" asked a district health officer.
"Yes, we are ready to help, but you must first prepare a short document showing how you intend to run the service to ensure confidentiality and sustainability."
"OK, we'll do that."
They never did.

Is it any wonder that international NGOs are tempted to muscle in and take over direct management of projects in Nepal, rather than seek to develop local capacity?

One influential man who had a vision for government and NGOs working in collaboration, was the Director of the National TB Centre. Key players on both sides came together every 4 months to discuss progress across Nepal. On one occasion, I made an appointment in advance to see the Director and arrived at the Centre with guests from our Paris headquarters. "Yes, the doctor is expecting you, please take a seat for a moment." We took off our shoes and entered his large carpeted office. While he continued his phone conversation, we were shown to low, cushioned seats. He called for a tray of tea, and moved out from behind his imposing desk to sit alongside us. During a warm-hearted discussion, he made a deliberate point of thanking us for our contribution to TB work and praised the Programme's community approach.

I had frequent contact with this energetic man. On one occasion he travelled by plane and car from Kathmandu to join us at a regional TB meeting. We rose to our feet as his entourage arrived. His time was short, so he immediately proceeded to quiz participants about the state of the TB programmes in their districts. For one, where the TB case-finding rate was poor, the doctor persisted in interrogating the district TB assistant. By the time the meeting was over, the man's hands trembled, and his head hung low. It was not unlike the humiliation that my student friends and I suffered at the hands of surgical consultants on medical school ward-rounds.

Dr Robert Koch announced his discovery of the TB bacterium on 24th March 1882. The TB Centre promoted World TB Day each year. In March of our final year in Nepal, the Centre's Director invited the Palace to attend a Kathmandu event. He was in his element. Fully attired in formal Nepali dress, he proudly escorted Crown Prince Paras around the exhibition hall. I felt nervous as I presented our organisation's work to the Prince. I also felt uneasy, as many Nepalis were opposed to the reigning royal family's heavy-handed role in governing the nation.

The Director was a model of determination and commitment. He had remained in post since the inception of the TB Centre three years previously. In the same period, no fewer than six directors of the National HIV / AIDS Centre in Kathmandu had been appointed. Such a high turnover meant that it was not possible to foster HIV networking between government and the non-government organisations. I could never quite understand what accounted for the demise of so many directors in such a short space of time. Admittedly, the style of the Director of the TB Centre was autocratic; but with passion and tears, rebuke and encouragement, he inspired government players and a wide spectrum of non-government agencies. And this led to the development of high-quality TB services in Nepal.

## The Umbrella and French organisations compared... chalk and cheese

Nick –

Thirty nine Christian agencies worked together as the Umbrella Organisation in Nepal. Its headquarters are in

Kathmandu. The French organisation is an international humanitarian aid agency based in Paris.

It was ten years ago that we started working with the Umbrella. 18 adults arrived in Nepal that spring, and we spent the first five months doing full-time language study. Six years later, at a farewell party for a family from the group, we met up again. Nine of us were still serving in Nepal. Things were very different with the French organisation. During my three and a half years working for that body I had an expatriate colleague for only half of the time. Those appointed to the post of administrator stayed between two and seven months. My first colleague arrived on a one-year contract. After only two weeks in Nepal he was told that lack of funds meant he would have to return to France. I encouraged each administrator to learn Nepali, but the organisation assigned no time to language acquisition.

Rapid immersion is one thing; being thrown in to sink or swim is another. We had supper with an American who had lived in Nepal for 18 months. After five months language study he started to lead the community health department at Tansen Mission Hospital. He admitted the placement had been difficult for a newcomer to Nepal – he had to operate in the Nepali language and negotiate with local officials, as well as develop the work and the staff team. His department ran well. But I think someone with more experience of Nepal should have taken the lead. Each of my short-term colleagues with the French organisation, and two more who have come to Nepal since my contract ended, arrived with little orientation training, and no understanding of the Nepali language. They were expected to assume key responsibilities in the programme on day one. Numerous organisations operating from offices in Kathmandu follow this emergency assistance model. Strings of short-term expatriates with no experience of Nepal arrive and struggle with government officialdom. After five months (the maximum time allowed on a tourist visa) they leave, discouraged that they have not achieved very much. It's almost comical. But what a waste of human and financial resources.

## Human being or human doing?

Nick –

We knew a two-doctor Finnish couple at Amppipal who regarded 'being' as of much greater value than 'doing'. The husband was a great believer in giving time to his patients, even if he got behind with his clinics. His wife stopped practising medicine, and allowed their home to become a place of refuge for their Nepali neighbours. Their children became virtually indistinguishable from their Nepali playmates. They saw 'living with the people and learning from the people' as the first step to finding opportunities to serve. By contrast, many expatriates in Nepal seem to be wholly focussed on 'doing', striving to justify their presence through frenetic activity. Several short-termers who have worked with us in Tansen have fallen into this trap. There is not much for a single person to do if it's not possible to socialise in Nepali. To stave off boredom, some have worked independently in the evening and at weekends, tapping on their computers to produce a plethora of documents on various programme initiatives.

With a minimum of local orientation, humanitarian aid workers love to jump into new placements and implement change. They don't speak the local language, so they tend to direct activities rather than collaborate with nationals. Another thing that can seriously hamper community development work is a rapid turnover of expatriate staff. A new broom tends to sweep clean, and this often results in projects being curtailed or significantly modified. National personnel feel let down and lose the will to think creatively.

The Umbrella's health project directors met each year for a week's conference. We learned about the organisation's strategy, and played a part in developing future policy. We confronted many issues that we faced day-to-day. For example, how could we justify calling the Umbrella a Christian organisation, when many of those working in its programmes were Hindus? The organisation aims 'to serve in Nepal in the name and spirit of Jesus'. But what did this mean in practice? Christians within it are free to communicate about Jesus by their words and their work[23]. After discussion, those of us who were Christians resolved to make our lives 'salty' for Jesus – seasoning the places we live and work with the attitudes of Jesus. We all agreed that prayer in Jesus' name – bringing our daily concerns to God – should be an explicit element in the daily life of the organisation's projects.

Each year the French organisation's project co-ordinators attended a conference in Paris. We ate and drank well, and I discovered that this organisation's members are emotional, strongly political, quite disorganised, but immensely sociable. On evenings off I ambled around the Arc de Triomphe and Eiffel tower or tiptoed into the lofty church of Montmartre.

The formal content of our meetings was translated from French into English and Spanish. This was a new experience for me. I found that those of us who relied on translation were at a slight disadvantage at question-and-answer times, since French speakers had a 5-second lead to jump in with their ideas. However, the facility meant I could participate fully, and I was even able to lead small group sessions. Each year, the conference coincided with the organisation's annual general meeting, so internal politics tended to dominate. We debated the pros and cons of shifting the organisation's focus to crisis alleviation rather than development projects. We looked at the three elements that comprised programme leadership: a volunteer doctor in France, who gave direction to the work; a salaried administrator at headquarters, who provided management support; and a co-ordinator on the field, who implemented the programme. We rarely addressed more practical issues. I perceived a yawning gap between theory and practice. The dreaming, philosophising and politically active hub often seemed far removed from the isolated field-based projects.

The Umbrella provided banking services, sent and received post, assisted with customs clearance and arranged accommodation for its many appointees. By contrast, since there were only one or two expatriates working in Nepal, the French organisation relied on us to take care of all these practical arrangements for ourselves.

When I worked with the Umbrella I became familiar with its employment policies and procedures. These had been shaped and re-shaped over 40 years of working in Nepal. In 1992 the government adopted a new labour act. As the organisation compared its policies with the legislation, we could see that the Umbrella gave more annual leave than the law required, but was stricter than the law in other areas. For example, we viewed theft from an employer as a serious offence, whereas the government had a more lenient attitude. As we worked at adapting our own employment policies I gained a working knowledge of Nepal's labour act and rules.

Arriving in Nepal with the French organisation, I inherited employment guidelines prepared by the outgoing team a year before. I resolved to develop these in conjunction with Nepal's labour laws and my experience of working in the Umbrella. As I did so I created a generic national staff post list with clear definitions of the grading levels. This proved useful when we appointed and promoted staff. To encourage equity, I set a salary scale whereby the rates paid to the highest-level national staff were only five times greater than those paid to the lowest grades. Most organisations have much wider pay differentials.

## Support from seniors

Nick –

When I worked as Director of Gorkha Community Health Programme, my line manager in Kathmandu knew Amppipal well. She regularly visited the project, and always thanked me for documents I sent. It was clear that her principal concern was to see an effective team delivering quality services. During the three and a half years I led the French organisation's Nepal programme, I sent reports to France each month. Most were never acknowledged. Generally, when we made enquiries to headquarters, they were slow to respond. The volunteer doctor in France did not appear very interested in the work. He visited twice. Three different administrators at headquarters provided management support, and one came to Tansen. When visiting, most of their time was given to office-based review, rather than witnessing programme activities or evaluating quality. The headquarters' team had little understanding of Nepal, because their attention was divided between numerous projects world wide. In spite of all the hammering I did on the doors of government offices every week, trying to secure a second expatriate visa, all I received from Paris were pithy emails saying I should 'push harder'.

Within the Umbrella, financial accountability was stressed. We had to make clear justification for over or under-spending our budgets. However, in practice money followed work and never became an all-consuming issue. The Umbrella's focus was on long-term development in Nepal. So few resources were needed beyond the modest salaries of national staff.

At my appointment interview in Paris with the French organisation, I asked to see the accounts of the previous

Nepal programme. I was struck by the huge amounts that had been spent. I explained that I would hope to operate a much less expensive programme. That November, the agency sent me to Nepal with an administrator, fully anticipating the launch of the work. We could not begin because there was no agreement with the government, but the organisation pressed us to spend designated funds before the end of the year. A month later, shortage of money resulted in my colleague being pulled back to France.

We searched Kathmandu for new sources of funding. We approached various embassies. Non-government health programmes competed with each other for limited funds. Every project had to show that it would achieve measurable and cost-effective health gains. We teased out the 'most attractive' elements of our proposals in order to solicit support. I did not feel comfortable with this approach.

During that first year we established low cost patterns of operation. At a later stage, more than adequate European Union funding became available and we consistently under-spent our annual budgets. I tried to justify our position, but headquarters informed me that under-spending placed them in a poor light in the eyes of fund providers. This could jeopardise future applications for financial support. The appropriateness or quality of our work in Nepal appeared to be less important than spending the budget fast enough.

When I went to the Umbrella's Kathmandu headquarters, senior colleagues always made time to listen to me. Each year I received an appraisal of my work. Ros' contribution was valued too. Indeed, she played a vital role as an ambassador of the Umbrella. When I went to the headquarters of the French organisation, staff generally seemed too busy at their computers to give much time to talk. My work was not regularly appraised. And Ros was never invited to join me in Paris.

I'd be wrong to depict the Umbrella as a perfect organisation. I think it also recognised some of its own shortcomings. To some extent we were sheltered from the real world. When we worked for them in a remote corner of Gorkha, I was under the impression that, with the exception of a similar Pokhara-based organisation, no other agency gave useful service to Nepal. While it is true that there are thousands of ineffective national and international NGOs throughout the country, I now realise there are many others of a high calibre.

We greatly appreciated all the services provided by the Umbrella, but being 'cushioned' in this way meant that we had no idea how to handle routine procedures, such as exchanging currency or applying for a driving licence. And when we worked in Tansen we discovered that the Umbrella had a bureaucratic face we'd not seen before. As 'outsiders', it proved difficult to enrol our girls into Tansen's mission hospital school, although we had personal links there. Looking back, I realise that I was a bit unfair in my criticism of our French organisation. There is enough Anglo–French animosity without my adding to it. I was at fault in making little effort to improve my own French language skills, and, when receiving communication in French, quite enjoyed adopting the mentality 'if you don't understand it, just brush it aside'. Having complained about the lack of support that I received from France, I have to admit that I revelled in the opportunity to work independently in Nepal. I pioneered a new programme, assembled and built a new team, and, in consultation with Nepali colleagues, developed the work. Had the French organisation been more involved, I might have had less freedom. And Ros did appreciate the generous Christmas hampers and the Bordeaux wine and Camembert I brought back from the annual Paris conferences.

Our four and a half years with the Umbrella gave us rich insights into Nepali life and exposed us to a style of working that matched our ideals. I did not entirely fit in to the French organisation. But I cannot say I had not been warned. Even my appointment letter hinted at the mismatch.

"…we would like to confirm our interest in your application for the position of Medical Coordinator in Nepal. Nevertheless, wishing to be frank, we have the impression that you might not be completely convinced by 'our approach', but we might be wrong, therefore we leave it up to you… We are waiting for your answer."

I accepted the post. The experience of working with the French organisation was challenging and rewarding. But there was a clash of cultures as I tried to operate the new programme in the style of my previous experience. In the end, headquarters shortened my contract to make way for someone whose leadership style might suit them better. But I'm jumping to the end of the story. After working for nine long months to obtain government agreement to work in the fight against TB and HIV, we were ready to launch the new programme.

## Launch of the TB and HIV / AIDS programme

Nick –

As I entered this new phase, I drew on much that I had learned from my Master's course in London. I applied epidemiology concepts when analysing the impact of drama on knowledge about TB. The family planning module I'd studied matched our approach to HIV / AIDS. And I utilized my learning about teaching health workers and health management.

## Appointing Staff

Nick –

If you want good staff, first select the right people.

The most rewarding aspects of my work in Nepal were end-of-month reporting and planning, and staff recruitment.

We initially chose seven Nepalis to launch the new TB and HIV / AIDS programme. Two and a half years later we had a team of 25 national staff.

When we advertised for health trainers, 80 people applied for two vacancies. Among the questions on the application form were: "From your previous experience, what special contribution will you bring to the programme?" and "Why are TB and HIV major public health issues in Nepal?"

Members of the senior staff team and I short-listed eight candidates. We used our tried and tested selection system. We decided what we were looking for: relevant experience, qualifications etc, and drew up a table for recording marks for each attribute. We eliminated most candidates on the basis of insufficient experience or lack of imagination in answering the questions.

On the selection day, the eight candidates interviewed one another in pairs and then introduced their partner to the whole group. They also sat a written test. One question was "You are conducting four days of training. The local village leader threatens to stop the course if you don't include his wife as a participant – what do you do?" In the afternoon the candidates were given a problem that they discussed in small groups. We wanted to observe how individuals functioned – did they facilitate one another, or were they dominant or passive? Finally, each candidate had to draw and present a health promotion poster.

By the time we reached the actual interviews, we were almost sure whom we would choose. The process also enabled candidates to make their own evaluation of each other. All the interviewees – both successful and not – said afterwards that they'd enjoyed and benefited from the day.

Neighbours and church friends were eager to find employment with us. "It's your duty to appoint one of us," they would say, when we met them on the path. This made me feel awkward afterwards when I saw disappointment in their faces. I sensed relief – both in our neighbours' expressions and in myself - when, in our final year in Tansen, we appointed a man from the house below ours to the staff team. Giving top priority to your 'own people' is a convention that chokes progress in Nepal. Many organisations are stifled by it. Office heads feel obliged to appoint and promote their own family members. Those who saw themselves as 'our people' could not understand when we insisted on making appointments on merit alone. One young man sought to impress me by coming to help build rabbit cages at the weekend. However, he was 'all fingers and thumbs', he had too many suggestions, and was a bit slapdash. So his overtures backfired.

One day when we were interviewing, I had the clear sense that a somewhat older candidate was the right man for the job. Among other things, he had government experience that would be valuable to the programme. On his first day at work, however, the local authorities telephoned us. They wanted him for questioning: they suspected that he was involved in subversive political activities. Something didn't seem right. They were branding him a criminal... but on what evidence? By association, the legitimacy of our programme and our work were under suspicion too. After 24 difficult hours, the poor man was cleared and released – one moment a perceived threat to society, the next pushed away and ignored. He remained nervous of uniformed authorities. My intuition at the interview was rewarded over the forthcoming months as he developed his skills in leading a fieldwork team.

Numerous local people asked us for manual work, so how should we go about appointing an office cleaner? Existing programme staff and our neighbours suggested names of poor people they considered suitable for the job. We put all the names into a hat and drew one out at random. I was conscious of God's hand, even in this process. Three people had independently recommended the woman whose name we picked. She worked well and served us tea every day with a broad smile.

We held a practical selection day for a driver-cum-mechanic. Two candidates seemed suitable: a high-caste man, who was qualified and articulate; and a low-caste man, who had the practical skills but lacked confidence. We decided to appoint the latter, reasoning that the job could make a big difference to his family. Just under a year later he resigned, as he knew we were not happy with his conduct. Even though it was the more articulate man that eventually got the job, I was pleased that we had given the poorer man a chance.

## Team building

Nick –

From the start of our programme I wanted the team to share a common vision. So we translated basic information about the French organisation into Nepali. We looked at terms and conditions of employment, office and fieldwork patterns, and individual job descriptions. Taking turns, each morning one of us presented a 'value' from a list we had drawn up: 'Love and service,' 'Promoting participation,' 'Integrity,' 'Forgiveness,' 'Witnessing to injustice,' etc. Presenters had to explain why that day's value was an important one for us to live by. We then identified those we considered integral to our work and recorded them for future reference. They proved particularly helpful when we gave orientation training to new staff.

The team's first task was to devise, test, and carry out a community survey of knowledge and attitudes to TB and HIV

/ AIDS. We presented our findings to government officials at district and regional levels. They helped shape our future work. We drew on existing sources for local information about TB and HIV and used UNDP's excellent publication 'Tools for community participation'[24]. We drafted and redrafted training manuals for different levels of health personnel, government staff, volunteer actors, and teachers. At my farewell event, a colleague recalled those creative early days. "We needed survey tools and training manuals... so Nick guided us to make them for ourselves," he said.

My colleagues requested more feedback; and I resolved to give it whenever possible. I sat in on training sessions they gave, and took notes. I organised a review meeting at the end of each training day. We usually remembered to follow the golden rule that you must find something positive to say before making a criticism.

I have a bad habit of wanting to put my oar into everything. I could have kicked myself for interfering too much. I gradually learned to give staff more time and not be so untrusting. Over the months, as I released the reins, I observed them doing tasks much better than I could have done.

The whole staff team gathered each month for three days' reporting and planning. Each day began with someone telling a story, a joke, a riddle, or perhaps singing a song. Even our part-time cleaner took her turn. This created a good atmosphere as we moved on to administrative tasks. We held reporting and planning meetings in a big group and applauded each presenter to say "well done" or "go for it" We established patterns of working that brought out the best from each other.

Each year we had a staff picnic which lasted all day. A goat walked there, but didn't walk back. We prepared snacks, peeled vegetables, cooked over open fires, played games and ate together. Picnics were great for team building.

A year into the TB and HIV Programme, I felt challenged by God to use opportunities with colleagues to speak about my faith. They heard me pray when we ate together; they sometimes discovered me bringing difficult situations at work to God in prayer. However, the Nepali authorities frown on explicit evangelism. Moreover, our French organisation took a specifically non-religious stance. However, we gave an open invitation to my colleagues to watch 'The JESUS Film'[25] after work one day. Most of the team came, and this gave an opportunity for them to learn more about the man who is central in my life.

Ros and I prayed each day for the ongoing work of the Programme, and for its staff. Two of them were believers. I sensed that we might see two or three more of my colleagues becoming Christians, but during our three years in Tansen none of them professed faith in Jesus. God alone knows people's hearts, and I am trusting that some were drawn nearer to him.

# Chapter 10

# LIFE IN TANSEN

## Health training

Nick –

You can't make a maize seed grow, or a fish swim, or even a horse drink. Likewise, we could only provide the right conditions for others to do the active work of learning when we undertook training.

We structured our five-day courses for health workers like a sandwich. The first and last days (the bread) covered broad facilitator skills; the middle days (the cheese and pickle) dealt with specific TB and HIV / AIDS issues. One of our general topics was 'team building'. To illustrate this, we devised various activities to show how it is possible to achieve more by collaboration. For example, we equipped groups of four people with newspaper, a pair of scissors, a stapler and a tube of glue and gave them ten minutes to make paper chains. Participants had fun. Our objective was to bring them to the 'ah-ha' of discovering the point of an exercise for themselves.

We gave priority to 'training of trainers'. Senior government health workers attended courses as participants. Then they worked with our programme staff, to train their juniors. Junior staff in turn helped facilitate health volunteer courses. We bent over backwards to fit in with the government hierarchical approach to training. Sometimes partnership between

*Community health volunteers employed their creativity to retrieve a kettle from a 'crocodile-infested lake'.*

government staff and my colleagues worked well. But it was a struggle. We taught high-school teachers how to engage teenagers in informal activities. In one game, we gave students sweets to share with one another. We discreetly told two of them not to share. After a few minutes each student noted who had made contact with whom. They found that the networks of people linked to one another by sweet swapping were large. We then likened sharing sweets to having sexual contacts. Sexually transmitted infections, like HIV can quickly spread in a group of young people. Saying 'no' to sex, or using a condom, limits the spread of HIV. A few teachers went on to apply what they had learned, but we later discovered that many did not. I never fully understood why.

## Role-play and street drama for health promotion

Nick –

The 1990's strategic thinking for HIV / AIDS prevention in Nepal gave priority to female sex workers and intravenous drug users, to the exclusion of almost everyone else. I am glad that the present strategy embraces everyone. Mass strategies for health promotion aim to induce small behaviour changes in many people[26]. This is generally more effective, in population terms, than focussing on a relatively small number in the highest health risk category. We sought to influence a wide range of people through community level drama productions. To maximise the impact in four districts around Tansen, we commissioned 11 street drama teams to perform plays about TB and HIV/AIDS, over a 2-year period.

Both programmes I worked with engaged in raising awareness of health issues. But there's little point in my knowing about cholesterol if I still eat pizza and chips every night. The bottom line of health promotion is behaviour change. We can make dangerous assumptions when we promote health. For example, we assume that humans are rational, that they have similar capability to change how they live, and that the desired results can be achieved simply by feeding people's minds with relevant information. In promoting health, we also need to keep on thinking

*Men discussing health after a street drama show.*

'upstream' to tackle politically determined health factors, rather than focus solely on the 'downstream' prevention and cure of disease.

A woman's baby had diarrhoea. A friend advised her to take the child to the traditional healer. He heard half a sentence of her story and examined the baby's wrist pulses. He then declared that the child was possessed by an evil spirit. Beating on a drum, eyes closed and with his whole body shaking, the healer chanted an exorcism and banished the spirit to a local river. In the middle of the performance the mother urged him to do his job well. He declared that the healing would be confirmed if the woman returned the next Monday with a cockerel for sacrifice. Before she left, he gave her some ash to apply to the child's forehead.

The woman met her friend again. As the baby was not any better, the friend suggested a visit to the health post. They greeted the junior health worker – "Doctor sir" – and sat down. The worker showed a withered plant that she'd forgotten to water, and said that the baby needed water most of all, or it could die. She went on to examine the child with a stethoscope, and demonstrated how to make up a packet of salt and sugar solution. "And do you have a spoon at home to feed it to the baby?" she asked.

We used puppet shows like this one to good effect. Participants in health or literacy courses took roles in drama performances. I believe they learned much through the experience. People can let their hair down and engage deeply when disguised behind a make-believe role.

We sought to make learning experiences practical and fun. On a first-aid training day for community health volunteers, we made up life-like wounds for the women to treat.

On another occasion we hosted a meeting for community health staff from different Umbrella projects. The previous week, our sewing lady had expressed surprise that I'd cut out material for dungarees with a large hole in the crotch. Three of my female colleagues were embarrassed when I suggested that these dungarees could be worn, over a pair of ordinary trousers, with a doll concealed under the front panel. Then the wearer could be 'delivered' of the doll through the appropriately positioned opening. They practised the new method, but allowed only other women staff to attend the delivery. The final verdict was positive - this method was more realistic for training village midwives than using a hole in the side of a cardboard box.

I watched my new colleagues present a street drama to highlight the HIV issue for migrant labourers and their families. A Nepali who'd worked in India for the past ten months returned home for the big Hindu festival, Dasai. He was weak, had lost weight and had sores in his mouth. At the end of the play the man wept with regret as he realised that he had contracted HIV from visiting prostitutes. Villagers in the audience cried too – aware that their sons and husbands lived abroad in similar circumstances.

## Positive feedback

Nick –

A seminar at the annual coordinators' workshop in Paris prompted me to commission a 'process evaluation' of our programme. Two Nepali consultants with different backgrounds spent a week with us.

They found that all our Nepali staff understood the Project's vision and goals. Relationships in staff teams were good. They suggested that the team leaders' skills could be improved. They looked at the quality of our partnerships with district officials and village people. Government health staff who had planned and implemented activities with us, viewed our work positively; but they didn't feel a sense of ownership of the programmes that we coordinated with them. Village people were enthusiastic about using drama.

The consultants commended us on our training programmes and manuals. They recommended that private pharmacy owners should be trained in counselling skills to care for people with sexually transmitted diseases. They suggested we should refer to our 'project' as a 'programme' – in order to sound less imposing. So we changed our name, and began planning for a new component that would include private pharmacy workers. We continued to develop our own staff skills. Overall I felt buoyed up by the evaluation.

Around the same time, a senior staff member from Paris visited to observe and document our achievements. She noted that the Programme aimed to complement the government's health activities and emphasised prevention and community responsibility rather than technical care of patients. She also documented how the programme had not followed some elements of its funding proposal with the European Union. She pointed out that I was spending time on day-to-day management tasks better done by an administrator. That prompted the organisation to recruit a second expatriate. We weren't spending our European Union grant fast enough, so she also recommended that we expand the national staff team. She commented that the Programme was doing a great job coordinating its activities with local partners. Moreover, she was impressed by the training activities we were conducting. I felt encouraged.

Around World TB Day that year, we conducted a study of community people's knowledge about tuberculosis. We used a simple questionnaire with 127 respondents in three villages. Drama teams then put on plays about tuberculosis. We followed up 122 people. 50% of them had attended a play. At ten weeks there was a very significant improvement in knowledge about TB. On the basis of these results we expanded our drama programme with confidence.

## Rosalind's role in the office

Ros –

I dropped in on Nick's office a couple of times a week. One afternoon, as I was leaving, I dug to the bottom of my rucksack to find a parting gift. I had only one satsuma left. "Oh," said Nick's colleague with a smile, "having the last one means I'll get a daughter." The saying was new to me. Sometimes I took some garden flowers for the reception desk, or a chocolate cake for the expatriate administrator. Occasionally I listened to the secretary's woes, commiserated with someone about a difficult journey from the field, or just joked about 'our' difficult boss. It was easy for me to go in to the office when I went to pray with Nirmala. I looked in on the different rooms, and chatted with anyone who was around. The office staff knew me, and I felt part of the scene.

To celebrate the official launch of the programme, we invited the staff for a rice meal at our home. Five colleagues brought their spouses and children, so we were fourteen people. After the meal we played games together: we pulled wooden blocks from the stack and balanced them on the top until the pile teetered; then we played 'Pit' and 'Uno' – card games that require little English. Over the years, as staff numbers increased, we repeated this kind of party. They were good times for building friendships.

One day when our two girls accompanied me to the office, we were unexpectedly invited to stay for a welcome party for some new staff members. The girls tucked into the beaten rice and goat curry with greater relish than I did. They also enjoyed the annual picnics with Nick's colleagues. Nepalis are warm and easygoing with children.

French visitors also came to our home for meals. One brought a bottle of wine. We searched in vain for a corkscrew. Nick ran out to one of our expatriate neighbours, a Catholic nun, who lent us one. The cork broke in two, and Nick ended up digging it out with a screwdriver. I was embarrassed. Imagine working with a French organisation and not having a corkscrew.

I enjoyed giving hospitality to short-term personnel. I offered to help as an interpreter when they went to look around flats, or needed a new worker to set up their kitchen. I showed them where to find groceries, and how to have clothes made at the tailors.

Sometimes it was hard coping with Nick's hectic schedule. He frequently travelled out to the districts to encourage field workers and meet with local officials. This kind of work was more stimulating for him than office administration, so he usually returned worn out but enthusiastic. I had to develop a less ambitious programme when he was away. I was often tired and irritable at the end of the day, so needed to start the girls' bedtime routine earlier. We both played contrasting, but complementary, roles in the launch and life of the Programme.

## The girls had the time of their lives

Ros –

"How can you do this to your children?" my grandmother asked us. "It's all very well for the two of you to go, but you shouldn't risk the children's safety and development by taking them overseas."

Elizabeth was six before she learned to ride a bike. Both our girls lagged behind their British peers at swimming and roller-skating. They missed out on children's TV, soft play areas, and trips to the library, museums or seaside.

But they had the time of their lives growing up in Nepal.

We played board games, threaded beads, learned to do cross-stitch, built up stamp collections, and watched tadpoles develop. Lydia and Elizabeth grew close together, and invented imaginary schools, orphanages, toys' hospitals, and shops.

One day our helper brought a baby myna bird for the girls to feed with caterpillars. On another occasion, after watching a local woman form mud bricks in a wooden mould, the girls asked for matchboxes, and imitated the process on a smaller scale. I remember when Elizabeth came home from school clutching a leaf plate sewn together with bamboo needles; a Nepali friend had shown her how to make it.

Days out were cheap but priceless. For the cost of a picnic and a hired vehicle, the delights of a natural aqua park were ours. At the river we let the current float us downstream, or sat on a ledge beneath a miniature Jacuzzi jet. We devised our own games of ten-pin bowling, knocking down piles of stones with pebbles.

The girls were sheltered from peer pressure to buy the latest brand of trainers. They were not exposed to TV or the Internet. But they saw chickens and rabbits being killed and cut, even when we wanted to protect them from such experiences. For them chicken- meat came wrapped in feathers, rather than on a polystyrene tray.

When we left London at the beginning of November for our third stint in Nepal, the girls were disappointed to miss the school bonfire and firework display. On our arrival in Kathmandu, we found that friends had already purchased tickets for us all to attend the British Embassy Guy Fawkes' party – complete with hot dogs and homemade toffee.

We celebrated birthdays in style. The birthday girl chose the theme: we held a jungle party, an elephant party, and a dinosaur party. Nick and the children spent the morning of the 'space' party decorating our front room with silver foil. We played planet bobbing, musical stars, and ate moon cheese shapes.

One monsoon holiday, with two and a half weeks of rainy days to fill, the mums pulled together to run a kids' club. We organised flapjack-making, winding wool pompoms, playing on scooters, trampolining, watching videos together and going out for picnic walks.

The school day was from 8am to 1.30pm, which left plenty of time for play, even after homework. Musical expatriates volunteered their skills, and children were given lessons in succession on Wednesday afternoons. Nick taught keyboard, and even, reluctantly, the violin. Later he began to learn the fiddle himself. Lydia developed her skills on the keyboard, and Elizabeth started playing the violin too.

## Schools came in all shapes and sizes.

Ros –

Missionary families often find themselves torn between wanting to serve God and to do the best for their children. We faced the same dilemma. We forget that our Heavenly Father is even more concerned for our children's welfare than we are. And so we proved his faithfulness time and again. During language and orientation in Kathmandu, we stayed in a guesthouse and could hear rote-chanting going on in a nearby 'boarding' school. 'Boarding' in Nepal does not mean residential; it is shorthand for English-medium. The names of schools in Kathmandu tickled us: 'Future Stars Academy', 'Rosebuds Boarding School'... Our home in Amppipal was on a main path to the high-school. During their midday break, children stared in through our windows. We resorted to closing the curtains. When we had a look inside their gloomy classrooms, we saw nothing but rows of wooden benches on the cement floor, and a blackboard across the front wall. No wonder the local children were fascinated by glimpses of our daughters' toys. Nepali students walked for up to two hours to get to their classes, which started at 10am. Our hearts went out to these children, when on some days they swarmed back along the paths toward home, after spending just half an hour in school. Older students, in their early twenties, were politically active and frequently called strikes. These increased as the Maoist 'People's War' gained momentum, and jeopardized the education of many Nepali children. Schools also shut for long periods of 'study leave' prior to exams, and at these times students sat under trees, bent over their textbooks mumbling as they learned them, word for word. We did not consider it appropriate to send our children to a Nepali school.

When we arrived in Tansen, we assumed that it would be relatively straightforward getting our girls into the Umbrella

Organisation's primary school. But it was not plain sailing. After bureaucratic delays and manoeuvres, they were eventually enrolled. To help offset the added pressure on teachers, I taught for three mornings a week. This was a big commitment, but having previously discovered how difficult home schooling was, I was convinced that pooling resources and working together benefited everyone.

## The Tutorial Group

Ros –

Tansen Tutorial Group then comprised 15 children, aged 5-11, of six or more nationalities. The international flavour was exploited in a musical play the children performed, entitled: 'A small part of the world'. In the production, they sang the Australian 'Waltzing Matilda', the Scottish 'Ye cannae shove yer Granny off a bus' and 'London's Burning', as well as songs in Finnish, Nepali, and Spanish. One November we celebrated St Martin's Day as they do in Germany. The children took candle-filled lanterns to friends' houses, and sang of the saint who cut his cloak in two for a beggar. In physical education lessons, the children learned a Scandinavian version of hockey, played with an air ball on the tennis court.

Each child followed an individual programme of learning for maths and English. But projects often inspired collaboration. One monsoon, a 'snake' project proved a great success. The gardener killed a snake, a mum put it in the fridge overnight, and the teacher dissected it in school the next morning. The climax of the project was a snake hunt. One father jokingly gambled a token fifty rupees that the class would not spot a snake that day, but he lost the bet.

The Tutorial Group led some English services using puppet shows, rap, and drama. They made a video of a Viking story they wrote together, and put on a Nepali version of the Bible story of Esther. A school sleepover in the teacher's house, where they dressed each other up as aliens, using newspaper, marked the end of one term. One night I found a restless Lydia unable to get to sleep. She was thinking about her role in a class drama, and complained that school was 'too fun'.

One potential weakness of the tutorial group, which our girls have since labelled 'the best school in the world', was its small size. To counteract this, once a year all the Umbrella's primary school pupils gathered (political conditions permitting) for a larger scale children's conference. This provided our girls with their first taste of being away from home.

After the age of 11, there were various schooling options. A family we knew well chose to send their eldest daughter to a Christian school in South India, but the train journey took five days. Some children attended school in Kathmandu. An impressive American family home-schooled their two teenagers in Tansen. We celebrated their 'graduation' one year - a bit like a school prize giving, with certificates and an iced cake. We acknowledged the hard work that this mother-cum-teacher had been putting in quietly in the background to keep her family together.

Some people have the impression that teachers of mission children are not 'real missionaries'. This could not be further from the truth. Missionary teachers are vital members of the team; without their input many parents would find it extremely difficult, if not impossible, to serve abroad.

## Ros teaches at Tansen

Ros –

When I started teaching in the Tansen Tutorial Group my role was flexible. Sometimes I would supervise a group doing a scientific experiment, or teach the five year olds physical education. A number of children were limited in their understanding of English, and I provided regular support to a Swedish girl. I was also able to develop the children's computing skills, using a somewhat neglected PC. They had to grasp basic mouse skills, handling CDs, and some simple word processing to pass their computer 'driving test'. Typing with one finger proved painfully laborious. We obtained a second computer and each child spent five minutes a day learning to touch-type.

I often led the daily half hour of devotions. I tried to link it into the class topic. When the children were studying space, I based my devotions on stars in the Bible. We looked at creation, the promise to Abraham and the star over Bethlehem. One day the children were thrilled to see a frog in the playground. So was I. My devotions that morning just happened to be on 'frogs in pharaoh's bed'.

'Tell the story of the Bible in ten minutes' a lecturer had challenged us at a theology summer school. It was a hard task. Giving children an overview of the Bible was also difficult. They knew lots of Bible stories, but had only a hazy idea how they fitted together. We made booklets from colour-coded pages linking creation with the new creation; and the history of Israel with the history of the church. This visual aid helped us see the overall shape of the Bible.

The pupils prayed with confidence, as children do, and saw amazing answers. We heard that one of the expatriate team, a Catholic sister, had been critically ill and died.
"Let's pray for her," one child piped up next morning.
"Well, there is a time for everyone to die," I hesitated. But the children insisted, and the next day we eard that the lady was alive! There had been a communication mix-up. As we continued praying for her, she gradually recovered.

During school devotions, Elizabeth was captivated by her teacher's story about George Muller. She informed me on the way home from school one day, that he had founded orphanages, told people about Jesus, and that he went to bed one evening and died in his nightie. Later, over the dinner table, she repeated the story to her Dad. This time Lydia butted in, "No, he didn't die in his nightie, but in his *nineties*."

At the end of our time in Tansen I put my professional skills as a foreign language teacher to work, mentoring the children's Nepali language teacher. We worked together to teach speaking and listening skills, using everyday vocabulary. The pupils learned to say whether they were feeling hot, cold, hungry, thirsty, happy or tired. I introduced the use of flashcards, real objects, and simple games. On the last day of 'shopping', the children returned from the bazaar proudly clutching the bananas and pencils they had bought using their language skills and a ten-rupee allowance.

## Remote living

Ros –

Email only became part of our lives when we moved to Tansen, but the connection via Kathmandu was slow and unreliable. It was frustrating to download attachments larger than 50kB – especially when the power failed mid-process. However, we started sending out monthly prayer points by email to a handful of people who requested them. We produced our newsletters in Tansen, and emailed them directly to supporters, and to church representatives who distributed paper copies.

The electricity and telephone line frequently failed when we had an important message to convey. I remember praying over the computer while the 'sending' indicator moved fitfully along its progress bar. We realised that even in this small matter we were entirely dependent on God.

In Tansen we had the luxury of a phone in our home, although it could be hit and miss trying to make connections. After storms one March, it was out of action for five days. Soon after our arrival, I was taken aback when a family of four appeared on our doorstep, asking if they could use our phone to receive a message they were expecting. I felt uneasy about allowing strangers to go to our upstairs bedroom, so gave some excuse and apologised. They walked away, apparently unperturbed.

It was great to experiment with new ways of communicating. My niece sent 'Flat Stanley' (a cut-out paper doll) for a week's visit to Tansen. We photographed him at school with the girls, eating Nepali food, visiting the Bazaar and meeting Nick's work colleagues. He returned (by post) with a diary of his exploits. Another friend sent us a disposable camera – I took photos, and then sent it back to her. The only problem was that she saw the photos before we did.

## Medical and dental problems. Weren't you scared when your children took ill?

Ros –

We lived near hospitals and doctors throughout our stay in Nepal. When Lydia cut her chin, a friend applied a sterile strip, and a surgeon later confirmed that she didn't need stitches. However, when Elizabeth had an ear infection and required intravenous antibiotics, there was no paediatrician at hand. The infection spread rapidly towards her eyes, and her face started to swell up. Nick was away, so I took local advice and set off on the tiresome day's journey to see a specialist in Kathmandu. Fortunately the roads were open that day, and we were able to travel. Elizabeth recovered quickly. It took me longer to recover from the stress, sleeplessness, and having to act as a single–parent in a crisis. I was thankful for the many people who prayed for our health and safety.

Virtually all Nepal's dentists work in Kathmandu. Tansen boasts the best dental clinic outside the capital. A Finnish dentist inspected the school children's teeth and recommended that Lydia see an orthodontist for a brace to widen out her steeply arched top palate. We managed to fit in an appointment when we travelled to Kathmandu for a conference. The orthodontist was most accommodating, and fitted an appliance for a fraction of what it would have cost in the West.

When local people were afflicted by typhoid and meningitis, I was so thankful for the vaccinations we had endured before travelling to Nepal. We bribed and cajoled our girls into taking the jabs, but injections still hurt. At the international health clinic in London the experienced nurses administered inoculations simultaneously in both arms, which was one way to reduce the trauma.

I honed many of the skills I had learned in Amppipal, including treatment of common infections, and how to add variety to our diet. Small cuts or bumps quickly became infected in Nepal. Boils and sores appeared. I learned to put antibiotic cream and a plaster over cuts, as a precautionary measure. I found mosquitoes particularly troublesome. When I had a cluster of bites on my chin, one became infected through constant scratching. It meant a visit to outpatients to have it lanced and drained.

## A diet to suit

Ros –

A healthy varied diet was crucial to well-being, I discovered. In Tansen, school started at eight, so there wasn't time for morning rice. Western cereals were available, but at an extortionate price. Indian cornflakes were cheaper, but unappetising, especially with buffalo milk. One of our girls liked porridge; the other did not. One fancied semolina; the other hated it. Our home-helper transformed Indian cornflakes and not-so-crisp rice crispies into delicious muesli, baked in the oven with molasses. But the girls found this too hard to chew in the morning. So I resorted to cooking eggs, or French toast, to give them a nutritious start to the day.

I cultivated a ginger beer plant, feeding it daily with ginger powder and sugar. Each week I harvested the yeast mixture to make a refreshing fizzy drink. The pressure in the bottles built up, and you could easily end up with the drink being sprayed all over the place.

To camouflage the strong-tasting buffalo milk I made custard or angel delight. We always boiled our milk. I collected the thick skimmed cream for a few days and froze it with condensed milk, salt and flavourings, to make ice cream. The girls' favourite was mint choc chip.

CHAPTER 11

# HEATH ROBINSON
## AND STAYING HEALTHY

Ros –

We raised rabbits to enhance our diet. I was uncertain the first time whether I would be able to swallow a casserole made with a creature I had fed and nurtured. But the unaccustomed taste of tender meat won me over.

Nick –

When we lived in Amppipal, I was intrigued by the rabbits at Pokhara's leprosy hospital rehabilitation farm. I dreamed of keeping them too. Our first pair travelled to Amppipal in a simple wire netting cage, on top of a wicker basket, on the back of a porter. The doe delivered her first six pink babies on the day we returned from a weekend away. She'd not made a nest in the wooden box we'd provided for her, but had given birth on the cage's cold, wooden floor. We arrived home to a sad scene. As I held the lifeless babies, I resolved that we should try to be at home for the next litter and give the mother more seclusion from the buck.

That litter thrived. I followed their weight gain, which amounted to about 250g per rabbit kitten per week. They reached 2 kg within three months.

It felt as though I was betraying a friend when I killed the first one. As I skinned, gutted and jointed it, Lydia, aged 4, looked on, fascinated and eager to see everything. Rabbit casserole was a treat. Elizabeth also took great interest in them from a young age. As a typical 3-year-old, she had a short concentration span. But she'd happily sit for half an hour holding a baby rabbit. With each new litter, the girls could hardly wait the 12 days for the kittens' eyes to open, after which we allowed them to be handled.

*Their noses twitching, rabbits won their way into our lives.*

Once, at the end of the long journey to Kathmandu, we arrived to find our hosts leaving the house on their way to a meeting. "Don't worry," they assured us, "We've left a chicken casserole in the fridge. Just re-heat it and help yourselves." The meal was delicious, and it got me thinking – what could we say to guests if *we* had to go out? There was no electricity or fridge in our home. The best I could come up with was: "We've got to go out, but don't worry, there's a rabbit in the cage. Just help yourselves!"

In Tansen I built wooden rabbit cages. On days off, Mohan and I worked on them together. I measured and marked; he did the sawing. When my father-in-law came out to visit us, he helped build a small shelter to house the cages. However, rabbit keeping in Tansen proved more difficult than at Amppipal. The does' ears became infected from time to time and needed to be cleaned. This required warm water, tissue paper and plastic tweezers; and I would carry out the procedure sitting on our front step, with the animal between my knees. Local bucks failed to perform well, so litters didn't follow. A pack of jackals visited every few weeks. I'd go down to the cages in the morning to find the hallmarks of their attack – whole panels of wood chewed away, and one or more rabbits dead. Undaunted, we strengthened the cages and their shed. Month by month the defences increased, until, with barbed wire all round and solid doors at the front, we finally defeated the dogs.

We were also troubled by a rat snake. It curled itself in a nesting box inside a cage on the day of Lydia's eighth birthday party. The children shrieked when they found it. A brave dad lifted the box out onto the grass and the beautiful, but scary, snake slithered away. It had squashed to death three babies. Towards the end of our stay in Tansen, the girls kept one adult rabbit each and we didn't breed them any more. Keeping them as pets was less complicated than running a farm.

Ros -

I have always been afraid of snakes. When we lived in Amppipal I never saw one. I think it was one of the ways God cared for me. In Tansen I summoned up the courage to look at an expatriate's collection of bottled specimens. One day I went to feed the rabbits and noticed something move below the cages; it was a bright green viper.

I rushed back up the steps and called out to the neighbours,

"Help, there's a snake. Can you kill it?"

No one dared.

"Nag ho," they protested, "it's a serpent deity. We can't kill it".

We watched from above as, a little later, the snake darted across the grass. Nevertheless Nick was a local hero when he killed the green viper. He struck it behind the head with a heavy metal pole. He later stalked the six-foot rat snake, and hit it a third of the way down its body, where its heart is supposed to be. I dared not watch even from the safe distance of an upstairs room. Though rat snakes are not poisonous, I was not happy to go down to the garden, or to let the girls play there, when I knew one was around.

One day when Nick was away, I noticed a man ploughing our neighbour's field with two bulls. I decided on the spur of the moment to ask him to plough our field too. I enlisted a curious neighbour to help me clear away the stones on the surface of the soil. A couple of hours later the field was a spread of beautiful rich brown furrows. This small episode was my biggest contribution to gardening, and it gave me a sense of achievement, as the garden was predominantly Nick's domain.

Nick –

This incident made me picture Ros as the noble wife described in the book of Proverbs: 'she considers a field and buys it; out of her earnings she plants a vineyard'[27]. But, as Ros said, I was generally the gardener.

The garden was a place for me to unwind between the responsibilities of work and home. I took ten minutes there most days, pulling weeds, watering, or training peas to their sticks.

Ploughing by bulls tickled the top six inches of soil. So I set about preparing deeply dug raised-beds. I used a spade for the job, brought all the way from England. A pickaxe and long crow bar were useful to dig up boulders, which were large enough to bend even sturdy tools like these. I crisscrossed the plot with grass paths, hoping they would prompt visiting children to stay off the beds. Being an enthusiastic compost maker, I piled anything remotely biodegradable on to the heap, fed in our waste kitchen water, and turned it from time to time. It bred thousands of earthworms.

En route from our Tansen home to work, I passed a neighbour who had an especially productive garden. So I offered her an hour's employment each day on our plot. She was skilled at tending Nepali varieties of vegetables, like garlic, spinach, ginger and potatoes; and made light work of hoeing using local tools. Between November and May she watered by hand and picked peas, beans and lettuce each day. I appreciated her wisdom and advice. Neighbours would stroll over to have a look and comment:
"You're crazy trying to dig while the soil is dry."
"I'd pick those bananas now before someone pinches them."
"It's good to see you digging out stones – I wish my sons would help me do that."
"You're always busy, not like us lazy Nepalis."
"My potatoes are much larger than yours."

The garden was where I met our neighbours – especially the men.

In the dry season, we spread out soya-beans and maize on straw mats in the sun. We also dried turmeric, tomatoes and hibiscus flower sepals, and used these to make excellent fruit juice and jam. During the monsoon we grew vines – cucumbers, pumpkins and bitter gourd, intercropping them with maize and climbing beans. Roses grew easily from cuttings, and we feasted our eyes on sunflowers and marigolds.

I rigged up a swing on a length of galvanised pipe suspended between two trees. Little tots and teenagers played on it all day. It was so well used by local children that we had to resort to locking it up occasionally to get some peace.

The garden had its problems too. Children climbed in the fruit trees to pick unripe guavas and peaches. At the end of a weekend away we returned to Amppipal to find the previously green garden completely bare. Free-range goats had eaten the lot. I felt we deserved a portion of the goat meat. Squirrels and crows tucked into our maize. The neighbour's chickens scratched up bean seeds as they were germinating. One day I found monkeys eating off the compost heap. Ants infested the potatoes, and the monsoon humidity rotted the marrows. I learned that local varieties of vegetables were generally more reliable than imported seed.

## Black-outs, bats and bins

Ros –

In Amppipal we enjoyed 'open air living' and a simple lifestyle. No running water, electricity or telephone gave a curious freedom. In Tansen, our home benefited from these utilities, so we relied on them… and were exasperated when they failed. We grumbled at the frequent power cuts and kept a box of matches and a candle on top of the light switch in every room.

One Saturday DVD night we started to watch 'Gosford Park' with two friends. Shortly after the film began the electricity cut out. The back-up power supply box sounded its piercing bleep; we had just enough time to shut down the computer. I lit a candle and we waited. When would the power be restored – in ten minutes, or the following morning? It returned later that evening, and we continued to watch. A detective film is the worst kind to leave unfinished. When the power failed again we knew our guests would have to leave before seeing the end of the film, to reach home before the 9pm curfew. It took us two more attempts, later in the week, to find out 'whodunit'.

To cope with power cuts in the kitchen, I gave our Tansen cook two sets of instructions. Instead of baking biscuits in the electric oven, she could fry 'nimki', a savoury snack, on the gas. Sometimes the power failed once the bread had risen in the loaf tins. In this event, our cook would transfer the dough to the 'miracle oven' – a ring-shaped tin designed to heat food on top of the gas – to finish the baking.

One Friday in May a gale blew up. Spring storms could be dramatic. The power went out and it turned cold. Wind whistled through the mosquito mesh on our window frames. We huddled around candles and listened to the thunder, and the rain drumming on the tin roof. About midday, we ventured out in wellies through the puddles. The electricity was not restored. The fridge began to drip. We kept the freezer door shut and hoped for the best.

Tansen had three sources of energy. The storm had damaged one, and it was reported that the other two power houses had been ransacked by Maoists. The town stands on a hill; all its water is pumped up by electricity. By the third day water supplies were running low. Beside the public tap, rows of assorted water pots queued, abandoned by their owners, as the supply was reduced to a feeble drip. With the utmost care, we filled a drum from the residue in our tank as a reserve drinking supply. Imagine my shock and disbelief when the hose pipe filling the barrel became dislodged, and some of the liquid gold flooded out on to our concrete kitchen floor.

That night I heard, almost audibly, a verse from the book of Exodus. 'He who gathered much did not gather too much and he who gathered little did not have too little' (Exodus Ch.16 v.18). In the morning light, I looked up the text. The

Israelites grumbled against Moses because they were starving in the desert. They remembered all the good things about Egypt. However God provided food for them each day, by giving them 'manna' (a kind of bread) to eat. This passage reassured me that God sees our needs, and provides for us on a daily basis. The familiar words in the Lord's Prayer, "Give us this day our daily bread", took on a new meaning for me.

On the evening of the third day the electricity came on again, and the following week our water tank was full. The incident brought home to me just how fragile and vulnerable we were. We resolved to set up a plastic tank to collect the rainfall from our roof as a backup supply.

Small bats thrived in our Tansen roof. They chirped like birds. Each evening at dusk they streamed out of a hole under the eaves. There was no way to block their entrances to the roof, so I had no option but to settle for an uneasy truce. It meant regularly sweeping up the noxious guano. Once or twice bats fell into the house. I found their low dipping flight unnerving, and shouted for help. The girls were fascinated. I relied on them to follow each bat's course, so we could locate them when they landed. Once grounded, bats are quite helpless. A friend explained how to sweep them into a dustpan, and gently hold them in place with the brush. They can then be taken outside and launched to freedom.

How to dispose of rubbish is a major issue in Nepal. There was no adequate local waste removal system – no 'bin man'. Until a few years ago most refuse in a Nepali village was biodegradable, and was eaten by the goats. Nowadays garish instant noodle packets litter the pathways as you approach a village. Nepalis are house-proud and regularly sweep their courtyards, but public paths resemble a dumping ground.

Nick turned biodegradable waste into compost. But that left tin cans, bottles, and plastic. Empty milk powder tins were good for storage, and resourceful neighbours used smaller cans as water dippers. I kept a supply of containers by the door for anyone who asked for them. Items that could not be composted or burned were stored and later buried in a pit dug in the garden.

Taking waste disposal seriously proved a bit burdensome, so we began to think more carefully about what we bought. I tried to reduce the number of tins we used, and purchased oil and washing up liquid in bulk. Our cook was always keen to take away with her the stronger and larger cooking oil cans to use for water storage. This might have accounted for our curry being a little oilier than some.

Nick –

The main water supply pipe to our home in Tansen was laid in shallow soil in the garden. One day, when digging, I punctured this pipe. Heath Robinson[28] got to work with some super strong sticky tape, but this proved absolutely useless. So he resorted to the tried and tested method - a short length of inner tube from an old bicycle tyre, deftly wrapped around the offending hole. This soon sorted it.

Elizabeth inherited a bike. We always had to borrow a pump with the right sized adaptor for her tyres. Old Robinson felt sure that his adaptor could be made to work by cannibalising an audio jack from some defunct headphones. But try as he may, it was all in vain.

## Keeping fit - socially, mentally and spiritually

Ros –

The expatriate teams where we lived (augmented by a few close Nepali friends) substituted for family. We marked one team member's 40th birthday with a progressive supper. An imaginative friend had secretly obtained photos of the birthday girl as a baby and teenager, and these were revealed, a few at a time, at each location.

The expatriate team members cared for one another at times of sadness. When my grandmother died, aged 90, we felt such a long way from our family in England. On hearing the news, the Finnish teacher who was taking devotions that day, sensitively changed his plans, to allow our girls to share their memories and grief. They choose a song to sing for Gran Gran.

Expatriates are renowned for being patriotic, and none more so than the Scots. This was certainly the case one Hogmanay. We all sniffed a lump of Isle of Harris peat, and savoured homemade Christmas cake, before dancing a reel by moonlight. In honour of Australia Day, an enterprising antipodean family presented each member of the team with an Australian vegemite sandwich. On March 17th, wearing our greenest outfits, we offered the Irish schoolteacher green iced cakes, and potatoes wrapped in green tissue paper. Each nationality brought its own distinctiveness to the team.

We discovered the freedom to share rather than compete; we prayed for others to succeed and rejoiced when they did. We were never conscious of any group attempting to 'patent' a project, so as to prevent others knowing the inner secrets of its success. As an 'unassigned spouse', I never felt less valued as a team member than Nick who held the official visa post jobs.

Farewells have been a recurrent feature of our life. They inspired us to write songs and skits. But at each parting we felt emotionally drained. One consolation of these comings and goings is that we now have a network of friends all over the world with whom we 'click' almost immediately, because of our shared experiences in Nepal. We feared that when we returned to England we would not find the level of trust, self-giving, and availability to one another that we'd grown accustomed to.

Staying mentally and spiritually fit was as much a challenge as keeping physically healthy.

Wherever I live, I designate a 'prayer chair': a quiet place where I can sit on waking, to pray and read my Bible. In Amppipal I crept downstairs, hoping not to disturb the children. I had frequent interruptions from callers at the door, but even a few moments of prayer at the start of each day helped me to quieten my mind before God. 'Patterns not Padlocks'[29] hinted how a mum with young children could experience spiritual refreshment during the busyness of the day. As I drank my morning cup of tea, I found it helpful to focus on Jesus, and to think of his presence in my life, warming and refreshing me.

Each night, Nick and I would pray in bed for our family and colleagues. In Tansen, we used a liturgy for evening prayers. If we had guests we invited them to join us as we went to the attic, lit a candle, and prayed together. I find punctuating the day with times for prayer very helpful, and have enjoyed the practical advice given in David Adam's book, 'Rhythm of life'[30]. As a family, we observed the church's seasons, particularly Advent and Lent.

At Tansen, my relationship with Nirmala continued to grow. We met several times a week to pray. I can vividly recall when Nick travelled out by motorbike to a district town, and we were concerned for his safety. He was not an experienced motorcyclist, and the thick dust covering the road concealed boulders that could easily have unseated him. Nirmala and I prayed for his journey. He arrived back rejoicing in God's care. When he had faced oncoming vehicles on a rutted road, there had always been a clear route he could take. Nirmala and I prayed for visas, the appointment of staff, and for obstructive government officials. We remembered staff members by name. When Nirmala was disturbed by dreams about her mother, we prayed for her family. Week by week God heard our prayers. I truly valued Nirmala as a friend.

I studied theology by correspondence. Despite the lack of certain books, and no internet access, I found the coursework stimulating and worthwhile. Study was spiritually and mentally challenging. Biblical studies, ministry and mission, and church history broadened my understanding. I made time for some study each morning while the girls were at school.

## Never stop language learning

Ros –

In Tansen, the family found it difficult to cope with church services conducted in Nepali. We wanted to be part of the church, and for the girls to have a positive experience. If we concentrated hard, Nick and I could take in what was going on, and understand most of the sermon. The girls took shakers, and sometimes joined in with the singing. Once Lydia could read she used the transliterated songbook I'd compiled. Sometimes they would interest themselves with colouring books or do puzzles from their 'church bags'. I often accompanied the girls to the children's class, not only to help with translation but also to give moral support. Integration was not easy for them. I tried to overcome the problem by prompting their Nepali teacher to get them to sing the church songs in their weekly language class. On the way home from church, the girls chose a special treat – a one-rupee wrapped sweet from a roadside shop. However, throughout our time in Nepal we appreciated English worship with expatriate groups. When in Kathmandu we attended the International Church.

We joined the weekly English Bible studies in Amppipal and the fortnightly English services in Tansen.

I never stopped learning. I negotiated with our milk lady to bring some ghee. I assumed she would deliver it the next morning, as she was usually keen to earn extra cash. But it did not arrive. The reason she gave baffled me: "We *fence* on Wednesdays". I understood the word, but had no idea what it meant in this context. So I asked my patient language teacher. He explained that out of superstition, many people will not give or sell their property on three specific days - Wednesday, Saturday, or the day the man of the house was born. The word 'fence' is used because of the limits that have been set.

I went to the supermarket to order some buffalo mince for the following Thursday. The shopkeeper checked his calendar and explained that it was the full moon on Thursday and animals would not be slaughtered on that day. So I had to place my order a day earlier. I was a little surprised by this, as I knew that meat was not usually cut on the *new* moon day or the eleventh day in the lunar calendar. My teacher explained that it was an exception, as the full moon that month happened to coincide with a festival day.

During our entire stay in Nepal, I continued with language lessons for an hour a week. What I enjoyed most was the chance to read some Nepali literature. My teacher recommended some short stories from the School Leaving Certificate syllabus. The language was antiquated but they gave fascinating insights into some of the issues faced by a second wife; family dynamics regarding inheritance; and quarrels about farming.

In one story we read how a father sometimes took his son to the Hindu holy man.
"They would eat *carrots* together", my teacher continued.
"Carrots?" I questioned, "but carrots have only recently become available in Nepal, haven't they?"

"It was forbidden to grow them in large quantities, as the sap is potent, and can be confiscated by the police," my patient teacher explained.

"What?!" Finally the penny dropped when I discovered that the words for carrot and marijuana are nearly the same.

Operating in a foreign language gave us little cause for pride. We were constantly reminded of our inadequacies, in expressing ourselves and understanding others. It was not until our third term that we began to reap the benefits of the thorough grounding we had been given. We began to build deep relationships, were able to contribute at house-group, and to behave in a way that was more socially acceptable. People warmed to us because we made an effort to speak their language, and they loved it when we asked questions about their cultural practices.

Nick –

I too aimed to keep spiritually fit. Every morning I sat up in bed under our red mosquito net, with a mug of tea in one hand and my Nepali-English Bible in the other. I read and prayed for 20 minutes. The most fruitful times were when I had to prepare a Nepali church sermon, or material for an expatriate team fellowship. In our final year I found a prayer partner. He was a short-term surgeon at the mission hospital. Every two or three weeks we met to bring matters before God, and to share triumphs and failings along our spiritual journeys. On Wednesday mornings I usually attended the Nepali church prayer meeting. I never felt like going, and this was all too evident, as I often arrived 15 minutes late. Praying in a foreign language is one of the greatest challenges a missionary has to face. As I look back, I am thankful to God for helping me persevere; I have certainly grown spiritually through the experience. One thing I did learn is that God is not put off by poor Nepali grammar. Each week as I left the meeting to set off to work, I rejoiced, glad that I'd gone.

I heard that Bhim, a friend of Ram's, had been jailed in Gorkha, because his brother was a known Maoist. I'd met Bhim at a biogas office in town a year earlier. Just before going back to the UK for two months, Ros and I attended the Umbrella's conference in Kathmandu. During that time, I had sensed a voice in my heart from God telling me to visit Bhim. But how could I? Gorkha is a day's journey from Kathmandu, and we had no free space in our timetable. Moreover, I wondered how the authorities would view such a visit. It could so easily have been seen as a demonstration of sympathy towards the Maoist movement. I thought of the impact a visit might have in relation to my family's visas and the registration of our organisation with the government. Two years previously, a mission expatriate had been arrested when he befriended a prison in-mate and unknowingly carried a packet of illegal drugs to him. Rational and irrational questions crowded into my mind. We left for the UK, but I had a heavy heart.

A month after our return, I extended the journey from Kathmandu to Tansen by a day and travelled to Gorkha. I bought some soap, a tee shirt and shorts and some noodles. I met Bhim's sister at a shop near his old office. She showed me the way to the jail. I was not permitted to meet Bhim, but I was able to chat to the police and guards. They inspected my parcel and conveyed it inside. Ten minutes later I received a short, hand written note of thanks from Bhim, listing all the items I'd given. We walked away, up the steep hillside. At a high point overlooking the prison, his sister stopped and pointed down into a corner of the jail's high walled courtyard. I could just make out two or three men. One of them was Bhim. He smiled and waved to us.

A few weeks later, Bhim suffered from a sudden illness that necessitated his transfer to the local hospital. Thankfully, not long afterwards, he was released from jail and came to Tansen with Ram to return my visit. He was radiant. Ram never stopped telling him about Jesus. I am trusting that Bhim will become a Christian believer one day.

As we built up contacts at Tansen, and our lives became more and more busy, we struggled to make enough time for rest. We both found it hard to slow down. The more tired we were, the less we planned days out, or days off. This vicious cycle soon spiralled to crisis point.

# Chapter 12

# REACHING CRISIS POINT

## Sarah's appointment

Nick –

'People are like tea bags - you have to put them in hot water before you know how strong they are.'

As I start to recall this episode, I feel a strange surge of emotion. There are elements of the story that I have never fully resolved. With hindsight, I see that Sarah arrived at a difficult point in the Programme. Several factors combined to undermine our working relationship.

I was the sole long-term expatriate leading the TB / HIV Programme. During the first 2 years, I had very little support from France. So I developed strategies and activities with my Nepali colleagues. The volunteer doctor in France, who was supposed to give direction to our work, opted out of close involvement with Nepal. Communication between us proved difficult. My French was virtually non-existent, and his English was far from fluent. He became critical of our programme, maintaining that it had diverged from the concepts he had in mind when he co-wrote the proposal three years previously. He expressed his views to headquarters. It was only later I learned that the programme evaluation I described in chapter 10 had been conducted specifically to investigate my varying account of developments. The exercise was positive. A principle recommendation had highlighted the need for a second expatriate to carry some of the administrative load.

I was under increasing pressure. Our staff team size was steadily increasing, and new initiatives were absorbing much of my time. I juggled many roles. Apart from giving direction and leadership to the Programme, I also acted as senior administrator and government negotiator. Although I had no experience in accounting, I'd worked with our Nepali administrator to make some fundamental changes in our record keeping. We were in the process of shifting from cumbersome spreadsheet-based bookkeeping to new accounting software. We were half way through the change over, when Sarah's five-month placement began.

She was new to Nepal, and came fresh from a French course in administration for development agencies. Paris had informed her that there were some administrative irregularities in the Nepal programme that needed to be looked at. She was keen to apply herself to the task. But in my haste to get on with what I felt were more pressing duties, I failed to give time for Sarah's orientation. Misunderstandings led to tensions, and soon we clashed.

I had anticipated that Sarah would observe office practices for a month, before making recommendations. Instead, she quickly informed Paris about inadequacies she observed, and implemented improvements without reference to me. Our new accounting programme was abandoned.

I felt undermined and completely let down. It seemed that all I had contributed over the years was under threat. I was angry too.

Around this time, the French volunteer doctor came to visit us. Headquarters knew he was a critical man, and decided to send someone to accompany him. But the nominated person dropped out at the last minute because of a heavy workload. The doctor spoke openly about his views in front of Sarah. We entered a destructive spiral that ended in confrontation.

The outcome was that Sarah, with barely three weeks experience in the country, was promoted and given equal status with me. I was threatened with dismissal.

My effectiveness as team leader plummeted. My desk piled high with disordered papers. Confusion and worry jostled in my mind. I reacted out of all proportion when an item was cut off my monthly expenses claim. I anticipated criticism in emails before opening them, and so read them in a negative way. I feel ashamed as I look back and see how I failed to support Sarah. But I knew there was no way she and I could co-lead the Programme.

Our Nepali coordinator decided to celebrate his recent promotion by throwing a picnic for the staff team. I attended in the morning, Sarah in the afternoon. I sat on the edge of the group. My Nepali friends expressed their appreciation by offering kind words, and by serving me with the sweetest tea and most tender meat. My eyes welled up with tears. I sensed a surge of love and care when I most needed it.

At the Wednesday morning prayer meetings at Nepali church, the once confident and supportive Programme Coordinator became a downcast lad who wept and needed bags of encouragement. This marked a turning point in my relationship with my Christian brothers and sisters in Tansen. We became mutually interdependent – much more than we'd ever been before.

Sarah alerted the personnel team in Paris about the crisis. Between us, we generated an impressive international telephone bill that month. Headquarters planned to send officers to Nepal, but subsequently reversed their decision; and Sarah and I went to Paris instead. By God's grace, we managed to remain calm sitting next to one another for six hours on the plane from Doha to Paris. It was a relief to be in the process of resolving our difficulties.

The headquarters' team managed the problem well, although I was disappointed that our volunteer director was unable to come to Paris. It had been more than two years since I had had a work review, so the personnel staff hardly knew me. They listened to us, as we expressed our different points of view. As a group, we agreed a new structure of accountability for the Nepal Programme: Sarah was to manage specific administrative matters, while I was to take overall charge. If only this basic assignment of responsibilities had been clarified before Sarah arrived, things might have turned out very differently.

## The ups and downs of relationships

Ros –

While Nick and I were trying to make sense of unfolding events with Sarah, I developed a new friendship. A German family had arrived in Tansen, and I seized the opportunity to refresh my German language skills. The mother of the family began meeting with me for one to two hours each week to chat and pray. When Nick was summoned at short notice to Paris, she suggested we pray together every day. For my sake, she was prepared to forgo the precious hour she normally reserved between her children going to school and her house-worker's arrival. She not only provided spiritual and emotional support, but also gave practical help. Our younger daughter caught an ear infection, which spread alarmingly close to her eye. My kind friend alerted me to the danger it posed, organised intravenous antibiotics for us, and let us stay overnight in her home. I tried to translate 'A friend in need is a friend indeed' into German a few weeks later, and we laughed together as we came up with unlikely rhymes.

Nick –

After the conflict resolution meeting in Paris, Sarah and I returned to Nepal, less stressed and with clearer minds.

I had learned that I should not hold on so tightly to what I regarded as 'my baby' – the Programme that I had launched. After all, I would have to let go of it altogether one day. I worked out with Sarah specific areas of responsibility for her remaining time in Nepal. Ros and I took two months in the UK as planned, which gave her some freedom to work independently.

During that short time away, we crammed eight church visits into as many weeks, spanning Bristol, York and Norwich. We covered more than a thousand miles. Our first meeting was exactly a week after we landed, and our final one the day we flew back to Nepal. The only Sunday we did not take a leading role in any service was when I was in Paris for a coordinators' conference. I think we failed to learn from our previous mistakes, and were pushing ourselves too hard again.

Ros –

During that deputation period we focussed on 'how we live out our faith'. We feared that some supporters viewed missionaries as remote and not living in the real world. We wanted them to understand that we faced many of the issues that they encounter too. To open discussion, we asked some key questions: What difference does it make to be a Christian at work? How can we connect with our neighbours? How can we communicate the gospel at festival times? How can we love aliens and strangers who live near us? Two Nepali Muppet puppets helped us introduce the issues as we found them in Nepal.

The routine was time-consuming - packing, unpacking, repacking, sorting, working out what items were needed where and when, and how to get them there. It would have been simpler to travel light, but we needed displays and literature, and we took crafts made by Nepali friends to sell. We also prepared Nepali gifts for our hosts. I saw it as a small personal triumph, that most of the time we ended up dressed and ready for the next event.

Countless people asked, "How are the girls coping back in the UK?" We struggled to decide how the children should be involved in deputation. At times they protested when we shared news about them. We did not require them to 'perform' in front of congregations; nor did we put words into their mouths in newsletters. We were pleased when they opted to wear their Nepali outfits for church visits. They were usually part of the family group when churches prayed for us in services. We felt proud of the girls when they showed supporters their personal photo albums of Nepal. Sometimes they stayed with grandparents, instead of trailing along to meetings where they did not know anyone.

Nick –

We returned to Nepal for a short time of hand-over, before Sarah left the programme. I felt apprehensive, but I was pleased to find that things were really running quite well.

## Short-term or long-term?

Ros –

A new short-term expatriate wanted me to accompany her on a search for accommodation, but it clashed with the office day-off when I would have preferred to spend time with Nick. I reluctantly volunteered, and we traipsed all over town to view three available flats. I patiently negotiated with the landlords, asked about water supplies, and translated the newcomer's questions. She needed time to think things over. I returned home tired, to a somewhat restless family, who'd clearly needed mum to facilitate their day-off activities. Up until then I had been positive about short-termers.

We ourselves had benefited from this kind of help. When we first arrived in Kathmandu, an energetic host and hostess welcomed us to the guesthouse. The next day they took us out for a walk to mission headquarters. After showing us the bank and post office, they treated us to coffee at a western-style café. Several weeks later we were surprised to discover that this retired couple, who seemed so at home, were on a short-term placement and had only arrived in Nepal two weeks before us.

Short-termers also enriched our team life in Amppipal and Tansen. One couple showed us great kindness. They invited us for meals, gave us half of their ginger beer 'plant', and babysat so we could both go out to house-group. The husband was a surgeon. He filled in for a few months while another medic was on home assignment. As surgeons do not require advanced language skills to operate in theatre, he could be effectively deployed almost immediately.

We welcomed a team of young people from New Zealand who came out to explore what mission is about. They organised the children's programme at our agency's bi-annual conference; and brought energy and new ideas, glitter glues, guitars, and crazy games.

However, we also witnessed ineffective short-term work. Eager and able volunteers staffed a two-week medical camp, offering glasses and dental care. The logistics were impressive and there were opportunities for Christian outreach. But sadly the camp was not giving essential services to an isolated population. The organisers had not researched the local situation, nor sought to work in harmony with existing long-term health players. Their outreach took place just down the path from Amppipal hospital.

There were hidden costs to short-term work. Long-term personnel had to arrange transport, accommodation, language lessons, orientation, and deal with the fall-out from culture shock. Short-termers came with high hopes, often expecting to contribute some kind of useful service from day one. Thirty years ago a 'short-term' assignment would have lasted three years; today it's as short as three weeks. I am fully convinced that short-termers can gain valuable experience from an appropriate placement; but I also feel that there are times when the energy expended by permanent team members to support them might be better used elsewhere.

'Long-term' service is shrinking too. A previous generation spent 20–30 years or more of their lives on the mission field. After nine years in Nepal we had out-stayed all but one family who started language and orientation with us. I recall a passionate talk by a veteran overseas worker at Bible college, who appealed to us to accept the long haul challenge. To illustrate his point, he held up a worn pair of running shoes used in a marathon. But longevity of service is not in itself a virtue. It can lead to unhealthy patterns of dependency, and rutted thinking.

The crisis with Sarah had knocked us for six. But little did we know that a further upheaval was looming.

## Insecurity and Stress… Maoists and the Monarchy

Ros –

At a quarter to ten that autumn evening I sat at my desk in the 'long room' of our home in Tansen. An enormous boom rocked the house. I shook. Nick thought it was a bomb. We retreated further inside, and phoned some friends. They had all heard the explosion. We knew it was nearby, but could obtain no definite information. There was not a sound from our Nepali neighbours that night. But the following morning they told us an army truck had been ambushed on the road about 100 yards below our house. Two soldiers had died immediately and five others had been taken to hospital with serious injuries.

As we walked to school we saw the shell of the vehicle, surrounded by onlookers. It was hard to know what to say to the children, who had slept through the blast. I tried to explain what had happened in a gentle and reassuring way. If our girls didn't hear a measured account from us, they would pick up rumours, and concoct their own story based on playground banter. The teachers dealt sensitively with the children's fears. Life went on.

A few months later another bomb close to home impacted our girls much more forcefully. The girls and I had eaten an early evening meal with our German friends on the hospital compound. As we walked home with Ram and his wife who were visiting from Gorkha, a loud blast stopped us in our tracks. Ram picked up a trembling Elizabeth in his arms. I took hold of Lydia with a firm grip. We returned to our friends. Had we left them any sooner, we would have been much closer to the explosion, which had occurred just a short distance above our home. The Lord protected us. We sat down ashen faced in our friends' lounge, waiting for news. We prayed together, and when it appeared safe, we made our way home as quietly and quickly as we could. The next morning we learned that the bomb had shattered the door and windows of the local sports hall. No one was physically injured. But the psychological impact on our girls was significant. They found it hard to get to sleep, constantly telling us about their fear of bombs. We made sure we allowed plenty of time to talk things over with them, and gave them lots of hugs and reassurance.

Nine years previously, when we first came to Nepal, it appeared to be a peaceful Himalayan kingdom where the many different tribes and ethnic groups lived together in remarkable harmony. The Kingdom's first democratic elections had taken place in 1991.

## A People's war

Ros –

During the spring of 1995 our language classes were interrupted by 'strike' days when shops shut and public transport came to a halt. Teachers did not travel on these days; neither did our home-helper. Strikes were the way political parties showed their strength. If the strike held, the party claimed support for its cause. Those who wished to work felt intimidated. Shopkeepers and bus owners feared their windows would be smashed or their vehicles damaged if they did not comply.

On February 4th 1996, a year to the day after our arrival, the Nepal Communist Party - Maoist - declared the start of its 'People's War'. We were unaware of this at the time, and had no inkling of its future impact on our lives. The Maoists' aims were to abolish the monarchy and establish a people's republic.

The district where we first lived was the homeland of the movement. One of the Maoist leaders hailed from Gorkha, and had attended a mission school there. We heard rumours of brutal attacks on community figures in remote villages. Our lack of Nepali language prevented us understanding the gory details. In February 1997 we passed a well-known local leader on the path. Within 12 hours, an armed mob had murdered him in his home. Outrage reverberated through the community.

One morning I felt a shiver of apprehension as a friend told me that Maoists had erected a red flag on the summit of Liglig Mountain, half an hour's walk from where we lived. They were staking out their claim to the territory. Groups of insurgents were reportedly seeking donations door-to-door. We were uneasy – we wondered when they would visit us. The day arrived. Two Maoist representatives appeared on our veranda and asked for a donation of 5,000 rupees (about 40 pounds). I quickly made cups of tea, while Nick engaged them in conversation. As I prayed fervently inside the house, he courageously told them one of Jesus' parables. Nick said that the only fruit that he had seen from the Maoist tree in Nepal was fear, so the tree sounded like a bad one[31]. "Given this start, will the Maoists ever be able forge a good future for Nepal?" he asked them. When Nick refused to give money they became aggressive, and said they could not guarantee our safety. As they walked away Nick was emboldened to speak a blessing in Jesus' name over them. They were dumbstruck – so he repeated the blessing and invited them back for more conversation. They never returned. The episode unnerved us. We also discovered something of the fear that our Nepali neighbours' felt. The police seemed powerless to discipline Maoist fundraising.

We'd watched a Nepali film at the cinema during our first few months in Kathmandu. The audience cheered when the police, the obvious 'goodies', appeared on the screen. But the reputation of the police declined. We heard that their record for infringements of human rights was no better than that of the Maoists. An expatriate colleague and neighbour witnessed the police's heavy-handed abuse of a girl suspect as they marched her to the police post.

Wealthy villagers and community leaders were especially vulnerable to threats and demands. A pillar of the community fled to the capital after his rice mill was smashed down. A Nepali doctor and a shopkeeper friend received repeated threats. Villagers with means retreated to the security of Gorkha town, or moved to Kathmandu. Maoist committee members filled the local leadership vacuum.

From then on the expatriate team at Amppipal observed a curfew. We no longer walked the paths after dark. Regular evening activities, like the prayer meeting and Bible study, were re-scheduled to the afternoon. The curfew limited our social life. I had begun to wonder if the precautions were really necessary, when on the eve of district elections, at about nine at night, we heard the tramp of boots on the path outside. Men chanted Maoist slogans, and brandished flaming torches. We turned out our lights and sat tight. We heard rifle shots and the blast of mortars. The group marched off into the darkness.

## A false hope

Ros –

Soon the Maoists' visible presence subsided, and six months later, in May 1999, I remember a carnival atmosphere on general election day. Women abandoned their household chores to parade the paths in their brightest, most glittery saris. They sauntered along, chatting with neighbours. Nepal had endured a string of ineffective coalition governments. We hoped that a Nepali Congress party majority would bring stability. But it too failed to deliver.

Periodic strikes continued and became more ambitious. In May 2001 Maoists called a three-day stoppage. I was surprised to see people queuing for vegetables the day before. The vast majority of Nepalis could never afford to stock up reserves of food. Many live on a day-to-day, even meal-to-meal, basis. I wondered what the long-term consequences of the unrest would be. We had already sensed decreasing levels of trust in the community. You could not be sure if the stranger you met in the teashop was a Maoist, or a plain-clothes policeman. After another strike, oranges doubled in price, and bananas became unavailable. The poorest and weakest members of society suffered most. The implications were far reaching. I often wondered how many women in labour failed to get to hospital on strike days;

and how many daily waged porters went hungry because the shops they serviced were shut.

If you put a frog into a pan of hot water it will jump out. If you put a frog in a pan of cold water and gradually increase the heat it will eventually boil alive. We knew that the political temperature was rising. We prayed that we would know when to jump out.

The royal massacre of June 2001 rocked Nepal. The king was considered an incarnation of the god Vishnu. Most offices and many homes displayed framed photographs of the monarch, King Birendra, who was active in public life during his reign of 26 years. He was popular. He permitted the transition to democracy in 1990. His death further undermined the country's fragile state. Many men shaved their heads that week in mourning for their 'father'. Photos of the late king and queen were erected outside the municipal buildings in Tansen. When I signed the condolence book I was number 3001.

## 'Go bags' for a Red zone

Ros –

Crown Prince Dipendra, who was blamed for the massacre, automatically succeeded his father as king. However, he died several days later from a bullet wound infection, and a further 5 days of official mourning were announced. The new King, Gyanendra, younger brother of the late Birendra, came to the throne. Radio Nepal issued little information. It warned citizens not to believe seditious rumours about the assassinations, but to await the results of the enquiry set up by the new monarch. The truth was obscure. We relied on the BBC World Service and the British Embassy for our updates. The Embassy advised us to pack a small 'go bag' in case we needed to leave quickly. This contained important documents, water purification tablets, maps, torches and medicines. As I put our go bag together, I felt a little more at ease.

In July 2001, the Prime Minister announced a truce with the Maoists. Our Nepali pastor urged us to persist in prayer for Nepal, and he set up an ongoing 24-hour vigil of intercession for the nation. Then in November, over four cruel days, Maoist attacks shattered the peace. A bank in Tansen was bombed - a family who lived near it spoke in church about how their bedcovers had shielded them from flying glass. The King declared a state of emergency, and ordered the army to suppress the rebels. Large gatherings were forbidden, and a 9pm curfew was imposed. Cautious local people did not want to be questioned by police patrols on their way home, so observed the curfews rigorously. One evening at 7pm I walked along the main shopping street in Tansen, and it felt like midnight. Every shop-front was shuttered. Only a few stray dogs were brave enough to show their faces in the litter-strewn street.

The political temperature rose. We set our radio to come on regularly for the 8pm English News. We became numbed to the daily reports announcing the numbers of Maoists and national troops killed. Each day we heaved an inward sigh of relief when our district, and those immediately surrounding us, were not mentioned. Rumour had it that the statistics were manipulated, and that most 'Maoist' casualties were innocent civilians. When the Prime Minister sought help from the United States to fight the rebels, President George W Bush pledged 20 million. We feared repercussions for our American colleagues. (However Nepali kids made no distinction – they often called out 'Americanee' in derision, at anyone with a white skin. One American colleague, originally from India, had a good sense of humour and said that at least *he* wouldn't be accused of being American.)

The Maoists started to target infrastructure. In summer 2002 the BBC reported that 16 districts were without electricity because of the bombing of hydroelectric plants. Telephone and water installations were also hit.

I vividly remember a holiday morning that October. As we sat drinking tea in a shack on the edge of Chitwan National Park, our guide alerted us to the voice of the King on the radio. We heard him using the elongated royal forms of speech as he dismissed the Prime Minister, postponed the elections planned for November, and took the leadership of Nepal into his own hands. Surprisingly, the Nepalis around us seemed relieved. They hoped the King would give credible guidance to their nation.

In January 2003 a ceasefire was declared. We prayed that peace talks would start. Students became vocal and protested against the marginalisation of political parties. That April, on a journey from Kathmandu to Tansen, I sat with the girls for five hours at the roadside. Students in the next town were holding a rally and blocking all through traffic. In August the rebels pulled out of peace talks, and violence resumed. The cycle of making and breaking ceasefires had begun again.

Like the frog, it was hard for us to gauge a gradual deterioration in security. The Umbrella formulated a sliding scale of security levels. Level five signified a complete breakdown of law and order. At level four (due to crossfire risk and loss of control by police and army) expatriates were expected to evacuate. While we were in Tansen the situation fluctuated around level three. The ambush of the army vehicle near our home jolted us up a rung. We continued to observe the 9pm curfew. There was tension and confusion, disruption of services, particularly transport, and we were cautious about having visitors to stay.

National instability inevitably increased stress, even though we were not always conscious of it.

CHAPTER 13

SURVIVAL

**We had to work at taking time off**

Ros –

Ensuring that we benefited from our rest days was far from easy. We first had to recognise that we had different ways of relaxing. Having spent a full week in the office, Nick looked forward to pottering in his garden. Caring for the children had restricted my movements, so I longed to get out and about on our days off. We both enjoy walking. But wherever we went we could not escape people. We found what we thought was a secluded spot for a cup of coffee from our flask, but within a few minutes a group of women, who had been cutting grass nearby, gathered round and began to ask: "Where have you come from?" "How old are your girls?" "Do you like living in Nepal?"

Sometimes we took trips down to the river to swim - about an hour and a half's walk from Amppipal. We hired porters to carry the girls, packed up a picnic and set off. Clambering over huge boulders we reached a gorge where a waterfall cascaded into a deep pool. For the sake of decency, I put loose drawstring trousers and a t-shirt over my swimsuit. The icy water was refreshing. But by the time we had trekked two hours uphill to get home, we were bathed in sweat again.

Pokhara was a weekend break destination. From this lakeside resort in mid-Nepal, tourists set off on treks into the Annapurnas. On our first visit, we were taken aback by the shabbiness of the waterfront, not unlike a British seaside resort in winter. The whole length of the lakeside road was under repair. When we ordered omelette and honey curd at one ramshackle eatery, the proprietor slipped off to buy eggs and honey. But breakfasts in a garden restaurant, with the sun glinting across the lake, were magical. Stately egrets perched in the trees; a kingfisher flashed by. We grew to love Pokhara, and returned habitually to our favourite eating-places. Chicken in a basket at Moondance, and cheesecake at Joe's were two of the specialities we savoured. When one of the lakeside hotels built a swimming pool, we became regular patrons. Between dips, I browsed the second-hand bookshops, looked at ready-made western garments, and got t-shirts embroidered.

We also escaped to Chitwan National Park on the flat plain in the south of Nepal, bordering India. We saw rhino, and kept on dreaming that we might see a tiger. Leeches were rare in Tansen. When we came across one at Chitwan National Park, its graceful head- over-heels movement fascinated the girls. Smaller creatures seemed to appeal to them more than the big game. Safaris lost their thrill after a while. I remember one of the girls moaning, "not another elephant ride".

As the political situation deteriorated, Pokhara lakeside attracted fewer and fewer tourists. It was no longer possible to blend in anonymously among crowds of visitors. As we walked along the lakeside road, proprietors pleaded with us to come and eat at their restaurant, or look at their trekking gear shop. The district headquarters of the health ministry were in the town, and Nick was tempted to spend time networking with officials. These reasons prompted us to take holidays outside Nepal. The French agency paid us a more generous maintenance allowance than our mission agency had, which helped to cover the extra costs.

Good friends had moved to Bangkok, and we went to visit them. We sunned ourselves at a coastal resort. It was a different world. The streets were clean, the food tasty and diverse, and we appreciated the chance to go out to a wide-screen cinema. For the first time in years we had a real holiday.

Although we thoroughly enjoyed our trips back to the UK, we always had a long and busy schedule of visits to make and friends to see. In Thailand we could relax with the children, spending time building sandcastles, or playing a board game. The ice cream was safe to eat, and the seafood appealing. The only problem was our limited language. We stayed in a Thai resort where few spoke English. The food was spicy, even for Nick's taste, so he indicated with gestures that he'd like a *little* chilli in his pork stir-fry. To his dismay, they misunderstood what he meant by 'little', and he found the dish laced with finely chopped chillies.

Nearing the end of our time in Nepal, we plucked up courage to visit North India. We had heard horror stories about taxi drivers who charged too much and took you where you didn't want to go. So we decided to link up with another family for moral support. The dads went ahead and negotiated rickshaws or rooms, while the mums and children kept each other company. Finding non-spicy food for the children was a challenge; even pizza came with chilli topping. The highlights of our trip would surprise a tourist coming from the west. They included eating out at a fast food chain, and travelling by train - things we couldn't easily do in Nepal.

Holidays in Thailand and India were exotic, but they were less expensive than returning to Europe.

We had been living in a 'red zone' for three years. At a mission conference I heard 'red zone' defined as an area where there is intense stress on a regular basis through perceived or actual threats to one's safety. Examples included curfews and travel restrictions, strikes and student violence, random attacks, and shootings. Red zone stresses add to the normal pressures of cross-cultural living and can precipitate burnout. Consequently, our mission agency offered its partners an allowance to pay for an annual break outside Nepal. I applauded this development, although I respected those who felt reluctant to spend mission money in this way, arguing that some supporters gave at great personal cost. The fact that Nick was under huge stress in the responsibilities he bore, convinced me that we needed to leave Nepal to get a worthwhile break. I welcomed the provision for other mission colleagues to do the same.

Nick –

We dropped everything for a week to attend mission conferences most years. The times for worship, Bible study, and meeting friends were uplifting. Over the years, our vision expanded as we listened to speakers from widely differing backgrounds. A Sri Lankan missionary challenged us about abandonment of security; a Scandinavian pastor explored the spirituality of the desert fathers and a Scottish doctor stirred us to look again at the reasons why we'd come to Nepal. I felt honoured to lead worship. I drew from my student experience as a church worship-group member. We used voices and instruments, old and new words, and silence...

There's a point in sailing up into the wind when, with the sails sufficiently filled, a yacht suddenly comes alive and lunges forward. Worshipping God can be like that. I love it. Leading worship is challenging musically, and invigorating spiritually. So at the end of mission conferences I felt both refreshed and exhausted.

Ros –

One year I was upset to think we would not be able to travel to the Umbrella Organisation's annual conference, which

I had been looking forward to for several months. A 15-day transport strike had been called, that coincided with the conference dates. We prayed. Some colleagues planned to leave Tansen before the strike. Nick's work did not allow that. We waited and packed half-heartedly. I never thought I would be pleased to hear the grating sound of bus brakes, and the toot of strident horns. But on the morning of the first day of the threatened strike, those sounds were music to my ears. The strike had been unexpectedly disbanded. It was a resounding answer to prayer, and we relished our time at conference all the more.

## Travelling was never stress-free

Ros –

Some expatriate colleagues said they preferred to stay at home for holidays than face the hassle of travelling in Nepal. I half agreed with them. We came straight back down to earth after a holiday abroad. The flight we had booked from Kathmandu to Bhairawa (two hours drive from Tansen) was cancelled because of fog. It took Nick an hour to find alternative tickets to Pokhara. That flight was an unexpected joy. Visibility was excellent and we surveyed the whole Himalayan range. We even identified Gorkha town and Liglig Mountain from the air. We landed at 5pm and tried to negotiate a taxi to take us the four hours to Tansen. By this point we had been travelling for 20 hours, and were desperate to reach home. School started the next day, and Nick was expected in the office. An older driver agreed to take us. His mates urged him to make good speed, as the curfew in Syanga, an hour into the journey, started at 7pm. We made it through Syanga. But at the next town a squad of armed police stopped us. They intimidated the driver with a barrage of questions. Our luggage was inspected. Nick wisely did not intervene. I sat tight in the back, with both girls lying across my lap asleep. I heard the sound of gunfire nearby and froze. I prayed fervently for protection. Eventually they let us through. We reached Tansen at 9pm, and helped our driver find a bed for the night. Looking back, I think we should have allowed ourselves more time for the journey.

*Every summer, monsoon landslides
disrupted journeys by road.*

Nick –

On our last but one visit to the UK from Nepal, we had a morning flight from Kathmandu to London. Check in was 6.30am. I'd sped around town throughout the previous day, wanting to get as much done as possible before our holiday. Government offices and an air-conditioning workshop had been among the many places on my itinerary. At half past nine in the evening we made the final checks to our packing – books for the journey, some Sterling, tickets, passports… "Oh no! Where's my passport?" We turned the room upside down in a frantic search for it. Our hearts sank. I was sure that I had put it in my pocket that morning – but where was it now? The British Embassy couldn't help at that time of night. "Please phone back after nine in the morning," they advised. We were due to spend a weekend with two other families in London. My parents had offered us their home as a base, while they were away. Ros quizzed me on London's bus and train routes, fearing she might have to stand-in as the tour guide. I told Ros to trust that it would be all right. We prayed. But we both tossed and turned through the small hours of the night. At five o'clock I set off into town on my moped mascot. I stirred up the night watchmen at several government offices I'd visited the day before. They hunted around for keys, and I looked on the floor and down the backs of seats where I'd sat. Unsuccessful, I returned to try the shops I'd been to, but no one was up. I tried to contact the manager of a de-humidifier supplier. At six I got through to him on the telephone... and he had my missing passport. How had I been so stupid as to lose it there, or anywhere for that matter? I went to pick it up. By this time Ros and the girls were at the airport, bracing themselves for a flight and a holiday in the UK without me. I managed to get to the airport at about 6.45 am. I was amazed, relieved and thankful; no less was Ros, of course.

## Threats to our work colleagues

Nick –

How did the security situation affect community health work? At Amppipal, the Programme began work in a new area. Locally elected dignitaries welcomed us with enthusiasm. We looked around to identify the most needy communities. We were heartened to find that our assessment matched the opinion of the local leadership, and so we undertook a baseline survey of health and economic status in 15 selected communities. Around this time the political climate began to change. When visiting the area, our staff were accused of being Maoists by some, and criticised for not being Maoists by others. Staying overnight was difficult, as it was always assumed that we were in sympathy with our host's political alignment. Often my colleagues would be quite unaware whether the hospitality they were receiving was from supporters or opponents of the radical party.

The survey highlighted local needs. We started work. In each place we used participatory methods over four days to raise villagers' awareness of problems in their communities, and motivate them to find solutions for themselves.

By this time a 'Maoist court' had replaced the elected village leaders. It wanted to be perceived as the body that maintained law and order in the area. Towards the end of our appraisal process we reached strongly Maoist communities and encountered opposition. Maoist representatives warned us that unless we stopped activities, not just in their villages, but in the whole of our new area, our staff would be at risk. Some sympathetic communities continued to request our presence, but assertive young radicals drowned their voices out. As representatives of a 'Western' organisation, did we 'smell of capitalism'? Were we threatening their authority by encouraging people to question the situations in which they found themselves, with a view to improving their lot? Did our proposed community health messages run counter to Maoist rhetoric? For whatever reason, we were not welcome to pursue health development work in that Maoist area.

My Nepali colleagues were well paid by local standards, and particularly liable to be approached by Maoist fundraisers. We explained that our organisation had a strategic role in serving the community. But that seemed to carry little weight. They demanded a month's salary as a 'tax' for the year. Those who refused to pay were visited at their homes in the middle of the night by up to a dozen armed men. No one was foolish enough not to pay. The staff of Amppipal Hospital channelled their corporate donation through one staff representative. Some days later, the man concerned was hauled into police custody and questioned for nine days.

Thereafter, the hospital Director advised everyone wishing to make donations to do so independently. The police offered protection to people who were prepared to report harassment. But everyone, including the police, knew that such protection could last only a few days, after which the threats would resume. As a result, the Maoist movement gained the upper hand, holding much of rural Nepal in its grip.

We conducted training courses in isolated, vulnerable locations. We paid a modest training allowance to participants on the final day of each event. My colleagues were anxious that Maoist fundraisers might take the money that had been set aside for this purpose, so they concealed it in socks, pillowcases and under their beds. One day they told me they had been warned that they would be visited, and lay awake all night in fear. Thankfully, that encounter never materialised.

*Although I witnessed direct combat between Maoists and government forces on only one occasion, heavily armed police and troops were a common sight.*

On one journey from Tansen to Butwal in our project vehicle, the driver and I had to stop and wait, before proceeding in convoy with armed 'protection'. Non-uniformed, but armed, young men climbed into taxi-jeeps with canvas hoods. One man who was in military uniform appeared to be in charge. In the queue were fuel tankers, returning empty after defying a Maoist transport strike. I felt uneasy – army personnel in civvies somehow lacked legitimacy. Contrary to their assertions, it seemed that we were in the convoy to provide protection to our guards.

Towards the end of our time in Nepal, local Maoist leaders exerted increasing influence over the health programme. Our training courses were frequently cancelled or re-arranged at the last minute to fit in with strikes called by the Maoists. Every day we discussed the safety of our field staff, jeep and motorbikes. With humour and tact, my Nepali team maintained informal relations with local Maoist cadres, as well as with government officials. It was a difficult juggling act. Maoist representatives pressured us to register with the local section of their organisation, to pay contributions from programme funds, and to coordinate our activities through their bureaucratic channels. We couldn't comply. When at the end of my assignment with the French organisation, I said goodbye to staff of the government district health offices, I learned that we were the only remaining international health agency working in those remote districts. It was not only Nepalis who were fleeing to the cities, but humanitarian aid agencies too.

# CHAPTER 14

# WAS IT ALL WORTH IT?

## Delegating at work, and seeing programmes flourish

Nick –

A short-term expatriate administrator was sent out from France to take over Sarah's responsibilities. He had an easy manner and was not in a rush to transform administrative systems. I was in a better frame of mind to accept suggested changes than I had been when Sarah came. We formed a good working relationship and led the programme together for seven productive months.

They were difficult times politically. The Maoist insurgency continued to develop strength. Its leaders, together with local and regional government officers, all wanted to have their say in directing our operations.

Despite this, our tuberculosis and HIV/AIDS control activities flourished. In coordination with government health staff, we conducted training courses that encouraged and motivated health workers and community people. Drama teams and 'peer communicators' proved popular in getting our message across. Female sex workers began to trust the staff of a pilot programme we'd launched to meet their needs.

While our French administrator worked at giving more autonomy to the Nepali office-based team, I sought to empower the field leadership. We appointed a very capable, but rather young, woman to be a second field team leader. She thrived in the role. I was struck by the confident and yet polite way she dealt with older government staff. The Nepali field coordinator delegated duties to the team leaders. His role developed as he relieved me of some of my responsibilities – higher-level government liaison; and coordinating and documenting our monthly reporting. I didn't find the hand over easy. At first, I expended as much energy in checking and following him up, as I would have done in undertaking the jobs myself. Towards the end of that final chapter of working in the TB and HIV / AIDS Programme, I could see that the Nepali team had the capability to run it independently. This was just as well, since after both expatriates left, there was a gap before others came.

## A bold and purposeful Christian church

Nick –

We gradually found our places as members of the Christian church in Nepal. But it took five years. The main hurdle was language. I guess most people are faster developers.

A small crooked woman, who belonged to our fellowship, passed our home one day and called out to Ros for a glass of water. As they sat together on the step outside, Ros asked about her day. "Oh I haven't done much. I cleaned some rice, cooked, read my Bible, and prayed," With a radiant face, she added, "I'm terribly weak. And although my body is getting limper, my spirit is growing stronger," A neighbour who was leaning over the wall had heard a more eloquent testimony from this diminutive saint, than she would ever have heard from Ros or me. When she had finished drinking the water, the dear lady reached for her stick, and, with her broken flip-flops fastened to her ankle with string, quietly set off again.

Leaders in the church taught from the Bible, and were always ready to witness for Jesus. As well as testifying to their families and neighbours, they would walk for many days to take the good news of Jesus to remote locations. They set an example in their devotion to prayer, their concern for the sick and bereaved, and in striving for justice and social action. They regularly expressed gratitude to God for many of the things we so often take for granted: safety in travel, recovery from sickness, a meal, or just a glass of water.

Courage was a quality that was not in short supply. The assistant pastor returned from a visit to support believers in two neighbouring districts. He told how the police had arrested three brothers because they spoke about Jesus, and carried tracts and Bibles. He had encouraged them from the scriptures, and said that he too was willing to be imprisoned for his faith.

One summer we spent two months in the UK. Returning to Tansen, we attended the Saturday morning service. It began with the usual format: a welcome, songs (while the congregation continued to drift in), notices, the reading of a psalm, and 'open worship'. During open worship some people sat, others stood with arms raised. We prayed aloud, altogether. I knelt down and wept for joy. Seeing our family and friends in the UK had been good, but now I felt I was 'home' again.

During one of these chaotic times of praise, I remembered Doug. He had prayed for us every day since we'd gone to Nepal, and we had received recent news that he was dying of cancer. I prayed in Nepali, in English, in tongues. As I bowed my head, I could see Doug in my mind's eye. He seemed to be there with us as a fellow believer, worshipping Jesus. I sensed God saying that Doug would not be healed, but that He was calling him home.

## Taking a stand for Jesus

Nick –

On 7th November 1992, in the sky near Tansen, an image of Jesus appeared in the clouds. Many Hindu people, including some from a village called Mashyam, reported that the spectacle lasted for several hours. This led a small number of people to believe in Christ. One woman began to pray regularly for her village. Nothing more happened immediately.

Twelve years later, 30 people from Mashyam village turned to faith in Jesus Christ. Neighbours and community leaders criticised them harshly. Nevertheless, they began to meet each Saturday for Christian worship, and during the week for Bible study and prayer. A group of these new adult believers attended baptism preparation at Tansen. After the four-day course, 23 people were baptised. It was a moving event. Two pastors climbed in to the church's concrete baptism tank. One at a time the candidates joined them and confirmed their faith. Then each was tipped back under the water. As they emerged, an established member of the church prayed that they would know the power of the Holy Spirit working in their lives, and have strength to live for Jesus through adversity.

## Two telling symbols

Nick –

During our Tansen years, I had gained sufficient confidence in using the language and was invited to speak at church every 3 months or so.

One year, I was asked to take the Good Friday service. I borrowed two pieces of heavy sawn timber from a furniture maker and lashed them together to form a wooden cross. I couldn't easily carry it, so flagged down a truck to help me. It was a golden opportunity to speak about Jesus' death and resurrection to the lorry driver who was both delighted to help and amazed by my story. That Saturday, I brought the cross to church and left it on the ground for everyone to trip over as they came to the service. It certainly produced a sense of anticipation, and gave me a head start for my sermon, about Jesus' death on a cross.

After Easter, I embarked on an ambitious series tackling the seven letters in Revelation, chapters 2-3. It took almost two years to complete. Just a few weeks after looking at the letter to the church at Smyrna, which speaks about believers being put in prison, the three evangelists that our pastor visited were jailed for six months. The next letter, to the church in Pergamum, ends "To him who overcomes... I will also give a white stone with a new name written on it, known only to him who receives it." I thought and prayed long and hard about what this verse might mean. What name could Jesus give that would only be known by the receiver? In the middle of my talk on that letter I gave a white stone to Rani. This is her story.

Rani had been a believer for about 12 years. At the time of her baptism, in Tansen, she suffered severe persecution from her family and feared for her life. As she fled from her pursuers, she took shelter in an unoccupied house. Her would-be killers made a relentless search. While Rani was hiding, she heard God's voice speaking clearly in her heart – "You are *God's beloved daughter*, no harm will come to you".

Several years slipped by, and she had all but forgotten the event.

And then I gave that talk... I spoke about Christ giving those who persevere in faith a white stone with a new name written on it. Hidden in my pocket I'd prepared such a stone with the words *'God's beloved daughter'* written in Nepali. I looked for someone who would stand up and say that they were persevering in their Christian faith. Very timidly, Rani came forward. I took the stone from my pocket and gave it to her. When she read the inscription, she immediately knew that this was a personal encouragement from God.

A day or two later I met Rani on the path. She wept. I apologised for having asked her to come forward in front of the church. "Oh no," she said, "I must tell you my story."

The following week, at our morning service, Rani confidently explained what had happened to her. She explained about the persecution she had suffered as a new believer and about God speaking to her at that time. She recounted God's faithfulness, and how He had spoken to her again through the inscription on the stone I had given her. I learned to take prayerful care in what I said in my sermons; and I began to recognise that God was prepared to speak to others even through me.

## House-group

Ros –

Rani was a member of our Nepali house-group. I found a role there. One Thursday evening I arrived at her home, stepped up on to the mudded veranda, took off my shoes and edged into a bed-cum-sitting-room. The door would not open fully, as it hit the end of a single bed, shoved against a metal wardrobe. I was early, so found somewhere to sit on the lower tier of a bunk bed, along with two other women. As more people arrived, I squashed on to the back row, and leant up against the wall. A group of women perched on the edge of the mattress in front of me, and others sat on cushions on the lino floor. The leader occupied the room's only wicker chair, which was jammed between the end of the bunk bed and a wooden staircase. Under the chair, in a basket of straw, a hen minded her chicks. About 20 of us, including a two-year old child, somehow managed to squeeze into that small room. The little boy was passed from one lap to another during the evening to keep him happy. We were just about to start singing when the lights went out. In the pitch black, someone put on a torch, and our hostess lit a candle. We sang 'Give me oil in my lamp'. As we were singing a second hymn by heart, the power came on again. Individuals requested favourite songs.

"You each have the opportunity to share one blessing and one prayer request," said the leader.

It was helpful to be challenged to remember the ways God was at work in our everyday lives.

"I had a safe journey to my parents' home – praise God".

"My son is struggling with exams".

"I have had a bad stomach, but am feeling much better now".

One girl was near tears as she shared her struggles: "In my work with students on the campus this week, I was strongly opposed by a loud-mouthed young man."

Someone prayed, and we then started a Bible study on James chapter 3, which speaks about suffering for doing good. Half an hour later, our hostess brought in trays of tea and salty crackers. We thanked the Lord for the snacks, and chatted together.

The house-group met at different homes in rotation. One Thursday it was due to meet in our front room, but no one turned up. Two key leaders had moved away. Subsequent meetings were somewhat disorganised: no one knew what we would study, or who would lead; and there were long pauses, and even longer monologues. I took a deep breath, and suggested we make a rota to show where the group was to meet, who would lead, and what passage we would study. We spent the remainder of the evening compiling a timetable. The group gradually regained momentum and enthusiasm.

Later I recommended a published Bible study guide in Nepali. With the aid of prepared questions, even the less experienced members dared to lead meetings. More people contributed their ideas. The expatriates who took the time to check vocabulary ahead of the meeting, found they could contribute more meaningfully.

Every three months we held a house-group social, for games, a video, or to eat together. One evening we hosted a 'momo' party. Together we rolled out the stretchy flour and water dough, and pressed it out into small circles. We blobbed a spoonful of spiced mince on to the discs, and then wrapped them into neat parcels. After steaming the dough momos, we ate them with thin tomato soup and chutney. When Nick scurried into the kitchen to attend to the steamer, someone hid his plate behind the curtain. Returning, he protested humorously. Everyone laughed.

A highlight was the house-group Christmas 'picnic' in our garden. Early in the afternoon three of the group arrived with rice, vegetables, oil and spices. Sitting on straw mats, we chopped vegetables, peeled garlic, and pounded ginger. I admired the speed and dexterity of my friends; I seemed to be all fingers and thumbs in comparison. Some lads brought large cooking pots, the outsides of which they smeared with mud. They dug a fireplace in the turf, gathered wood, and lit a fire. The whole group assembled at six. In a large circle near the fire, we sang, told stories, and ate pilau rice and chicken curry by the light of a paraffin lantern.

New believers stretched us with interesting questions. One evening we talked about how sin and sickness might be related; the virtue of fasting; and the fallacy of purgatory. Another time we debated whether, on becoming a Christian, it was appropriate to change one's name. One lad in the group, Shiva, was named after a Hindu deity. He had kept his name, arguing, "Shiva needs Jesus too." Another girl was re-named 'Prisca' at her baptism. We encouraged her by looking up references to her namesake in the New Testament. Sometimes Nepalis appeared to understand scripture more clearly than we did. They readily appreciated the connection between Jesus' baptism and temptation, as this often mirrored their personal experience. When Jacob urged his family to get rid of their foreign gods, they handed him their idols and earrings[32]. The full impact of these verses is often lost on Western Christians.

The Nepalis in our group saw the idols in their neighbours' homes every day and Hindu sadhus wearing large gold rings in their ears. They knew the significance of these, and had no problem relating to the Genesis text.

It was a great joy to meet with Nepali believers who shared my desire to study the Bible and to live it out. It thrilled me to see friends developing leadership skills in our group. One timid, young female student, who led a Bible study, was almost swamped by a more confident lad. A few months later the same girl guided the group with assurance, maintaining momentum, and keeping the discussion on track. I was excited when a young man explained in a Saturday sermon what he had learned at house group a few days earlier. I contributed my time and ideas to the group, but it was God's Holy Spirit who nurtured these men and women towards Christian maturity.

# CHAPTER 15

# AGENTS OF CHANGE...
# OR CHANGED AGENTS?

## Exploring how Christians cope at Hindu festivals and weddings

Ros –

I hope I never stop learning. In a foreign country with rich traditions, there were always new aspects of culture to explore. Many questions arose, and I saved these each week for my language-cum-culture lessons.

Much of my curiosity centred on rites of passage and festivals. Nepali wedding processions are unmistakable. A cacophony of assorted traditional instruments can be heard wafting across the hillsides, as the groom and up to 50 supporters progress to the bride's house for the wedding ceremony. The following day they retrace their steps, carrying the bride aloft swathed in a red and gold sari, on a stretcher that looks more like a shopping trolley. I had to shield our anxious young daughters from the jocular crowd and the brash, discordant noise.

Elizabeth was born in Kathmandu during an auspicious month for weddings. When I was feeding her at night I heard the city version of the wedding procession: a noisy, jazz style brass band playing into the small hours. Wedding houses were draped with cascading strings of coloured lights. Red marquees transformed drab courtyards.

Friends and colleagues invited us to weddings. I never mastered the art of putting on a sari alone, so I would call on my nearest female neighbour to help me dress for these special events. On one occasion, a wedding family asked if I would be the official photographer, as they knew we had a camera. I readily agreed, and enjoyed the chance to see a Hindu wedding close up. The groom's mother showed me the sets of clothes she had prepared for her daughter-in-law.

But in this predominantly Hindu environment, how did Nepali Christians celebrate weddings? We experienced a model ceremony. The groom's Hindu parents and relatives felt able to attend. They even expressed their approval at the conclusion of the wedding. The Christian couple had made thoughtful preparations, and took care not to cause unnecessary offence. The ceremony took place in a small hotel, rather than at home or church. And the exchange of vows and rings replaced the Hindu wedding rituals. However, the groom took pains to show respect for his Hindu relations by kissing their feet.

*In keeping with Nepali tradition, the couple wore tinsel garlands, and the groom, a new Nepali cap.*

There was a feast afterwards. At the reception, I spoke with another Christian couple, who had been married in church. The groom's Hindu parents had refused to attend their wedding.

After Nirmala's parents insisted that they should have a Hindu wedding ceremony, Mohan and Nirmala eloped together. Nirmala became a Christian some months later. The church in Tansen, however, felt torn about their relationship. Nirmala resolved to be baptised, which opened the way for their marriage to be blessed in church. As a 'wedding gift', we arranged for the local bakery to make and decorate a three-tier cake. After the service of blessing, the couple cut the cake and served it to their guests. It was a day of reconciliation. We were delighted to attend services of thanksgiving for the birth of their daughter, and later their son. We informally adopted them as godchildren.

## Death in a Hindu family

Ros –

Nepali Christians are put in a difficult situation when a death occurs in their Hindu family. We were new to Nepal when the Hindu husband of a devout Christian died. The church insisted that she should not participate in the Hindu funeral customs, as they were considered idolatrous. If she did, she risked alienation from the church. If she did not, the village community would ostracise her. I did not understand what was going on at the time, and I don't remember how the issue was resolved. But I do recall that we interceded fervently for the widow at our church prayer meeting, and that she remained a member of the fellowship.

A few years later, I witnessed the anguish of our Nepali Christian friend, Mohan, when his father died. Mohan had visited his father during his final illness, and taken his leave. When he heard the news of the death, however, he pursed his lips and said he could not go to be with his family. He felt strongly that to do so would betray his Lord. He was adamant that he could not participate in the Hindu funeral rituals. He knew that if he went out of respect, he would be coerced into taking part. I asked him if he could show solidarity with his mother by writing a letter. That, he felt, would only rub salt into the wound. The situation raised many questions. How could Mohan show love to his family at the time of his father's death, without compromising his faith? How can Christians mourn Hindu parents, when they do not countenance shaving their heads or wearing white as Hindus do? I could not fully understand the dynamics of the situation, but wanted to support my Christian brother in his grief. His aunt, a staunch Christian, who had suffered persecution for her faith, vehemently rejected everything associated with Hinduism. Was it right to make a complete break in this way? There was no easy answer to this dilemma. It was a huge issue for the fledgling Nepali church.

I had a lot to learn. We tried to celebrate appropriately in the Nepali context during other special events. Friends and neighbours gave us plates of food at festival times; so we gave them star biscuits at Christmas, and hot cross buns at Easter. We planned the thanksgiving for Elizabeth's birth to take place when she was five months old, the time when Hindu families celebrate the first rice-feeding of their daughters. Though we were outsiders, I longed to get under the skin of my Nepali friends.

## Dasai - helping new believers face the challenge

Ros –

I had been studying theology by correspondence for several years. In Nepal it was difficult to access books and materials, and I felt at a disadvantage. When, however, I had to nominate a dissertation topic, I realised I could capitalise on my situation. I decided to tackle 'Issues facing Nepali Christians relating to the Hindu festival Dasai'.

In Nepal Dasai is the biggest Hindu festival of the year. I knew that many of the matters raised would overlap with those that Christians face at the time of weddings and funerals. So

I drafted questionnaires for Hindus and Christians, and researched the mythical background to Dasai. One October, before the festival, I interviewed 14 Christians of different ages and backgrounds, to find out how they felt about Dasai. I asked what they thought was appropriate for a Christian to get involved in; and, conversely, what was inappropriate.

The ten-day festival comes at the end of the monsoon. People whitewash their houses in preparation. My pious, elderly neighbour allowed me to see the corner of her kitchen, where she had sown barley seeds in sand around a water jug, representing the goddess Durga. Each morning I heard the tinkling of a bell as she offered flowers, rice, fruit and vegetables at her shrine. On the eighth and ninth days, our neighbours sacrificed goats and buffaloes and feasted on the meat. The festival climaxed on the tenth day, when senior family members blessed their juniors.

*They daubed red powder mixed with rice on their foreheads (a tika) and tucked the sprouted barley shoots behind ears or into hair.*

Children received a five or ten rupee note crumpled into their hands. Neighbours paraded the paths in their new clothes, with red blessing marks prominent on their foreheads. Meanwhile, shrieks of delight rang out as children played on makeshift bamboo swings and small, human-powered, wooden ferris-wheels.

The Christians I interviewed struggled with wearing the tika on their foreheads. They found it difficult to cope with the ritual worship that characterises the festival. Many felt they could not eat meat, as it had been sacrificed to idols. New believers were pressurised by their Hindu families to join in.

An only child of Hindu parents wept as she recalled:
"I had to receive a tika from my mother. She refused to eat until she had put the powder on my forehead. Am I a Christian any more? I feel that Satan is drawing me back. Please pray for me."

I was encouraged to hear how most of those I interviewed coped on the tenth day.
"I took photos of my family when it came to tika-giving," one young man reported.
"I brought a couple of friends from church along with me, and my family didn't force us to receive tikas," said another.

The findings I compiled showed that certain believers were more vulnerable to pressure at Dasai than others. I was keen to use the results to help generate dialogue in the church. So, with the help of my language teacher, I prepared a summary of my research in Nepali, together with some topical questions. When I presented my findings at various house-groups, it thrilled me to hear the animated discussion that followed.

"What was it like for you when you returned to your family at Dasai?"
"Is it good to have a programme at church so believers don't have to return to their families?"

"How can we show respect for our elders and demonstrate Jesus' love for them?"
"How can we support new believers at festival time?"
"What can Christians affirm at Dasai?"

As an outsider, I had been able to catalyse debate about a crucial issue for the Nepali church. This, to me, was hands-on theology. It was the culmination of nine years' experience of living and working in Nepal, achieving fluency in the language and gaining the trust of the church.

## Changed people

Ros –

During my nine years in Nepal, I had glimpses of how God was at work in the lives of ordinary people. While waiting in the lobby of Patan Hospital, near Kathmandu, a familiar voice greeted me. It was the one-armed sewing lady who had come persistently to our door in Amppipal, and who generated more work for me than for herself at times. Four years had passed since I last saw her, and she seemed so very different. Her face shone. This was not the cringing apologetic woman I used to know.

She told me her story:
"I moved with my husband to Kathmandu for work. We met some Nepali Christians here and because of their example came to know God for ourselves. We have now both been baptised".

We walked together to the hospital canteen for a drink. As we sat down, I suggested we could pray together. There was no doubting the genuineness of this woman's faith. She prayed fluently from her heart. Her eyes radiated light, and I was thrilled by the sense of hope and purpose she displayed. I felt privileged in having played a small part in the fulfilment of God's plan of blessing for her life.

# AGENTS OF CHANGE... OR CHANGED AGENTS?

I struggled to forge close relationships with Nepali women in Amppipal. They seemed so busy with their household chores. The problem was compounded when we visited them, as they then felt obliged to prepare additional food and drink to entertain us. I can remember the occasion when we were invited to the home of Nick's colleague – the Programme's coordinator. Sitting on the veranda, talking with 'the men', made me feel decidedly awkward. But I did not consider it right to impose myself on the women, in their domain around the fireplace. Besides, I had no idea how to clean rice or cut vegetables with a curved knife held under my foot. I do, however, recall the time when a break through occurred. After a meal, I joined the grandmother as she de-husked maize with her thumbs. She showed me her technique. I made everyone laugh at my cack-handedness. But I persevered, and the wife of Nick's colleague also joined the group. The shared task broke down some of the barriers between us. We joked together about the blisters on my thumb.

It was the Programme coordinator and his wife that Nick sought advice from when he was thinking of giving me a Nepali wedding necklace. He consulted them about how much gold he should buy, where to get it, and how to have the ornament made up. When Elizabeth was born, they arranged for a neighbour to weave a Nepali wicker cradle as a gift. I shall always remember them.

Several years later, this couple had an opportunity to travel to England for study. Our parents, who had received lavish hospitality from them during their visit to Amppipal, welcomed them as friends. It must have felt strange viewing pictures of their own simple Nepali village home, while seated in my parents' carpeted living room. On my parents' final visit to Nepal, there was a reunion with the family, and we again shared happy memories. We were overjoyed when they emailed us from England with the news that they had become Christians. Friendships like these have truly enriched us.

Nick –

Have we made an impact on the Nepali friends and neighbours we lived alongside for nine years? Yes, I believe we have, even if in some cases it has meant a growing dependence on us. We, of course, have benefited enormously from participating in the 'life journeys' of those around us.

At Amppipal, an auxiliary nurse-midwife worked at the Community Health Programme. She and Ros sometimes met to read their Bibles and pray, although she never declared her faith publicly. I valued her support at work – she was a 'big sister' who gave me wise advice. At that stage, her children were young high school students – we have a photo of her daughter on our veranda, holding baby Elizabeth. Our paths crossed again when we both worked for the TB and HIV Programme at Tansen. Her family had by then grown up. The girl who sat on our veranda now was working as a teacher's assistant at our girls' school. A year later, her son and I had trekked in the Himalayas in Gorkha district: 'brothers' venturing into the mountains together. All Nepalis have seen snow at a distance. But on this trip, he was able to handle it and to throw a snowball for the first time.

During the trek we also visited villages where the Gorkha Community Health Programme had worked five years previously. We washed our clothes at a water tap that the Programme installed. It had been constructed to last 20 years and was performing well.

When we lived at Amppipal, a member of the Community Programme staff invited us to his home so he could learn more about Jesus. Ros and I worked through a Christian basics course with him and his wife. Three years later, as a result of my laxity in monitoring the Programme accounts, and his falling prey to temptation, he misappropriated building supplies and had to leave the job. He moved on to a teaching job in Jumla. We met him again there, and he appeared bright and positive in his role. But there was rising political tension in the area, and the school closed. A year later we heard that our friend had died. He drank, and it was this that eventually ruined his life. We never had the opportunity to visit his widow again.

Mohan and I became good friends. He had come to Amppipal to be a flat mate for his uncle Padam – Director of the Community Programme. After Padam died, Mohan continued living in the village, where he received his schooling and was involved in church youth work. We tried to help improve his English skills, but he never succeeded in gaining the School Leavers' Certificate. When we gave him the opportunity to be a programme field worker for a few months, he thrived on the task. Soon after returning to Nepal to launch the French Programme, I tracked him down and appointed him as the 'do any practical job' man. This work experience proved invaluable for Mohan, teaching him many useful skills and aiding his development. Our friendship grew and we got to know his wider family. He and I travelled to far east Nepal on a 100cc motorbike to visit his mother, brothers and parents-in-law. Mohan's wife became a close friend of Ros.

While I enjoyed this friendship, I began to wonder if Mohan was becoming too dependent on me, and if I was acting as a barrier to him reaching his full potential. Men like Mohan are desperately needed to develop Nepal, but progress does not come without difficulties. The temptation for him to better his lot in the short term is very real. I was therefore not surprised when Mohan asked me if he could leave Nepal with us and come to live in the UK.

Another man worked as secretary in Amppipal. His life-journey also took him to Tansen where he continued working with the Umbrella organisation. Over the years he softened from being negative towards Christians and the Christian faith. I am trusting that one day, like Paul, he will become a follower of Jesus[33].

How can we measure the impact of our nine years in Nepal? It is impossible for us to do so. We don't know if or how the seeds we've sown will grow, or how the people we've touched will develop. Ongoing links with our friends in Nepal will be more distant. We leave them in God's hands.

## Agents of change... or changed agents?

Ros –

Foam cushions had been set around the edge of the biggest room in the office. We sat down on these and leaned over small stainless steel plates heaped with beaten rice and curried goat. This was the scene at an impromptu welcome party for four new members of the Tansen Programme team. It was a significant event, not only for the newcomers, but also for us, as it meant the 'family' size had increased to sixteen. Our Nepali coordinator joked that it was high time the Programme had a family planning operation.

The first annual staff picnic at 'Luv' Hill was an intimate occasion. I arrived with the girls after their morning-school, and initiated a game of 'Pit'[34] with the women on the team. The following year we had a much larger gathering, and the venue was Srinagar Hill. Wives and children accompanied their husbands, giving me the challenge of working out who belonged to whom. As we posed for the staff photograph, I gasped inwardly. For it dawned on me that we were making a big impact on the lives of these forty people. I could hardly believe that this had all happened within the space of eighteen months.

Three and a half years after arriving in Tansen, we set out mats in a circle on the grass terrace below our home. We resorted to flattening cardboard boxes to provide extra seats for the whole staff team. As dusk fell, staff in turn around the ring, solemnly put their hands together in a 'Namaste' greeting, respectfully addressing each member of our family. They spoke very warmly about Nick. Several said how much he had impressed them on field trips. One man saw him as 'the father of the Programme'. The secretary recounted a memorable trip he'd made with Nick by motorbike to the field. He outlined in copious detail the events they shared together - from a snake crossing the road to fractious negotiations with local officials. "Nick taught me a lot from those experiences," he added. Someone else praised Nick for treating everyone equally – "There are no big or small people in his eyes." Another pointed to our vegetable plot, saying 'You can even tell from his garden how hard working he is'. The Nepali administrator recalled how difficult it had been at the beginning, trying to balance the monthly accounts. With a smile he added, 'But look where we've got to now, thanks to Nick'.

Nick certainly gained skills through the multi-faceted tasks that exercised his brain. He has always regarded the establishment of a strong and healthy staff team as his single greatest accomplishment. He had invested an enormous amount of time and energy in many lives, and this had paid dividends. He discovered a latent talent in achieving positive outcomes from government negotiations. (Or was he just pig-headed and not prepared to take 'no' for answer?) When it came to programme design and implementation, he went to great pains to ensure that his sometimes-whacky new ideas would work. He honed his competence in staff selection, management, and training, and taught others a diverse range of skills – anything from wiring a fluorescent light, to handling statistics.

The Tansen team certainly thought Nick had what it took to start something new. They had heard reports about the enthusiasm with which he drove forward the Community Health Programme in Gorkha; and they had personally witnessed his commitment to the French project. Many wondered what he would tackle next.

When one becomes deeply engrossed in an overseas health development programme, it is all too easy to acquire an unhealthy sense of ownership. But we had to accept that we were not indispensable. Making the break proved difficult, but it did provide a chance to review our achievements, and express our appreciation of others. Often it's not until someone retires that they have the space to look back and reflect upon their life's work. We valued being able to assess our effectiveness every 3-4 years, as we moved from one location to another.

## Ros' new skills

Nick –

Tenacity is a vital component for anyone involved in world mission. There were numerous occasions when Ros could so easily have given up, but she doggedly stayed the course, keeping her focus. While month followed month as we sought government agreements and visas she, with Nirmala, prayed without ceasing.

Ros had the gift of being able to maintain family stability and a sense of calm, even in the midst of danger and uncertainty. Many times when I felt up against it, Ros was there to reassure me and restore my confidence. She was a power of strength when I clashed with the short-term programme administrator, Sarah.

Ros made a point of structuring her days, and pacing herself, and in so doing remained healthy. On Tuesdays Ros and other mums managed to 'keep fit' to an aerobics video… while the kids 'kept fat' in front of the TV. Wednesday afternoons saw her on the tennis court playing doubles with expatriate or Nepali doctors and medical students. When I was away, or had crashed after a spell of overwork, Ros always seemed able to cope, which was crucial for family survival. And as we faced unexpected change and crises, she could be counted upon to guide the children through.

Although the girls and I still seem to be as skinny as rakes, Ros has never failed to provide a good balanced diet for the family, giving us a substantial breakfast to start each day. As a capable hostess, she enjoyed entertaining those who visited our home. Superb Greek salads often featured on the menu, comprising (among other things) locally grown cucumbers, garlic and tomatoes, served with homemade yogurt. And somehow she'd obtained Kalamata olives.

Ros persevered through her correspondence study. Her dissertation was an analysis of interviews conducted with local Nepali believers about the Hindu festival, Dasai. She developed and presented findings that explored how Christians could support one another at Dasai.

Ros worked hard to understand and nurture our children. She developed imaginative ideas to satisfy their active young minds. Even though there were no libraries or museums, Ros was able to devise a myriad of crafty craft activities. She organised birthday parties on exotic themes - 'the jungle', 'space' and 'baby animals'. I can recall the girls being entertained on countless long journeys.

At home and at school, Ros led devotions. She learned the art of seeing the child's perspective, of making topics relevant, tapping into their imagination and keeping pace with their enthusiasm.

Ros chaired school committees, supported teachers, and filled in when there were gaps. With some reservation, she took on the role of computer trainer at Tansen for three years. She applied her teaching skills to train the school's inexperienced Nepali language teacher. Together they made flash cards, played games and took trips to the bazaar to help the children try out what they'd learned. Through her input, that teacher's lessons inproved.

Ros demonstrated practical skills in a wide variety of ways. She readily took to dealing with minor heath problems: removing leeches, and treating styes, boils and mosquito bites. When the children developed a fever, Ros would not only treat and comfort them, but would also pray to Jesus for healing. Our girls knew that mum's faith was real, as they joined in prayer for personal, local and even international issues. Lydia and Elizabeth are now quick to pray too, and have become expectant that God will answer.

Early on, Ros realised that she had more important priorities than washing-up or separating stones from the rice. Ordinary household tasks absorbed a vast amount of time. So Ros employed home workers, that benefited both them and us. She set them realistic daily tasks, was fair in her dealings, and sought to minimise any tendency towards dependency. When poor people asked for help at our door, Ros knew that their difficulties would not necessarily be alleviated by a gift of money. So although she would sometimes give food or second hand clothing she was much keener to help by buying craft items or offering employment. But she admits that wise giving is easier said than done.

We remember that when we lived in Amppipal, an experienced expatriate who'd been an encourager of Nepali Christians for several years stressed the value of making disciples of new believers. Ros tried to follow this advice. She spent many hours reading the Bible and praying with Nirmala. A level relationship between them emerged. Together they persevered in prayer, even in the face of disappointment.

Two years before we left, the church house-group that we attended reached rock bottom. There was no leader and no structure. Ros prompted them to find some ready-made Bible study guides and prepare a rota of leaders. Over the following months, the group blossomed, growing in confidence to the point where almost every member felt capable of taking the lead.

We tried to support Nepali student workers. Ros listened sympathetically to their troubles, prayed, and attended events they organised. On her insistence, they always brought receipts acknowledging financial support. Through regular contact, she and they established accountability, one for each other.

A large card file of names and addresses sat on Ros's desk. Her computer desktop displayed her email folders. She made a point of keeping friends and supporters up to date with monthly prayer notes, weekly jots and hand written letters. Though she has a natural flair for letter writing, to maintain it required a great deal of persistence. She also sealed every envelope with 'glue-stick' as Nepali envelopes had feeble glue.

Now that we are back in the UK, Ros wonders how many of the skills she has acquired are transferable. Not all, but many, I guess.

## Living in uncertainty had become normal

Ros –

When we met newcomers to Nepal, we realised how many skills we had learned. Living in uncertainty had become normal.

In the domestic realm, life was unpredictable. Our kitchen in Tansen featured numerous cooking options: sturdy square green kerosene stoves from Amppipal days, a two-ring gas cooker, an electric oven, and even a 15-year-old microwave. It may sound 'overdone', but having different cooking options was very useful. When the electricity unexpectedly failed, I would transfer the bread dough from the loaf tin to an ingenious ring-shaped 'miracle oven' which worked on the gas. When there were national strikes, however, gas became unavailable. I had to be creative and flexible, and learn to laugh and not cry.

I avoided promising things to the girls, as plans frequently failed. A trip to the river could be scuppered by a strike. We became experts at instant re-planning. We were travelling in a bus with friends. On reaching Mugling, Nepal's equivalent of a motorway service station, one member of the party called out that we should have our rice at Naryanghat – an hour's drive further on. However, landslide damage narrowed the road to one lane in places, and lack of policing created a major blockage, with long queues of buses and lorries. What should have been an hour's journey became a marathon seven hours. When we eventually reached Naryanghat, no one felt like delaying any longer, so we decided to forgo the rice and make do with a large bottle of cold coke.

As it was very rare for flights or bus journeys to run to schedule, I always took snacks, drinks, books, paper, pens, and 'Uno'[35] cards to keep the girls occupied. We endured long hours in Kathmandu's dreary domestic air terminal, reading aloud against the din of crackly announcements and trying to keep children and crayons off the dusty floor. Improvisation saved many a day.

We've never been under the illusion that we are in control of our lives. Even before the political unrest, numerous obstacles delayed our journeys: landslides, breakdowns, sickness or roadblocks. We had to rely on others for even the simplest things in life - cooking a vegetable we'd never seen before; or negotiating a price for rice bought on our veranda. I could not communicate with Nick when he was away on field trips, so I had to turn to those around me for advice. Dependency on others was new for us – we'd kidded ourselves that we were self-reliant. And of course this threw us back on God – trusting him to hear our prayers in both the big and the small issues of life.

# CHAPTER 16

## BECOMING A BIT NEPALI

### Breaking the rules

Nick –

"She's eating using a knife, it's in her mouth." "They're kissing and cuddling in the middle of the street." Do you wince when people flaunt social norms? In Nepal, when someone has started a plate of food it becomes 'unclean'. An equal, or more senior person, should not eat from it. As we sat around the veranda on straw mats, our village host offered us popcorn from a large metal plate placed in the middle of the floor. Each person took a handful in one hand and deftly tossed it with the other, piece by piece, into their mouth. Most of my helping flew around the room - so I resorted to putting my hand up to my mouth. But then I could not go back to the shared plate. The hostess said that the 'unclean' rule didn't matter, but she nevertheless slipped away and cooked some more, so she could give me a plate of my own.

It's not correct to give anything with only your left hand – that's your dirty hand, used when you go to the toilet. The right's okay, or both together, but not the left hand on its own. I expect I'll go on giving money at UK shops with two hands, even after we've settled back. And it's quite likely I'll be affronted if someone gives something to me using their left hand.

When I noticed foreigners, or so called progressive young Nepalis, 'breaking the rules' I felt offended, even more so than many nationals themselves. How easy it is to imbibe cultural norms. I drifted towards male chauvinism... I reached the stage where it no longer seemed unnatural for me to be served first or to be barred from doing the washing up.

Every day I would set off for work wearing my brightly coloured Nepali cap and strong flip-flops. These are symbols of the village Nepali. My colleagues used to grumble at me for not wearing proper shoes, so I tried to remember to change into lace-ups when attending official functions. I found flip-flops easier for walking on slippery paths; and there was no need to take them off to wade across streams or rivers. However, I have not mastered the skill of stopping flip-flops flipping and flopping mud up the back of my trousers.

My colleagues set off for a field trip with a neat satchel containing just one spare shirt, a razor and a toothbrush. I took an enormous rucksack for my sleeping bag and mat, spare clothes, books, torch and radio. Over the years my pack shrunk. As night fell during a field visit to Arghakhanchi, we searched for somewhere to stay. Householders baulked at putting up six strangers. Finally a woman welcomed us in. As I sat on the veranda in the dark, I listened to the BBC on short wave. Others helped prepare a meal. After eating, we went to bed. Four men shared two beds in one room; the women fared slightly better next door. I did not sleep well. Through the night a colleague's elbow poked in my back and my hand prodded his ear. I didn't look very fresh the next day, but my friends smiled and said I had become a 'real' field worker. These trips were opportunities for me to interact closely with those I worked with. We ate together, walked together and laughed together. We talked about the Programme, politics, village life, Hinduism and Christianity. We became good friends.

At our farewell, work friends said they'd heard of Dr. Nick before they joined the new Programme, through the project I had led in Gorkha. They had wondered what it would be like to work with a foreigner. Three years later, they admitted they had failed in their quest. "Dr Nick is more like a Nepali", they quipped.

For much of the last nine years, I tried to use the Nepali language at work. I often did not understand and I was not successful in communicating adequately with others; nonetheless, a fair bit of Nepali has diffused into my brain. Although I have now dispensed with my coloured Nepali cap and look English, the right words do not come easily; and I find myself following Nepali grammar, so that I at the end of a sentence the verb place.

On my very first day of language learning in Kathmandu, a gentleman who spoke with me challenged me. He sincerely hoped that my Christian zeal would not abate, but was also keen that I should take time to learn about Hindu philosophy. I confess I did not make much progress in this sphere, although I gained considerable knowledge about Nepal.

I had hoped to change this country, but I think the country has changed me. I may have given a little, but I've certainly gained more.

## Nepali thinking rubs off

Ros –

What does familiarity breed? Contempt, or numbness? Over time, I found that Nepal's endless traffic jams, lost baggage, and delayed journeys no longer made me hot under the collar. Maybe I developed some Nepali fatalism and accepted circumstances too readily – but I have more patience than I had ten years ago.

I also became sensitive about things that previously I would have overlooked, exposed skin, for example. Nepali women cover their legs with a sari or ankle-length trousers. I blushed inwardly when, at a roadblock en route to Pokhara, female tourists sauntered up the street in shorts, revealing flabby white legs.

But I never mastered the skills of village living: crouching on the ground to scrub fire-black pots with ash, threshing rice from the husks on a circular woven tray, washing clothes under a running water tap, or looking immaculate in a sari after walking along a muddy path.

Having returned to the UK, I appreciate creature comforts, like hot water for a bath and my bright bedside reading light. I am thankful for the weekly rubbish collection and it's a real treat baking large sized potatoes, rather than their tiny Nepali counterparts.

## Adjusting to a 'new' culture

Nick –

I realise that fitting back into Britain is not going to be easy. The spaces that people had for us in their lives ten years ago will no longer be there. The confidence we had in those we once knew well may need to be restored. No doubt we will miss social cues, and fail to catch the meaning of people's body language. We may be perceived as invading the personal space of same-sex friends, and standing back from those of the opposite sex. We will inevitably continue to use Nepali gestures, and puzzle our friends. When others come to our home, our style of hospitality is unlikely to match their expectations.

I may look the same on the outside, but inwardly I am different. Sometimes I feel like shouting aloud, "My heart is in Nepal". Our friends have changed. They've faced illness, bereavement, or an exciting job promotion, but we weren't there to share in their joy or sorrow. We were rocked by the massacre of Nepal's royal family, but I guess it hardly featured in the UK media. We followed international events through the radio and newspaper, but we missed out on the hours of television footage about Princess Diana's death, September 11, or similar news.

Invitations to local events in Nepal tended to be given at very short notice. We were hoping to attend one couple's engagement party, but it proved impossible, as they only asked us a matter of hours before the celebration was due to take place. Our friends in the UK have diaries that are full for several months ahead. We will need to readjust to the concept of forward planning.

We've relied on home workers to do the dishes, clean the house, wash clothes and prepare food. In Britain, our domestic helpers are inanimate machines.

Our children have seen almost no television. They were spared peer pressure and all that entails, but now the 'must have' society is encroaching upon them. Apart from acquiring an additional computer and a library of DVDs, our material possessions changed little in terms of quality or quantity over our nine years in Nepal.

Our paths have led in different directions to those who stayed in the UK. When we set out, we aimed to maintain close ties with our family, and the churches that sent us – distant limbs perhaps, but closely united in mind and purpose. Reintegration is a challenge. I wonder how far we will succeed?

## 'Called' back to the UK?

Ros –

Did we need a call back to the UK, in the same way as we had been called to Nepal? We had explored our dream of working overseas. But how did we know when it was right to go 'home'?

Practicalities prompted our return. Nick had completed his contract with the French agency. Our eldest daughter was unable to study at the local expatriate school beyond her 11th birthday. But we were not entirely sure what we were going back to. To stay in Nepal and take a new role with the Umbrella Organisation was a tempting idea – we had heard of vacancies that were a match for Nick's skills. But we were also aware of the potential problems that our girls could face. We had met grown-up children of missionary families who felt rootless. It was so sad to hear them express their dilemma - "We just cannot settle in our parents' home country." We wanted our girls to identify with our wider family in the UK, and to know what it was like to be 'English'. It was fairly clear that if we had lived abroad any longer, it would have made this process more difficult for them. Perhaps one day they will feel drawn to work overseas, and if that happens we will be only too happy to support them. But we firmly believe that at this stage in their young lives it was right to give them the chance to discover the UK.

Nepal has been our focus for the past ten years. It was liberating to abandon ourselves joyously to the tasks God had given us there. As yet we do not have a post-Nepal vision. Nick is qualified in General Practice (family medicine). We have a mid-terrace house in Norwich. These are our only fixed points. We are confident that God will keep us, just as He did during our 'pit stop' year in London.

There are a number of key decisions we will have to make: Should Nick return to work as a General Practitioner? What church should we attend? Should we move house? People are bound to confront us with awkward questions: Will you run the Sunday School? What are you doing for Christmas? Where will you be going on holiday? Lesser things will no doubt also exercise our minds: Is it practical to get a pet straight away? Which mobile phone should we buy? Ought the girls to have separate bedrooms? Deputation will help to cushion us for a few months. Whatever happens, we want to avoid making hasty decisions. We plan to give ourselves time to adjust, and to listen for God's prompting.

In many ways, we feel as though we are starting again as learners. I've not driven a car for four years, and am apprehensive about parallel parking. We will soon have to reactivate our bank accounts and learn our pin numbers. I am nervous about how to entertain others appropriately. There will be family pressure to conform, find a well-paid job, and settle down.

It is going to be hard coming to terms with churches that are reluctant to reach out in their localities, let alone reaching across cultures. When I think of the vibrancy of the church in Nepal, I feel vexed that so many congregations in the UK seem to be stuck in 'maintenance' mode.

## Torn between two worlds

Nick –

In Nepal we sometimes felt that we lived 'double lives': on the one hand we had a very basic home and ate a largely vegetarian diet of seasonal foods; but on the other, when we took a weekend break at Pokhara Lakeside, we splashed out more in two days than most Nepali families spend in a month. Some of our friends and neighbours could barely afford to buy enough food. Back in the UK we consume more rich food and wine than we need.

I look forward to a few days sailing on the Norfolk Broads, but I know that hiring a boat won't be cheap. How do we deal with this rich – poor tension? Will we regard our time in Nepal as a passing dream? Or will we fill our home with memories of Nepal and attempt to distance ourselves from UK culture? We know that the right course of action is to keep our eyes open to both worlds. The Apostle Paul summed it up so aptly: "I know what it is to be in need, and I know what it is to have plenty. I have learned the secret of being content in any and every situation, whether well fed or hungry, whether living in plenty or in want. I can do everything through him who gives me strength"[36].

Saying goodbye both to friends and neighbours, and to our familiar roles was difficult. We had come to love Nepal and its people. Over the years we sought to share our lives with individuals and families, and were touched by their care and concern for us.

Many things coursed through our minds as we thought about our return to the UK. What we looked forward to most were the re-unions with family and friends… and I relished the thought of getting my teeth into a Cox's apple, and having a brisk walk along a Norfolk beach, followed by fish and chips.

What is now my greatest concern? I find myself worrying on behalf of Lydia and Elizabeth, who are about to enter an enormous school. How will they adjust to life in the UK? I am anxious at the expectations of others – to attend events, to behave in a certain way, or to perform a particular role. In Nepal, we had been spared active participation in anniversaries, birthdays and family Christmas celebrations. It's not that I don't enjoy such occasions, but we've found new ways of celebrating. I know I'll have to adjust to a faster pace of life.

I am also apprehensive about returning to sleepy churches in the UK. Shortly before we left Nepal, we received an email from a friend saying his church would probably not support a new mission partner because they had struggled to make ends meet. Financial reserves had been used to pay central church expenses. Moreover, there were plans to redecorate interior walls, and they needed to repair the roof…

Jesus made an unbeatable offer to the church at Laodicea – He was prepared to enter fully into their lives[37]. If churches welcome Jesus first, they will discover God's passion for mission, both locally and worldwide, and they won't be consumed by financial concerns or re-decoration. Brother Yun, in his inspiring book, 'The Heavenly Man', suggests that some in Christian work are like the disciples who took Jesus in their boat, but struggled on their own against opposition, rather than calling on the master. "Too many churches and ministries have welcomed Jesus into their midst in the past, but today they are operating in their own strength and plans, while Jesus sleeps in their midst," says Yun[38].

Hebron church in Tansen was not perfect, but we saw new people being attracted to the main service every week. We experienced God's blessing through heart- felt open worship; we witnessed changed lives as evangelists took the Gospel message to nearby villages and towns; and there was a sense of joy and anticipation in a church literacy class, as believers longed for the day when they would be able to read the Bible for themselves. Members of the church faced persecution from their families and neighbours because of their faith, but the church kept growing. The fellowship was strengthened and emboldened as they supported one another in prayer. We only wish we could have brought Hebron with us to the UK.

## Loss and change – the process

Ros –

Six months before leaving Nepal, I feared that the 'wrapping up' might not go smoothly. I wanted to say farewells, pack up our house, and dispose of our belongings as I had planned. My readings about Solomon encouraged me. He was allowed to finish his work of building the temple. I felt reassured that we would also achieve what we desired to do.

We had seen many expatriate colleagues leave Nepal, so had a good idea of how we wanted to go about it. Some sneaked away, cheating friends of the chance to say good-bye properly. Others left expecting to come back, but never returned, so burdening the team with the messy business of tidying up. And there were those who unsettled the group, by talking for months on end about their future plans.

One exemplary teacher left unhurriedly. She placed notes of appreciation in each of our pigeonholes, and presented carefully compiled photo-albums to friends and pupils. I prayed and hoped that we would be able to finish in a way that was God-honouring: by tying up loose ends, saying goodbye, and dealing with our belongings appropriately.

We started the leaving process when Nick's contract finished earlier than anticipated. But I saw God's hand at work in this – especially as the girls had two weeks holiday starting the next day. We were able to go to Amppipal as a family to say farewell there.

The last weekend spent in our Tansen home was hectic. We hosted the Nepali house group meeting for the last time, held an early birthday party for Lydia, and invited all our neighbours for tea, snacks and a film.

We then spent three days packing up the house. I had prayed it would be hot and dry, so we could stow and transport our belongings easily. It was.

On our final Saturday Nick preached in church; leaders gave us local woven gifts and prayed for us. Over tea and doughnuts we said good-bye to individuals. That afternoon the expatriates arranged a special farewell and presented us with a beautiful book filled with entries by each team member.

We also went to the bazaar to give family photographs to several shopkeepers, and bid them goodbye. Our tailor emerged with a large framed photo of Tansen, asking if

I liked it. I thanked him very much for being so thoughtful, but had to explain that it would be too big to pack. Eventually he handed me an envelope with a photo of himself and a small picture of Tansen.

We felt satisfied that we had completed our round of farewells.

I read somewhere that it's important to say good-bye to places as well as people. So we asked Lydia and Elizabeth where they wanted to go on our final afternoon in Tansen. I feared our outing would be rained off, but the sky brightened, and we had a dry, if humid, walk to the disused helipad and through the forest. We finished off the day with a meal at the one western-style restaurant in town. The girls took snap shots with disposable cameras.

The next morning friends prayed over us, and our vehicle set off. The journey to Kathmandu via Pokhara was long, but avoided a section of road damaged by landslides. I was in a daze. I felt neither especially happy, nor sad. I did have a sense of completion. While Elizabeth laid her head on my lap, I quietly soaked in the stunning deep green of the monsoon scenery. It was a fitting farewell from the most beautiful country in the world.

In Kathmandu, Nick made arrangements for the freight. Meanwhile I went for a manicure, pedicure and hair cut - an affordable treat in Kathmandu - to smarten up before meeting the family. A New Zealand couple opened their home so we could meet up with friends who had moved to the capital from Amppipal. We were touched that Mohan and Ram, possibly our closest Nepali friends, travelled a day each way from their homes to be with us.

The adrenalin had been high during the two months before departure. After sorting, packing, and saying goodbye we were physically and emotionally drained. Thankfully, we had arranged a week's holiday in Thailand for rest and relaxation. This short breathing space was just what we needed. It is easy to start seeing Nepal through rose–coloured spectacles, and forget the strikes, power cuts and frustrating bureaucracy. It is also possible to exaggerate the comfort of UK life and underestimate the hassles of finding a parking space, paying bills and arranging car insurance. Someone told us of an exercise to help counteract such polarised views. We divided a sheet of paper into four squares, and labelled the squares: things we like/don't like about Nepal, and things we like/don't like about the UK. The family brainstormed each area in turn, as a way of gaining some perspective and balance.

We also played the 'transition game'. We had a pack of questions relating to life in Nepal, and at meal times we would work our way through some of the issues. One question was, 'Where's the best place to take a friend visiting Nepal from your home country?' Another was, 'What do you like about being a missionary kid?'

When we returned to the UK previously, I decided which toys I thought the girls needed rather than letting them choose. This time we squeezed the little shrunken plastic creatures they'd made at school into their travel knap-sacks. It meant that at least they had a few familiar things with them during the long journey back.

I prayed that I would show understanding towards the girls as we went through the process of loss and change together. I didn't want genuine grief to be smothered by all the good things that grandparents and supporters would lavish upon us. Happily, children have a knack of living in the present and adapting to new circumstances. The transition proved easier than I had anticipated.

On our final UK 'tour' we will be 'signing off', and saying thank you to our supporters. We will concentrate on handing the baton on, prompting churches to think how they can continue to support mission at home and overseas. We hope that those churches that helped us, will, in the future, redirect their energy to other mission partners.

How can we lead fulfilled lives in the UK, while still cherishing our memories of Nepal? The girls suggested we have a night a week when we eat curry and rice, and speak Nepali. Nick and I plan to remember our Nepali friends when we say evening prayers together. We hope to maintain contact by email, and keep up with news of the country on the Internet.

Although we are now freed from fears for our own safety, we are mindful of the Nepali friends and colleagues we have left behind, as they continually face the uncertain future of their land. For many of them, leaving the country is not an option. So we have an ongoing task to pray for our Nepali brothers and sisters and to advocate for justice and peace in Nepal.

# BOTTOM UP OR TOP DOWN?
# THINKING ABOUT DEVELOPMENT

Nick –

It has been said that 'development' is the biggest industry in the world. Certainly in Nepal there are many hundreds of organisations claiming to be doing it, and many thousands of Nepalis employed in it. What strategies undergird development programmes? Broadly speaking, there are two approaches.

*1. Develop trust and cohesion in communities and promote community empowerment.*

The Umbrella implemented a project committed to this strategy in Surkhet district, in Western Nepal. Critics said that mission staff went into communities with 'nothing to offer', just 'empty baskets'. But villagers learned they could tackle local problems using their own resources. They also discovered immense self worth and satisfaction. The process took time - many years - but the long-term benefits were significant. When external resources were essential, community members learned how to approach other agencies and request the help they needed.

*2. Deliver technological solutions through existing local and national leadership structures.*

It is paternalistic to try to disturb the patterns of community leadership in a developing country that have existed for centuries. Development agencies should serve the stated needs of community leaders and provide appropriate 'hardware', like water systems or mains electricity. The identification and provision of such primary facilities can result in rapid improvements to health and quality of life.

Which of these two approaches is better?
What is development, anyway? Is it about water, electricity and clinics? Or perhaps it's something social or spiritual? What might be a Christian approach to development?

Gorkha Community Health Programme (CHP) graduated through three phases of health activities. In the 1970's staff gave vaccines and other basic services to children through mobile clinics. In the 80's the government established health posts in each village, and CHP staff trained and supported the health workers. In the 90's we took a further step away from direct care and focused on health development committees in each village. We encouraged these committees to take responsibility for motivating local health post staff. These three phases tie in with the old adage about satisfying a hungry man. You can give him a fish, feed him for a day, or teach him how to fish. You might even go a step further and get him to consider the pros and cons of accessing a range of possible foods.

The fishing picture challenges development workers to foster a deeper level of participation by community members. The World Health Organisation endorses community participation for health-related activities, although local people's contributions are often sidelined in top-down health programmes. This is one of the reasons why many national and international programmes fail to deliver.

## What is 'Christian development'?

The Umbrella organisation in Nepal has mission and vision statements that are explicitly Christian. The French organisation is a secular humanitarian agency, with an entirely different ethos. For nine years, we lived in Nepal as individuals with a Christian faith. To what extent were we doing 'Christian development'?

Some writers suggest that Christian development is different from secular development because Christian workers operate with Christian *motives*, in a Christian *manner* consistent with Christian *ethics*. They suggest that it is not what Christians do that is different, but the way they do it. Christian and non-Christian development workers can share the same development goals and undertake the same activities. A 'Christian' drinking water project would look the same as a 'secular' one. This rings true. Certainly the skills required to fit taps, pipes and tanks are common to both.

Other writers say that Christian and secular work are different because their underlying assumptions about development are different. Christians believe that personal submission to Jesus Christ is essential for wholeness. Most post-modern thinkers affirm that humans are spiritual beings, but they see religion as a matter of personal choice. I imagine that they perceive a 'supermarket' of faiths in which different faiths are brands that are equally effective in satisfying people's spiritual needs. Lacking a particular spiritual conviction, secular development cannot ground itself in any one faith. In practice, this neutral attitude to religions leads secular players to sideline spiritual aspects of the health of an individual or a community. Instead they focus on physical, social and environmental health.

Historically, the Protestant church has debated the relationship between social action and evangelism. There has been a divide in the way that churches have approached the poor. Some promote social action, but ignore evangelism. Others seem to believe that bringing people to faith in Christ is all that God requires of them. Jesus preached the coming of the kingdom of God in a fuller sense, but each wing of the church has emphasised one part of his message to the detriment of the other. The Nepali government imposed limitations on the Umbrella Organisation, which served to open this split. As a result, the Nepali church has focused on evangelism - to be a pastor or evangelist is regarded as the highest calling for young Nepali Christians. The Umbrella, on the other hand, has majored on health care, education and rural and industrial development.

In other settings, 'holistic' missions have attempted both to serve people's physical and social needs, and proclaim Jesus as Lord. Some projects manage to hold these facets in balance[39], but many projects only 'paste together' the physical / spiritual divide – they double the number of activities they have to do, but fail to achieve integration.

There is a richer way to understand 'Christian development'. The 'ultimate goal' of Christian development is the total transformation of the *worldview* of communities to a biblical worldview. Worldview may be defined as the way a community views the larger world around it – including beliefs about physical and spiritual reality and humanity's place in that reality.

In the biblical worldview all people are made in the image of God; all have value and dignity. The Bible recognises corruption in people's hearts, but affirms God's love for us. Healing and forgiveness are available because of the death of Jesus on the cross. These are basic tenets of a biblical worldview. However, no one can claim a full understanding of how God intends the world to be. I perceive that God deals with communities of people in unique ways. I cannot assert that my culture has found God's definitive view and justify imposing my culture on others. Indeed there are many salutary examples from mission history of cultural imperialism to warn us against this. However, Christians believe that the Old and New Testament scriptures reveal God, and can correct and refine our worldview.

And what if a society in which Christians work does not acknowledge truth in the Bible? Jesus told his parables to anyone who would listen. They are radical stories that challenge our worldview. Bible stories are pertinent for all people, whatever their creed. God-ordained patterns for living, which we find in the Bible, can be the basis for development work that seeks to transform communities, even if people never hear of Jesus. Of course there is more to the Christian gospel than this, and no believer in Jesus will be fully satisfied while his or her friends remain outside a commitment to him. But the gospel is not only about spiritual conversion.

Secular development is based on the secular assumptions that prevail in the West. Biblical development challenges these assumptions. For example, Christians pray and look to God for supernatural intervention, for healing or guidance. Secular workers do not. Jesus' radical teaching about right conduct in the Sermon on the Mount[40] is a foundation for the Christian worker, but would not be even considered by secular thinkers[41].

I am discovering that Christian development workers can and should start out from the Bible's teaching on what God wants for humankind and for the world. We can expect God to direct our goals. We can pray and listen to God. Rather than focussing exclusively on the 'felt needs' expressed by those we serve, we can seek also to know God's desires for an individual or community. Local Christian churches, too, can and should be players in the process.

# NOTES

(Scripture references from New International Version (NIV))

[1] NIV: Deuteronomy, Chapter 10, verses 17–18.

[2] TearFund's *Footsteps* magazine – an excellent resource for development workers is published in many languages – Write to Footsteps mailing list, Resources Development, 100 Church Road, Teddington, TW11 8QE, UK or visit http://tilz.tearfund.org and select Footsteps.

TALC (Teaching Aids at Low Cost - source of books, posters and CDs about primary health) PO Box 49, St Albans, Herts AL1 5TX, UK (Tel +44(0) 1727 853869) www.talcuk.org

[3] *Pictures, people and power*. People-centred visual aids for development. Bob Linney, McMillan Education Ltd, 1995 (ISBN 0-333-60044-4).

[4] Centre for Disease Control and Prevention – Epi Info – www.cdc.gov/epiinfo

[5] The British Medical Association, Christian Medical Fellowship (CMF) and Royal College of General Practitioners have allowed me free membership during my years in Nepal. At considerable expense to themselves, they sent me their journals.

[6] NIV: Genesis Chapter 22, verses 1–14.

[7] NIV: Luke Chapter 15, verses 11–24.

[8] Adapted from Luke, Chapter 10, verses 30–37.

[9] Dave Titus 'The string man', United Mission to Nepal annual conference, Kathmandu, 1999.

[10] *'Good news down the street'* Michael Wooderson, Lynx, 1993.

[11] NIV: Matthew Chapter 11, verse 28.

[12] NIV: 2 Corinthians Chapter 12, verse 9 and Philippians Chapter 4, verse 13.

[13] Psalm 121, verses 1–2 & 8

[14] Myers Briggs personality type indicator tests. Many sites on the world wide web, or see: Gifts Differing, Understanding Personality Type, Isabel Briggs Myers, Davies-Black 1995, ISBN 0-89106-074-X

[15] Robert Chambers, Institute of Development Studies, University of Sussex, at a London School of Hygiene and Tropical Medicine seminar, May 2000.

[16] Nicholas Henwood, M.Sc. Dissertation, 2000, Community Health Development in Rural Nepal, *Who does what? The roles of community people and development agency staff*, London School of Hygiene and Tropical Medicine.

[17] For example Putnam RD, 1993, *Making democracy work*, Princeton University Press, New Jersey, USA, and Campbell et al, 1999, Social capital and health, Health Education Authority, London.

[18] Goulet D, 1995, *Development Ethics: A guide to theory and practice*. Apex press, London.

[19] Robert Warren, *An affair of the heart, How to pray more effectively*, Highland Books, 1994, ISBN 1 897913 09 5

[20] NIV: 2nd Corinthians, Chapter 13, verse 14.

[21] "Peace, perfect peace, our future all unknown?" Edward H. Bickersteth, 1875.

[22] Carl and Betty Friedricks founded United Mission to Nepal's hospital in Tansen in 1953.

[23] Nepali legislation forbids coercing people to become Christians – may God forgive us if our actions are perceived as coercion. I am just a poor beggar who's found a wide open door to the heavenly banquet and am running back to

tell my friends that the feast is delicious and the name of the door is Jesus.

[24] Srinivasan L, *Tools for Community Participation*, 1989, Published by UNDP, and distributed by PACT Publications.

[25] The JESUS Film Project is an offshoot of Campus Crusade for Christ. The film closely follows St Luke's Gospel. Go to www.jesusfilm.org and watch it in any of 800 languages!

[26] Geoffrey Rose, *The strategy of preventive medicine*. Oxford University Press, 1992. ISBN: 0192624865.

[27] NIV: Proverbs, Chapter 31 'The Wife of Noble Character', verse 10–31.

[28] Heath Robinson was an inventor of crazy contraptions. I believe they say a 'Rube Goldberg device' in the USA.

[29] *Patterns not Padlocks* by Angela Ashwin, Eagle. ISBN: 0–8634.7088–2.

[30] *The rhythm of life* by David Adam. Morehouse Publishing Group, (1997), ISBN: 0819217158.

[31] NIV: Matthew Chapter 7, verses 15–20

[32] NIV: Genesis Chapter 35, verses 2–4

[33] NIV: Acts Chapter 9, verses 1–30

[34] 'Pit' is a noisy trading card-game. To play it you only need to be able to say (or shout) the numbers from one to four.

[35] 'Uno' is not as noisy as pit… (you need to be able to say red, green, blue, yellow, and 'Uno').

[36] NIV: Philippians, Chapter 4, verses 12–13.

[37] NIV: Revelation, Chapter 3, verse 20.

[38] P.318, The Heavenly Man, Brother Hun and Paul Hattaway, 2002, Monarch Books, Concorde House, Grenville Place, Mill Hill, London, ISBN 978-1854245977.

[39] *Cup of Water, Bread of Life: Inspiring Stories about Overcoming Lopsided Christianity* by Sider, Ronald J, Zondervan Publishing Company, 1994, ISBN 0310406013.

Sider, author of the bestselling *Rich Christians in an Age of Hunger*, demonstrates in *Cup of Water, Bread of Life,* how to bridge the gap between evangelism and social outreach. He tells of ministries that not only led individuals to a saving faith in Jesus Christ, but helped them overcome social, economic, and political barriers.

[40] NIV: Mathew, Chapters 5 to 7.

[41] Ideas in these paragraphs came from - *Towards biblical world-view Transformation*, Stephen Thorson, 2002, United Mission to Nepal, Nepal. And, Justice, Mercy and Humility: the Papers of the Micah Network International Consultation on Integral Mission and the Poor, Ed Tim Chester, 2002, Paternoster Press. www.micahnetwork.org/integral-mission.

200592UK00001B/12/P